Evaluating health risks

An economic approach

Per-Olov Johansson
Stockholm School of Economics

Published by the Press Syndicate of the University of Cambridge
The Pitt Building, Trumpington Street, Cambridge CB2 1RP
40 West 20th Street, New York NY 10011-4211, USA
10 Stamford Road, Oakleigh, Melbourne 3166, Australia

First published 1995

Printed in Great Britain at the University Press, Cambridge

A catalogue record for this book is available from the British Library

Library of Congress cataloguing in publication data
Johansson, Per-Olov, 1949–
    Evaluating health risks : an economic approach / Per-Olov
Johansson.
        p.   cm.
    ISBN 0 521 47285 7. – ISBN 0 521 47878 2 (pbk.)
    1. Medical economics.   2. Medical care – Cost effectiveness.
I. Title.
RA410.5.J635   1995
338.4′33621 – dc20   94-21095   CIP

ISBN 0 521 47285 7 hardback
ISBN 0 521 47878 2 paperback

Contents

Preface   *page* ix

1 Introduction   1
Scope of the study   1
Important contributions   3
Plan of the study   5

2 Some basic tools and concepts   9
Utility maximization   9
A health production function   12
Intertemporal models   15
Introducing risk   17
Some further comments on risk   22
More complex intertemporal models   27
Appendix   30

3 Evaluating health changes in a certain world   33
Two money measures of a change in health   33
On the properties of compensated money measures   37
An example: using CV and EV   40
Overall versus instantaneous money measures   41
A health production function approach   43
Using market data to evaluate changes in health   47
Appendix   49

4 Money measures in a risky world   52
Introducing money measures in a risky world   52
A WTP locus   57
Evaluating changes in mortality, and the value of a statistical   59
  life
Endogenous risks and altruism   61
Changes in wealth and the value of health   63
Intertemporal models   65
Appendix   69

vii

5 Evaluating health risks: practical methodologies   71
  The contingent valuation method   71
  Closed-ended techniques   79
  A useful interpretation of WTP measures   83
  CVM studies of health risks   86
  The human capital approach   88
  Market-based estimation methods   89
  The value of a statistical life   93
  Appendix   96

6 Contingent valuation studies of health care   97
  Empirical studies of the WTP for health care: a brief review 97
  A study of high blood pressure   102
  The results   106
  Useful formulae for the computation of the mean WTP   113
  Appendix   114

7 Aggregation   115
  The social welfare function   116
  Project evaluations   119
  Pragmatic views on the aggregation problem   124
  An illustration: how to assess a treatment   126
  Altruism   127
  Altruism in cost-benefit analysis   130
  Appendix   134

8 Further evaluation issues in a risky world   135
  The value of information   135
  A health production function model   139
  Using the model to assess health changes   142
  On the value of changes in life expectancy   146
  Appendix   150

9 Concluding remarks on related approaches   153
  Qalys and hyes   153
  Risk–risk and risk–dollar trade-offs   158
  Cost-effectiveness analysis   160
  Appendix   163

  Notes   168
  Bibliography   171
  Index   185

Preface

For a person working with applied welfare economics and environmental economics, cost-benefit analysis plays a central role. In particular, much effort and time is devoted to examining the properties of measures which involve monetary benefits and improving existing techniques for the empirical estimation of benefits expressed in monetary units. When shifting one's interest and orientation towards health economics, it is somewhat surprising to find that most health economists work with other benefits measures such as quality-adjusted life-years (qalys) and healthy-years equivalents (hyes). There also seems to be no book available which defines and examines in detail the properties of money measures of changes in health risks and surveys the empirical methods which can be used to assess the economic value of such changes. The books by Jones-Lee (1976, 1989) and Viscusi (1992), though excellent, do not have this orientation. Books on environmental economics, for example Braden and Kolstad (1991), Freeman (1979) and Johansson (1987, 1993), typically devote no more than one or two chapters to (environmental) health risks. For this reason, and since economic evaluations of health care expenditures will come to play an important role in those economies where there is a growing awareness of the fact that resources are limited and hence must be allocated in a reasonable way between different and competing needs, I decided to write such a book. The aim of the book is to define money measures of changes in health (risks) caused by medical treatments or other 'factors' such as public safety programmes and pollution, to examine the properties of these measures in order to highlight their advantages as well as their weaknesses and limitations, and to present and discuss the methods which are most frequently used to calculate such measures in empirical applications.

The book is an advanced text in applied welfare economics and its application to health economics. It is intended for Ph.D. courses in health economics, environmental economics, welfare economics and public economics. The book should also be valuable as a reference text for those undertaking evaluations of projects involving health risks in government agencies and other organizations. In using the book as a textbook, it is recommended that the student should be familiar with microeconomics at the level of Varian (1992), Cowell (1986) and Kreps (1990). For the reader who is only interested in the more fundamental issues and wants to skip the more complex intertemporal models the following route is recommended: chapter 1; chapter 2, the first two sections, the fourth and fifth sections; chapter 3, the first–fourth sections; chapter 4, the first, third, fourth and fifth sections; chapters 5–6; chapter 7, the first and third–fifth sections; chapter 8, the first section; chapter 9.

Many people have contributed with comments and suggestions on previous versions of the manuscript. In particular my thanks go to Glenn C. Blomquist, Ingemar Eckerlund, Magnus Johannesson, Michael W. Jones-Lee, Bengt Jönsson, Göran Karlsson, Bengt Kriström, Karl-Gustaf Löfgren, Tore Söderqvist, Magnus Tambour, Niklas Zethraeus, and two anonymous referees provided by the Press. The manuscript was completed during a visit to the University of California, San Diego. I would like to express my gratitude to Richard T. Carson for his hospitality during my stay, as well as for updating me on the research frontier within the contingent valuation field. At the Press, my editor Patrick McCartan provided me with all necessary support, as usual. The English was scrutinized by Ann Brown, and the figures were drawn by Linus Jönsson.

The manuscript was written as a part of a project testing the usefulness of the contingent valuation method (CVM) for economic evaluations of health care. Financial support from the Swedish Council for Social Research is gratefully acknowledged.

I would finally like to stress that any flaws, errors and 'Scandinavianisms' which remain are the sole responsibility of the author.

1 Introduction

Scope of the study

A problem common to health economics and environmental economics is how to evaluate changes in morbidity and mortality; pollution often creates severe health problems which necessitate an explicit treatment of changes in mortality and morbidity risks. However, the approaches used in these two fields to deal with the valuation issue are very different. Most environmental economists have based their approach on mainstream micro and welfare economics, the purpose being to undertake a social cost-benefit analysis of environmental change. Since most environmental goods and services are not valued in the market, a lot of work has therefore been devoted to improving different empirical methods that can be used to measure the willingness to pay (WTP) for changes in environmental quality. In particular, environmental economists have developed and refined the contingent valuation method (CVM), a survey method which is used to measure the WTP for environmental quality; see, for example, Cummings *et al.* (1986) and Mitchell and Carson (1989). Environmental economists have also used what are known as hedonic price studies in order to isolate the WTP for quality attributes from individuals' actual behaviour in the market; see for example Blomquist *et al.* (1988), Brookshire *et al.* (1982) and Viscusi (1992).

In health economics the cost-benefit approach seems to have been largely ignored, although there are exceptions; see, for example, Eastaugh (1992). Most health economists appear to prefer cost-effectiveness analysis, where the health consequences are measured in physical units such as the number of life-years gained from a medical treatment; see, for example, Drummond *et al.* (1987). Much effort has been devoted to attempts to combine survival and quality of life dimensions into a single outcome measure to be used in cost-effectiveness analysis: some authors would speak of a cost-effectiveness analysis when the output measure is in natural units such as life-years saved or improvement in functional status, and a cost-utility analysis when utility change indices (combined survival and quality of life dimensions) are used as the output measure. The most well known outcome measures are

1

quality-adjusted life-years (qalys) and more recently healthy-years equivalents (hyes); see, for example, Klarman *et al.* (1968), Weinstein and Stason (1976), Boyle *et al.* (1983) and Williams (1985) for presentations and discussions of qalys, and Mehrez and Gafni (1989, 1991) for definitions of the hye measure. The reader is also referred to Culyer's (1989) review of health economists' work on the normative economics of health care.

The theoretical foundations of cost-effectiveness analysis (cost-utility analysis) are, however, unclear. For example, it seems to be somewhat uncertain exactly what costs should be included in the analysis. One can also find differences between studies in their treatment of the discounting of future health effects; see Johannesson and Jönsson (1991a, 1991b) for a discussion of these problems. The rationale from a theoretical perspective to maximize the number of qalys or hyes gained is also unclear. One possibility is to view cost-effectiveness analysis as a decision-maker's approach to economic project evaluation, and to maximize whatever the decision-maker views as important; see Sugden and Williams (1978). The decision-maker is, however, seldom explicitly identified in applied cost-effectiveness analysis. It is usually just assumed that the target of the decision-maker is to maximize the number of qalys gained or some other outcome measure.

These problems have led to renewed interest in the cost-benefit approach in health economics, and applications using the CVM to measure the WTP for health care are starting to appear. These applications include Acton (1973), Appel *et al.* (1990), Donaldson (1990), Johannesson (1992), Johannesson, Jönsson and Borgquist (1991), Johannesson *et al.* (1991), Johannesson, Johansson, Kriström and Gerdtham (1993), Johannesson *et al.* (1993), Thompson *et al.* (1982, 1984) and Thompson (1986). A further reason for the interest in the cost-benefit approach is possibly the fact that the costs for health care are increasing at a rapid rate in the industrialized countries. This increases the need for sound economic analysis of the benefits and costs of different health programmes.

There is no text available which presents in detail the theoretical foundations of WTP measures of changes in health risks or surveys the empirical methods which can be used to estimate a WTP for a change in health risks. Texts in environmental economics, in particular those concentrating on the valuation issue, typically include a chapter or so on how to evaluate health risks. See, for example, Braden and Kolstad (1991), Freeman (1979) and Johansson (1987, 1993). The excellent books by Jones-Lee (1976, 1989) are devoted to health issues, but provide no complete discussion of money measures or the empirical methods available in estimating the monetary value of changes in health risks. Viscusi (1992) provides an impressive survey of empirical studies aimed at valuing changes in health risks, but does not devote much space to health care.

The purpose of this book is to provide a reasonably broad coverage of the evaluation issues faced by health economists planning to use the WTP approach in their work. The main part of the book is concerned with the economic theory of health benefits: for example, what is meant by a money measure of the utility change caused by a health change in a certain world and a risky world, respectively, and what properties such measures possess. However, two chapters are devoted to empirical issues. One of these (chapter 5) briefly surveys the methods that can be used to assess changes in health and the available empirical evidence, for example, with respect to the value of a statistical life. The other (chapter 6) presents in more detail a particular empirical method, the CVM, and discusses with reference to actual studies of medical treatments many of the steps in an empirical valuation study based on the survey method.

Important contributions

There is a large body of literature on the theory and measurement of consumer surplus. The concept was first introduced by Dupuit (1933 (1884)), who was concerned with the benefits and costs of constructing a bridge. Marshall (1920) introduced the concept of consumer surplus to the English-speaking world. Marshall's measure, like that of Dupuit, was an all-or-nothing measure: 'The excess of the price which he would be willing to pay rather than go without the thing, over that which he actually does pay is the economic measure of this surplus of satisfaction' (Marshall, 1920, p. 124). Later Hicks, in a series of articles in 1940–1 and 1945–6, and Henderson (1940–1) demonstrated that consumer surplus could be interpreted in terms of amounts of money that must be given to/taken from an individual.

Measuring the consumer surplus as an area to the left of an ordinary or Marshallian demand curve yields what is known as the ordinary or uncompensated or Marshallian consumer surplus. The Hicksian or income-compensated consumer surplus is measured as an area to the left of a compensated or Hicksian demand curve where the individual through adjustments in his or her income is held at a pre-specified level of utility. The most well known Hicksian money measures are the compensating variation (CV) and the equivalent variation (EV). In the former case, the individual remains at his or her initial or pre-change level of utility. In the latter case, s/he is held at the level of utility s/he would attain with the considered change in, say, a price. Adding to a consumer surplus the amount of money that the individual spends on the commodity yields a measure of his or her WTP for the commodity.

For a long time there was a debate about the conditions under which different money measures coincided. The debate centred around the path-dependency issue, which had been introduced as early as 1938 by Hotelling.

The basic problem is that when several prices, for example, are changed, the order in which they are changed may affect the magnitude of the consumer surplus of the combined change in prices. The ordinary consumer surplus measure turned out to suffer from this problem, unless strong restrictions were placed on the individual's utility function (assuming it to be quasi-linear or homothetic; see chapter 3). On the other hand, the compensated or Hicksian consumer surplus measures do not suffer from this problem.

Uncertainty – or rather risk, since probabilities are assumed to be knowable – started to interest welfare economists at an early stage. Waugh (1944) showed that consumers facing exogenous random prices are better off than if these prices are stabilized at their arithmetic means. Later studies, for example, Samuelson (1972) and Turnovsky et al. (1980), have shown that the Waugh result is not generally correct.

In environmental economics, interest in consumer surplus measures in a risky world increased dramatically after the paper by Weisbrod (1964) where he introduced the concept of option value. The idea is that a consumer is willing to pay a sum in excess of his or her expected consumer surplus to ensure that a desired 'commodity', say a national park, is preserved. The argument seemed both novel and intuitively appealing but there has nevertheless been much discussion about the precise meaning of option value. The reader is referred to Johansson (1987) for a short summary of the arguments and the different interpretations put forward.

Jones-Lee (1974, 1976) provides a summary of a couple of early analyses of the value of life and safety improvements. The main contribution of Jones-Lee, however, is his own analysis of the value of life and safety improvement. This analysis is consistent with economic theory in general and the von Neumann–Morgenstern (1947) expected utility theorem in particular. In his analysis, Jones-Lee concentrates on the concepts of the CV and the EV, and uses these concepts to define money measures of changes in survival probabilities. A few years after the publication of Jones-Lee's (1976) book, Broome initiated a debate in the *Journal of Public Economics* about the possibility of meaningfully valuing life. Broome argued that you cannot meaningfully place a monetary value on the loss of a statistical life (see chapter 4), since, eventually, death probabilities translate into the death of actual individuals. This view was challenged by several other economists. The main argument seems to be based on the distinction between *ex ante* and *ex post*. In advance, i.e. *ex ante*, it is meaningful to look at trade-offs between changes in survival probabilities and (for example) money. On the other hand, *ex post* when we can identify with certainty the individuals whose lives are at stake, it is not meaningful to try to define the value of life (or we may say that it is infinitely high). See Broome (1978, 1979), Buchanan and Fair (1979), Jones-Lee (1979), Mishan (1981) and Williams (1979) for the value of life debate.

Important and early contributions on insurance include Arrow (1963, 1964) and Cook and Graham (1977); the reader is also referred to the short review from Bernoulli (1954 (1738)) onwards in Borch (1990). Two further contributions of great potential importance to health economics deserve attention. Arrow and Fisher (1974) and Henry (1974) focus on the irreversibility of many decisions and discuss the value of awaiting further information about the consequences of a project in a risky world. They define the (conditional) expected value of perfect information, sometimes called the quasi-option value in environmental economics. Graham (1981) shows that in a risky world there is possibly an infinite number of money measures of a unique change in expected utility (when the individual pays so as to remain at a pre-specified level of expected utility). Graham uses this fact to define a WTP locus. Though both these contributions relate to environmental economics, they are of great interest also to health economics, as will be evident from later chapters of this book.

There is a large empirical literature using different methods to estimate the economic value of changes in morbidity and mortality, though very few studies as yet relate to medical treatments. This literature will be considered in chapters 5 and 6. For this reason, it will not be discussed here.

Plan of the study

In order to derive money measures of the value of changes in health, a number of essential tools and definitions are required. Instead of waiting until these different concepts arise in the text before introducing them, chapter 2 presents the basic tools used in the subsequent analysis, and serves as a basic point of reference for the analysis in the remainder of the book. Although the chapter introduces some economic health models, it has no pretensions whatsoever to provide a full review of existing models. Rather, the chapter concentrates on a few simple models which are useful in defining and illustrating the properties of money measures of the value of changes in health.

In chapter 3, money measures of the value of changes in health are introduced, and their properties examined. In developing the theory it is as well to discuss the simplest considerations first, and for this reason, the assumption that individuals do not face any uncertainty is retained throughout the chapter. This assumption will enable us to point out central properties of money measures, properties which carry over to the more complex risky world money measures which are introduced in chapter 4. The bulk of the chapter is devoted to a digression on two so-called income-compensated or Hicksian money measures, the CV and the EV. The two final sections of the chapter, however, discuss the circumstances in which market data can be used to assess changes in health.

The interpretation of a medical treatment or a health policy measure as having a certain impact on the individual's health profile is questionable, to say the least. Rather, the future health profile can be viewed as stochastic, and a treatment will change the probability that the individual will experience a particular health status. Chapter 4 introduces risk, and the money measures derived for the certainty case are generalized so as to cover changes in probability distributions. In sharp contrast to the certainty case discussed in chapter 3, in a risky world there is in principle an infinite number of money measures keeping the individual at a pre-specified level of (expected) utility. This fact is used to derive a WTP locus, and to discuss the choice of money measure in a risky world. The chapter also discusses the circumstances under which it is meaningful to place a monetary value on changes in an individual's survival probability, and introduces the concept of the value of a statistical life. Further issues discussed are altruism and the possibility of using changes in expected income as a lower bound for the value of changes in health.

In the case of a commodity that is traded in the market, buyers and sellers reveal their preferences directly through their actions. Since health basically is a private good, one expects to be able to use market data to assess the value of health changes. However, in many countries, the government intervenes in the market or even runs the health care sector. Often, the price paid for a treatment is zero or fixed at an arbitrary level which is kept constant over long intervals of time. This makes it difficult to use econometrics to estimate conventional demand curves for medical treatments. There is also the further complication that risk plays a central role within the health field.

This raises the question of how to overcome the problem of preference revelation. Several different practical methods which can be used to measure WTP for health services have been suggested in the literature. Chapter 5 presents the three most frequently used and/or suggested methods: survey techniques, the human capital approach, and indirect methods using market data. The chapter also offers an overview of empirical studies using different methods to assess the value of health changes and the value of a statistical life.

Chapter 6 concentrates on the CVM. The chapter reviews studies using this method to value health care, and also discusses in some detail many of the steps in a CVM study of WTP for a medical treatment. This is done with reference to the procedures used in a 1991 study of patients' valuation of treatment of high blood pressure (hypertension): the central valuation question is presented, and the econometric procedures used to estimate the average WTP for the treatment are outlined. The chapter also presents some simple formulae which can be used to calculate the average WTP from discrete responses ('yes/no' data).

Chapters 2–6 are concerned with the definition and measurement of money measures at the individual level. In chapter 7 we look at the aggregation problem and examine the conditions under which the sum of WTPs for a measure indicates whether a proposed project is socially profitable. The reason for this exercise is that most empirical studies present the average WTP for the project or measure under examination. However, behind an average WTP there are typically both those who gain and those who lose. The chapter introduces the concept of the social welfare function and uses this (unobservable) function to derive cost-benefit rules for small and large projects, say medical treatments, in a risky world. This approach highlights the distributional aspects of a proposed measure. Empirical methods which can be used to stress a project's distributional consequences are discussed. The two final sections of the chapter address the important issue of how to treat altruism in a cost-benefit analysis. In particular, we discuss how to formulate the valuation question in a CVM study so that it will be useful in a cost-benefit analysis when people are altruists.

In chapter 8 we consider some further evaluation issues in a risky world. An important issue seldom touched upon in health economics is the value of information in a situation where a measure may have some irreversible effects. This kind of problem gives an extra dimension to the valuation issue: that is, how do we define and measure the value of the option to delay a decision when there is independent R&D going on which may reveal whether the consequences are in fact irreversible?

A second issue is to develop the health production function approach and further illustrate how an intertemporal version can be used to evaluate health changes. In particular, time used up in the production of health is now introduced, and the individual has a job, so that his or her health status can affect the number of hours s/he works or the hourly wage s/he receives.

The final issue considered in chapter 8 is how to define money measures when the survival probability is age-dependent but may be affected through investment in health capital. Parametric changes in the individual's age-dependent health production function and in the survival probability are analyzed using results on the envelope theorem in dynamic optimization; these results considerably simplify the derivations of the results in Rosen (1988), for example. As a by-product, one which should be useful for those working with intertemporal health models, we show how to solve an optimal control problem when the death probability depends on a state variable (health capital); this is not a standard optimal control problem.

It is outside the scope of this book to examine in detail the properties of the outcome measures typically used by health economists, i.e. quality-adjusted life-years (qalys) and healthy-years equivalents (hyes), but chapter 9 introduces these measures. The properties of these measures are indicated and, drawing on the results derived in the previous chapters, some similarities and differences between money measures of utility change and qalys and hyes are examined. Since qalys and hyes are used in cost-effectiveness analysis, the book concludes with a brief discussion of such analysis as compared to cost-benefit analysis.

2   Some basic tools and concepts

In order to derive money measures of the value of changes in health, a number of essential tools and definitions are required. Instead of waiting until these different concepts arise in the text before introducing them, this chapter presents the basic tools used in the subsequent analysis.

The chapter is structured as follows. The first section considers an individual's utility maximization problem within a single-period context. The individual consumes private commodities and values his or her health, and in this section, the health status is treated as fixed by the individual. In the second section, this assumption is abandoned, and a simple health production function approach is presented and discussed. The third section introduces discrete-time intertemporal models, and points out some of the complications which time adds to maximization problems. In the fourth section, risk is introduced, and basic concepts such as expected utility and risk attitudes are defined. The fifth section applies these concepts to problems such as insurance and utility maximization when the probabilities of different outcomes are endogenous. Finally, the sixth section is devoted to some more complex intertemporal utility maximization problems.

Utility maximization

Let us consider an individual consuming n different private commodities x_i, where $i = 1, \ldots, n$. These can be bought in non-negative quantities at given, fixed, strictly positive prices p_i. The individual also values his or her health status, which is 'normalized' so as to range between 0 and some finite positive level, which is often arbitrarily set equal to 1, where 0 is the worst possible health status and 1 is the best possible health status. The individual is viewed as being equipped with an ordinal utility function $U = U(x, z)$, where x is an n component goods vector and z denotes the individual's health status.

Health is here viewed as a homogeneous and well-defined 'commodity'. Alternatively, one may view z as a vector characterizing the individual's health status; see Lancaster (1966) for a presentation of the characteristics

9

approach to consumer choice. For example, the individual's overall well-being is affected by health characteristics such as age, blood pressure, capacity to hear and see, types and degrees of pain, presence of different kinds of infections, number of hours sleep per day, physical condition, mental status (which in turn is composed of different characteristics), and so on. A combination of such characteristics produces a particular level of utility. Viewing z as a univariate variable or an index thus means that the individual is assumed to be able to 'collapse' the different aspects of his health into a single dimension. This seems to be a quite typical assumption employed in health economics, for example when a visual-analogue scale (VAS) is used where the patients are asked to indicate their perceived health status between the worst possible health state (0 cm) and the best possible health state (say, 15 cm). The reader is referred to Drummond (1988, appendix 3) and Mooney (1986, chs. 3–4) for detailed discussions of the nature of the health commodity and how to measure health status.

The utility function $U = U(x, z)$ is assumed to be continuous, increasing in both of its arguments, twice continuously differentiable, and 'well-behaved' so as to generate an interior solution to the individual's utility maximization problem as well as demand functions for private goods having the usual properties. These assumptions are standard and it seems reasonable to employ them, at least for strictly positive z values. If $z = 0$ is interpreted as meaning that the individual is not alive, it does not make sense to define utility levels and demand functions. In what follows, we will assume that z is strictly positive, but in later chapters we will discuss how to define money measures when the individual faces a strictly positive death risk.

In this section, the individual's health status is assumed to be given. Similarly, income, net of any taxes, is taken to be fixed. The problem of utility maximization for the individual can therefore be written as follows:

$$\max_{x} U(x, z)$$
$$\text{s.t. } y - px = 0 \tag{2.1}$$

where y is the fixed income, p is a price vector of order $1 \cdot n$, and any symbol referring to transposed vectors is ignored here and throughout. Any cost of health care is here viewed as being covered by a tax on the individual's gross income; in the next section, we introduce the case in which health care is paid for by the individual.

According to (2.1), the individual is assumed to act as if s/he maximizes a well-behaved utility function subject to a budget constraint. S/he chooses a bundle of consumption goods so as to attain the highest possible level of utility subject to the constraint imposed by the budget in (2.1). First-order conditions for an interior solution to this utility maximization problem are stated in the appendix to this chapter. Solving these conditions for x in terms of prices, income and health yields demand functions for goods:

$$x = x(p, y, z) \tag{2.2}$$

where $x = [x_1(p, y, z), \ldots, x_n(p, y, z)]$ is a vector of goods demands. The quantity of a commodity demanded is a function of prices, income and health status. In particular, note that the individual's health status has an impact on his or her demand for different private goods.

Substitution of (2.2) into the direct utility function in (2.1) yields the *indirect utility function*:

$$V = V(p, y, z) = U[x(p, y, z), z]. \tag{2.3}$$

The indirect utility function expresses utility as a function of prices, income and health. Taking the partial derivative of the indirect utility function with respect to the ith price and income, respectively, and invoking the envelope theorem (see chapter 8) yields:

$$\partial V(.)/\partial p_i = -\lambda x_i(p, y, z) \quad \forall i \tag{2.4}$$
$$\partial V(.)/\partial y = \lambda(p, y, z).$$

Thus the partial derivative of the indirect utility function with respect to a price is equal to minus the demand for that commodity multiplied by λ. In turn, λ is the marginal utility of income; λ can also be interpreted as the Lagrange multiplier associated with the budget constraint in (2.1). Note that the utility derived from an additional dollar, i.e. λ, is a function of the individual's health, among other things. Dividing the first line in (2.4) by the second, one obtains (minus) the demand function for the ith good. This result, which is known as Roy's identity, suggests that a theory of demand may be constructed by making assumptions on the indirect utility function instead of on the direct utility function.

Taking the partial derivative of the indirect utility function with respect to z yields:

$$\partial V(.)/\partial z = \partial U[x(p, y, z), z]/\partial z. \tag{2.4'}$$

This yields the extra utility of a small *ceteris paribus* increase in the individual's health status (strictly speaking, if (2.4') is multiplied by dz for small values of dz). Note that demands for private goods are functions of z. There are therefore adjustments in purchases of goods following a change in z, but these adjustments 'net out' when prices and income are kept constant. This result can easily be verified by differentiating the budget constraint keeping all prices and income constant. The following should

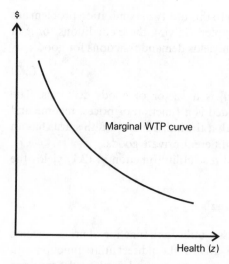

Figure 2.1 A marginal WTP curve for improved health

also be noted: dividing through (2.4′) by the marginal utility of income converts the expression from units of utility to monetary units. The right-hand side expression is then interpreted as *the marginal WTP* for health. A marginal WTP curve for improved health is illustrated in figure 2.1. The curve slopes downwards since the individual, by assumption, is willing to pay less for a marginal increase in health if his or her health is good than if his or her health is bad.

In general, we will use the indirect utility function to define money measures of utility change. Some authors, however, prefer to use the *expenditure function*. This function yields the minimum expenditure necessary to sustain a particular level of utility. The expenditure function is thus defined as follows:

$$e(p,z,U^R) = \min_{x} \, [px: U(x,z) \geq U^R] \tag{2.5}$$

where U^R is the reference level of utility, usually taken to be either the initial or the final level of utility. We will not investigate the properties of this function here, but the interested reader is referred to, for example, Johansson (1987) for a detailed discussion.

A health production function

In the previous section, health was taken as a datum to the individual. This is a questionable assumption, to say the least. In general one expects an

Health (z)

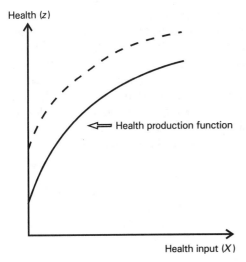

Health input (X)

Figure 2.2 A health production function when there is a single input

individual to have some influence at least on health status. For example, s/he can buy headache pills to relieve a headache, and reduce consumption of fatty foods to reduce blood pressure. One way of introducing such considerations is to view the individual as being equipped with a *health production function*. This is a function capturing the relationship between 'health' goods inputs and health status.

In the simplest possible case, we can view the health production function as follows:

$$z = f(X, z_0) \tag{2.6}$$

where X is a vector of health goods (possibly including goods which also serve as consumption goods), and z_0 is the initial (given) health status. Thus by purchasing health goods, the individual is able to improve his or her health. The health production function 'describes' how different combinations of health goods affect the individual's health. We assume that the health production function is strictly concave, twice continuously differentiable, increasing in all arguments, and that health cannot be improved without bound by increasing the use of a single input. These are restrictive assumptions, but they are useful in introducing the concept of a health production function; see, for example, Wagstaff (1986), Grossman (1972, 1982) and Becker (1965, 1975). In later chapters, the deterministic relationship between inputs and output is replaced by a stochastic relationship.

A single input (strictly concave) health production function is illustrated in figure 2.2. The more of the input that is used, the better the health attained, though at a decreasing rate. An increase in initial health shifts the function upwards, as is illustrated by the dashed line in figure 2.2. In some cases, for example a treatment based on headache pills, the relationship in figure 2.2 seems reasonable, at least if X is not increased so much that side effects occur and health starts to deteriorate. In other cases, say a medical operation, the notion of a health production function may seem hard to apply since there is basically only a binary choice: operate or do not operate. Nevertheless, the quality of the operation may be thought of as a continuous variable (and measured along the horizontal axis in figure 2.2). The concept of the health production function is thus, probably slightly more useful than a first impression may indicate.

When there are health goods the budget constraint of the individual is $y = px + PX$, where P is a vector of prices of health goods and services. Maximizing the utility function in (2.1) subject to the new budget constraint and (2.6) yields demand functions, which can be written as follows:

$$x = x(p, P, y, z_0) \qquad (2.7)$$
$$X = X(p, P, y, z_0)$$

where $X = [X_1(p, P, y, z_0), \ldots, X_k(p, P, y, z_0)]$ denotes a vector of demand functions for health goods and services; see also the appendix at the end of the chapter. We have thus arrived at the usual Marshallian demand functions for health goods also. This has the interesting implication that market demand curves for such goods can be estimated and used in an attempt to evaluate changes in health. A demand curve for a health good/ service is illustrated in figure 2.3. As the price of the good is reduced, demand for the good increases (unless the good is a Giffen good).

The indirect utility function is obtained by substituting the health goods demand functions into (2.6), and then substituting (2.6) and the first line of (2.7) into the direct utility function:

$$V = V(p, P, y, z_0) = U[x(.), f(X(.), z_0)] \qquad (2.8)$$

where we use the same notation as before, for example V still refers to indirect utility, in order to avoid unnecessary clutter. Thus (indirect) utility is a function of prices, income and initial health status. The interested reader may wish to check that the partial derivative of the indirect utility function with respect to the ith goods price and the jth health goods price yields $-\lambda x_i(.)$ and $-\lambda X_j(.)$, respectively, where λ refers to the marginal utility of income.

In the above model, there is no variable input of time in the 'production' of health. In chapter 8, pp. 139–46 pure leisure time is included as an argument in the individual's utility function, time devoted to health

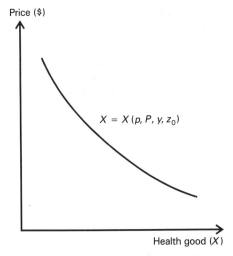

Price ($)

$X = X(p, P, y, z_0)$

Health good (X)

Figure 2.3 A demand curve for a health good

production is included as an argument in the health production function, and labour income is added to the budget constraint. The major difference between the indirect utility function of this problem and those considered previously is that the wage rate now shows up as a separate argument, i.e. $V = V(p, P, w, y^f, z_0)$, where w is the wage rate, treated as fixed by the individual, and y^f denotes his or her fixed non-wage income. A slightly different approach is to assume that the individual, in addition to fixed income y^f, has a variable income which is a (well-behaved) function of health, say $Y = Y(z)$ with $\partial Y(.)/\partial z > 0$. In other words, by improving his or her health, the individual can earn a higher income. According to this approach, the indirect utility function has the same arguments as the function in (2.8) since Y ultimately, i.e. through its dependence on z, is a function of prices, the fixed income and the initial health status.

Intertemporal models

The models considered thus far are atemporal or single-period ones. In order to be able to define money measures for treatments that change an individual's future health profile, we will need intertemporal models. In this section we will consider discrete-time models. A continuous-time model is outlined on pp. 27–30.

Let us consider a T-period model. Goods and services and health status are now indexed according to period. Thus, x_{it} denotes consumption of the ith good in the tth period ($t = 1, \ldots, T$), and z_t is health status in the tth period. In order to be able to compare amounts of money received or paid in different periods, we must introduce some assumptions about the working of capital markets. Here we simply assume that the individual has access to perfect capital markets in which s/he can borrow and lend any amounts at the prevailing market rate of interest. In order to simplify the presentation, this interest rate is taken to be constant over time and is denoted r. The *present value* at the beginning of period 1 of a dollar received in period t ($t \geq 1$) is thus $1/(1+r)^{t-1}$.

The present value of the individual's income is now $\Sigma_t y_{nt}[1/(1+r)^{t-1}]$, where y_{nt} denotes the current value income in period t. If the present value income is denoted y, we can preserve the notation used in previous sections. Similarly, let $p_{it} = p_{nit}/(1+r)^{t-1}$ denote the present value price at the beginning of period 1 of commodity i in period t. The T-period version of the indirect utility function (2.3) can now be written as follows:

$$V = V(p, y, z) = U[x(p, y, z), z] \tag{2.3'}$$

where $p = [p_{11}, \ldots, p_{nT}]$ is a vector of present value prices, y is the present value of all incomes in periods $1-T$, $z = [z_1, \ldots, z_T]$ is a vector containing health status in each period, and $x(p, y, z) = [x_{11}(p, y, z), \ldots, x_{nT}(p, y, z)]$ is a vector of demand functions for consumption goods. Thus we can use the same notation regardless of whether T is equal to one, as on p. 11, or exceeds one, as here. See also (A2.4) and (A2.5) in the appendix to this chapter. Note that the demand for a consumer good in a particular period (and the marginal utility of income) now depends on the entire health profile as captured by the z vector.

Matters are more complicated if we want to consider an intertemporal extension of the health production function model on p. 13. The basic problem is that we must somehow specify how investment in health affects future health. A possible generalization of the health production function (2.6) is as follows:

$$z_{t+1} = f(X_t) - \gamma z_t \tag{2.9}$$

where X_t is the input of, for simplicity, a single health good in period t, and γ is a depreciation factor. According to (2.9), by investing in health, the individual can affect future health status. To sustain a particular level of health s/he must invest so as to neutralize the 'natural' evaporation of health as covered by the depreciation term γz_t in (2.9). (2.9), which is a difference equation, can be interpreted as a health accumulation equation.

The reader may find it a bit disturbing that health is viewed here as being like any other consumer durable. A development would be to explicitly introduce ageing, possibly through a separate term in the health accumulation equation (2.9). One can also add a vector of time-dependent characteristics to either the health production function or the utility function. For our purposes, namely to derive money measures, it is hard to see what insights, if any, such extensions produce. The reader is however referred to p. 30 below and chapters 4 and 8 (pp. 60 and 146–50), where we discuss time-dependent health in a risky world.

Dynamic optimization problems involving difference equations such as the one given by (2.9) are relatively complicated to handle. For this reason, in this section we will consider only a two-period problem. Assume that the utility function is additively separable in time so that it can be written $U = u(x_1, z_1) + v(x_2, z_2)$; the separability assumption is not needed here but is introduced since it will be needed in later chapters. To solve the maximization problem, we use the method of backward induction. First, consider the second-period problem, which is to maximize $v(.)$ with respect to x_2 since z_2 is a datum to the individual according to (2.9); see (A2.6) and (A2.6') in the appendix. This yields second-period demand functions of the form $x_2 = x_2(p_2, y_2 + s, z_2)$, where a subscript 2 refers to the second period and s denotes a saving carried over from period 1. Next, substitute these demand functions into the period 2 utility function. The problem for the individual is then to maximize:

$$\max_{x_1, X_1, s} [u(x_1, z_1) + v_2(p_2, y_2 + s, z_2)] \tag{2.10}$$

subject to the first-period budget constraint $y_1 - s - p_1 x_1 - P_1 X_1 = 0$ and the health accumulation equation $z_2 = f(X_1) - \gamma z_1$, where z_1 is given for the individual. This procedure will yield the full period 1 and period 2 demand functions, and also define conditions for the optimal investment in health. The demand functions will have prices and income as arguments in a quite conventional way. See the appendix for further details.

Introducing risk

A typical feature of medical treatments is that their consequences are not known with certainty in advance. They rather shift the probability that an individual will experience one or another health state. In this section we will introduce some concepts which are needed in the analysis of health in a risky world. We will consider risk rather than uncertainty, i.e. the probabilities that different states of the world or 'events' will occur are knowable, and we will assume that the individual is an expected utility maximizer. The reader interested in the basic axioms underlying the expected utility theorem of von Neumann–Morgenstern (1947) as well as in other approaches to the modelling of behaviour under risk and uncertainty is referred to Arrow (1971), Arrow and Kurz (1970), Dobbs (1991), Hammond (1981), Kahneman and Tversky (1979), Karni and Schmeidler (1991), Loomes *et al.* (1992), Machina (1987), Sugden (1986), Ulph (1982), Viscusi (1989) and Weber and Camerer (1987), to mention just a few. See also the discussion following (2.22) on p. 25.

We have thus far assumed that the individual is equipped with an *ordinal* utility function. This means that if the utility function $U(x,z)$ is a suitable representation of his preferences, any other increasing function or monotonic transformation of $U(x,z)$, say $H(x,z) = h[U(x,z)]$ with $\partial h/\partial U > 0$, will serve equally well. To illustrate, suppose that $U = x^\alpha z^\beta$, i.e. a Cobb–Douglas function. Taking logarithms, which is a monotonic transformation, yields $u = \alpha \ln x + \beta \ln z$. These two utility functions can easily be shown to rank bundles, i.e. combinations of x and z, in the same way. Thus a monotonic transformation leaves the ordinal properties of a utility function unchanged. The signs of the first derivatives of an ordinal function are unchanged by a monotonic transformation, but the signs of higher-order derivatives can change since no restriction can be placed upon $\partial^2 h(.)/\partial U^2$. The definition of risk attitudes, however, is closely related to the signs of second derivatives. We therefore need a stronger assumption than ordinality in order to be able to say anything about an individual's risk attitudes.

Cardinality is such an assumption. There are various forms of cardinality, such as weak cardinality and strong cardinality, but we will not go into details here. The reader is referred to Morey (1984) for a detailed discussion of various forms of cardinality. We will just note that if the utility function $U(x,z)$ is weakly cardinal, any positive affine transformation of the function, say $G(x,z) = a + bU(x,z)$, where a and b are constants and $b > 0$, will serve equally well. Note that the signs of the partial derivatives of any order are unchanged by a positive affine transformation.

In order to illustrate the meaning of risk attitudes, it is useful to consider an individual who faces an uncertain income. There are just two states of the world: the individual's income is either high or low. Let π_1 denote the subjective probability that the high income state occurs; following Jones-Lee (1976) we will interpret our probabilities as subjective ones. The probability that the low income state occurs is therefore $\pi_2 = 1 - \pi_1$. The individual is assumed to be equipped with a well-behaved cardinal indirect utility function $V(p, y_i, z)$ for each possible state of the world where, in the example under investigation, $i = 1,2$, y_1 is a high income and y_2 is a low income. The *expected utility* of the individual is:

$$E(V) = \Sigma_i \pi_i V(p, y_i, z) \tag{2.11}$$

where E is the expectations operator. Expected utility is thus a weighted average of the utility attained in the different states of the world with the probabilities π_i used as the weights. Later, we will introduce a more general model generating the hypothesis of expected utility maximization as a special case.

Taking partial derivatives with respect to income of a well-behaved cardinal indirect sub-utility function $V(p, y_i, z)$ yields:

$$\partial V(.)/\partial y = V_y \qquad (2.12)$$
$$\partial^2 V(.)/\partial y^2 = V_{yy}.$$

An individual is said to be risk averse with respect to income risk if $V_{yy} < 0$. Conversely, he is a risk lover if $V_{yy} > 0$, and risk neutral if $V_{yy} = 0$. Let us consider a Friedman–Savage (1948) diagram such as the one in figure 2.4, in which utility is depicted as an increasing function of income while all prices and health status are held constant.

Figure 2.4a is drawn on the assumptions that $V_{yy} < 0$, while $\pi_1 = \pi_2 = 0.5$. The individual clearly prefers to get the expected income $y^E = 0.5(y_1 + y_2)$ rather than the 'gamble', since:

$$V(p, y^E, z) > E(V) = \Sigma_i \pi_i V(p, y_i, z). \qquad (2.13)$$

Such behaviour, i.e. preferring the expected value of the gamble rather than the gamble, is called risk aversion. By moving horizontally to the left from point A towards point B in figure 2.4a it can be seen that a risk averter is a person who would be willing to forego some part of his or her income in order to change a random prospect into a certain one. The utility function of a risk averter is strictly concave in income.

Figure 2.4b pictures the case of a risk loving individual ($V_{yy} > 0$). In this case the straight line between y_1 and y_2 is above the corresponding segment of the utility function. Thus the individual in figure 2.4b may prefer a risky prospect to a certain one even if the former gives a lower expected income. The risk lover has a utility function which is strictly convex in income.

Finally, a risk neutral individual ($V_{yy} = 0$) has a utility function which is linear in income. Clearly, such an individual will be indifferent between certain and risky prospects provided they yield the same expected income, as is seen from figure 2.4c.

The *cost of risk-bearing* is the amount of money a risk averse individual is willing to forego in order to turn a risky prospect into a certain one. In terms of figure 2.4a, the cost of risk-bearing is an amount of money such that the individual is moved from point A to point B. Denote this amount c. The individual is indifferent between having income $y^E - c$ with certainty and participating in the gamble whose expected outcome is y^E. The amount c is sometimes called the *risk premium* since it is the smallest compensation the individual needs in order to be prepared to choose the risky prospect. For a risk neutral individual the cost of risk is equal to zero since such an individual looks only at the expected outcomes.

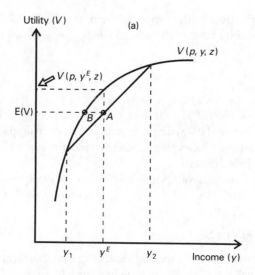

a Risk averse

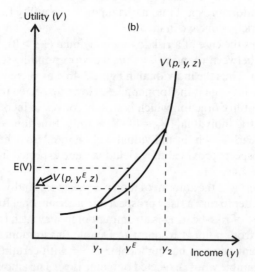

b Risk loving

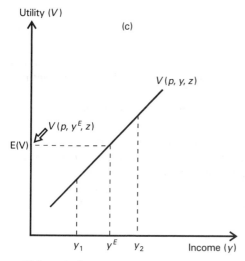

c Risk neutral

Figure 2.4 Attitudes to risk

The individual may of course be risk averse or risk loving with respect to health risk. For a risk averter with respect to health risk $V_{zz} = \partial^2 V(.)/\partial z^2$ is strictly negative, while it is strictly positive for a risk lover, and equal to zero for a risk neutral individual. The reader can get an idea of these concepts by letting z replace y along the horizontal axis in figures 2.4a–c. The reader should also note that a person may be risk averse with respect to health risk while being risk loving with respect to income risk, for example.

The magnitude of the second-order derivative V_{zz} (or V_{yy}) is not invariant under a linear transformation of the utility function. This is readily verified by multiplying the utility function by a constant and taking the second-order derivative with respect to health (or income). For this reason, V_{zz} is not a suitable measure of risk aversion. We can define an Arrow–Pratt coefficient of *absolute* risk aversion by normalizing by $V_z = \partial V(.)/\partial z$, and reversing the sign, to obtain:

$$R^A(z) = - V_{zz}/V_z. \tag{2.14}$$

Multiplying (2.14) by health status z yields a so-called Arrow–Pratt index of *relative* risk aversion:

$$R^R(z) = - z V_{zz}/V_z. \tag{2.14'}$$

In a cardinal world, the signs of the partial derivatives of these measures with respect to health tell us whether risk aversion (risk loving) is increasing or decreasing when health is improved. The reader can check that if the utility function (ignoring income here) is of the form $V = -e^{-\sigma z}$, where σ is a constant, then the individual has constant absolute risk aversion (equal to σ). See Arrow (1971) and Pratt (1964) for details on risk measures. The reader is also referred to the presentation and comparison of different risk measures in Varian (1992, ch. 11).

A final issue to be addressed in this section is how to define expected utility when the individual faces a strictly positive probability of death. If utility associated with the state 'being dead' is said to be undefined or $-\infty$, we are simply unable to proceed; we cannot define a meaningful overall utility function. Still, individuals seem to handle choices involving the risk of losing their lives, for example choosing to fly rather than travel by car in order to save time, quite rationally. The reader is referred to Viscusi (1992) for evidence in this respect. A possible set of assumptions, which will be used as the basic case in the remainder of this book, is as follows:

$$V(p, 0, z > 0) > 0 \qquad (2.15)$$
$$V(p, y, z = 0) = 0 \qquad \forall y > 0.$$

The individual thus prefers to stay alive (avoid health state 0) even if this virtually means a zero income, and no income, however high (and transferred to one's heirs), can compensate for the loss of one's life. In other words, the technically useful assumption (2.15) says that inf $V(p, y, z > 0) > \sup V(p, y, z = 0)$, where 'inf' means infimum and 'sup' means supremum. Alternatively, one may define an income y^* (given p) yielding the minimum survival consumption level. Then, $V(p, y, z > 0) \geq 0$ if $y \geq y^*$, while $V(p, y, z) < 0$ for $y < y^*$. Rosen (1988) shows that $y^* > 0$ produces a non-convexity in the expected utility function. As a consequence, risk averse people can actually prefer more life-risk gambles to less; see Rosen (1988, pp. 287–9) for details. The implications of (2.15) as well as of other assumptions for the possibility of defining money measures of health changes involving the risk of losing one's life are discussed in chapter 4. The reader is also referred to Jones-Lee (1976, 1989) for a discussion of this issue.

Some further comments on risk

In this section, we will use the apparatus just developed to examine a few problems such as the optimal insurance when losses of wealth and health, respectively, are at stake. We will also consider a few generalizations of the simple two-state expected utility model.

Let us start by considering the following experiment. An individual whose present health is z is asked to participate in a treatment yielding either health $z + z_1$ or health $z - z_2$. His present expected utility is $V_0 = V(p, y, z)$. Participating in the treatment yields an expected utility equal to

$$V_1 = \pi_1 V(p, y, z + z_1) + \pi_2 V(p, y, z - z_2) \qquad (2.16)$$

where π_i is the individual's subjective probability that he will experience health state i, for $i = 1, 2$, with the treatment. Differentiating (2.16) with respect to z_1 and letting z_2 adjust so as to keep expected utility constant yields:

$$dV_1 = \pi_1 V_z(p, y, z + z_1) dz_1 - \pi_2 V_z(p, y, z - z_2) dz_2 = 0 \qquad (2.17)$$

where $V_z(.)$ is the marginal utility of health. Suppose that we evaluate (2.17) for $z_1 = z_2 = 0$. Then the marginal utility of health $V_z(.)$ must obviously be equal in both states of the world. It then holds that $dz_2/dz_1 = \pi_1/\pi_2$. That is, by asking the individual about his or her trade-off between small changes in health, we can figure out the ratio of his or her subjective probabilities that the two health states will occur.

Let us next turn to the conventional insurance problem. The individual, whose state-independent income is y, faces a probability of π_1 of losing the amount L. The probability of 'no loss' is $\pi_2 = 1 - \pi_1$ in our simple two-state model. Suppose, however, that the individual is risk averse and can insure against the loss. The insurance premium is p_I per dollar insurance, i.e. paying $\$p_I$ entitles the individual to receive $\$1$ if the 'loss-state' occurs. The problem for the individual is to choose I, the insurance, so as to maximize his or her expected utility:

$$E[V] = \pi_1 V(p, y - L - p_I I + I, z) + \pi_2 V(p, y - p_I I, z) \qquad (2.18)$$

where E denotes the expectations operator. The first-order condition for an interior solution to this maximization problem is as follows:

$$\partial E[V]/\partial I = \pi_1 V_y(p, y - L - p_I I + I, z)(1 - p_I) \\ - \pi_2 V_y(p, y - p_I I, z) p_I = 0 \qquad (2.19)$$

where $V_y(.)$ is the marginal utility of income. If the insurance industry earns zero profits, i.e. $\pi_1(p_I I - I) + \pi_2 p_I I = 0$, so that insurance is actuarially fair, we can set $p_I = \pi_1$ and $(1 - p_I) = \pi_2$ in (2.19). It is then easily verified that our risk averse individual will completely insure against the loss, i.e. set I equal to L. In other words, s/he will buy insurance so as to completely even out the marginal utility of income across the two states of the world. This makes sense, since s/he can increase expected utility by reallocating income from a state in which the marginal utility of income is low (income or wealth is high) to a state in which the marginal utility of income is high (income or wealth is low). The insurance enables the individual to undertake such a reallocation.[1]

Is this result valid for health insurance too? In order to investigate this issue, let us assume that income is state-independent, while health can be either bad (z_1) or good (z_2). As above, the individual can buy an insurance which yields a sum of money if state 1 occurs. The problem is to choose I so as to maximize:

$$E[V] = \pi_1 V(p, y - p_I I + I, z_1) + \pi_2 V(p, y - p_I I, z_2). \qquad (2.20)$$

The first-order condition for an interior solution to this maximization problem can be stated as follows:

$$\partial E[V]/\partial I = \pi_1 V_y(p, y - p_I I + I, z_1)(1 - p_I) - \pi_2 V_y(p, y - p_I I, z_2)p_I = 0. \qquad (2.21)$$

If insurance is actuarially fair, the individual will once again insure so as to even out the marginal utility of income across different states of the world. Note, however, that if the marginal utility of income is independent of health, a risk averse individual facing the maximization problem in (2.20) will not buy insurance; without insurance, the marginal utility of income is equal in the two health states. Similarly, the individual will not insure if his or her marginal utility of income in the good-health state *exceeds* the marginal utility of income in the bad-health state. That is, if the marginal utility of income falls as income increases, buying insurance would further increase the difference.

For the individual in (2.21) it must thus be the case that $V_y(y, z_1) > V_y(y, z_2)$, i.e. the marginal utility of income in the bad-health state must exceed the marginal utility of income in the good-health state. Buying insurance evens out $V_y(.)$ across the two health states. However, it is not necessarily true that s/he insures himself fully in the sense that s/he redistributes income so as to even out *utility* across states of the world. This is the case in the conventional insurance case considered in (2.18)–(2.19), since s/he insures until $I = L$ and hence obtains the same disposable income (wealth), health, and utility in both states of the world. In the case of health risk, the outcome hinges on the second-order properties of the utility function; s/he may overinsure, underinsure or fully insure. The intuitive reason for this ambiguous outcome is that health in the two states influences the choice of insurance strategy: the insurance can even out the marginal utility of income, but cannot necessarily even out total utility between different health states. We will not elaborate upon this issue here. The reader is referred to Besley (1989), Cook and Graham (1977), Jones-Lee (1976), Marshall (1984) and Selden (1993) for detailed investigations.

Nevertheless, life and accident insurances can possibly be used to estimate money measures of the value of health, as will be further discussed in chapter 5.

On p. 16, a health production function was introduced according to which the individual could invest so as to change his health. In a risky world, it is sometimes more fruitful to view the individual as investing so as to change the probability that s/he will experience a particular health state. In order to illustrate this approach within a simple two-state model, let us assume that the individual can change his or her survival probability π by purchasing a health good X, assuming that $\pi = \pi(X)$, where $\pi(X)$ is a strictly concave bounded 'production' function. The direct cardinal utility function is written as $U = U(\pi(X), x)$, where the 'utility' of being dead has been set equal to zero. This is quite a general approach. Suppressing X, three special cases are as follows:

$$U(\pi, x) = \pi u(x) \tag{2.22}$$
$$U(\pi, x) = g(\pi)u(x)$$
$$U(\pi, x) = g(\pi)x.$$

The first line is the conventional expected utility approach. The second line yields the prospect theory model of Kahneman and Tversky (1979). The distinctive feature of this model is the function $g(\pi)$, which derives psychological 'decision weights' from probabilities. The final line presents a similar approach suggested by Handa (1977). The reader is referred to Machina (1987) for a good overview of expected versus non-expected utility theories.

The different approaches in (2.22) are shown merely to illustrate that the function $U = U(\pi(X), x)$, which is used at certain points in this book, is quite general. Nevertheless, there are other approaches to choice under risk such as regret theory, see Loomes and Sugden (1982), which are not covered by this book. We also avoid situations with 'ambiguity' where probabilities are not known, but lie somewhere between 0 and 1. In such situations people may learn more over time as more information arrives, i.e. they update or revise the probabilities according to, for example, Bayes' law. The reader is referred to Demers (1991) for such a model; see also Johansson (1993, pp. 174–7) who uses Demers' model to undertake a social cost-benefit analysis of the optimal size of a pollution treatment plant when decisions are irreversible and the decision-maker learns more over time.

Maximizing $U = U(\pi(X), x)$ with respect to x and X subject to the budget constraint $y = px + PX$, where P is the price of the health good, is assumed to yield an indirect utility function of the form

$$V(p, P, y) = U[\pi(p, P, y), x(p, P, y)]. \tag{2.22'}$$

We assume that this function is well-behaved in the usual sense for $\pi \in (0,1)$. Thus the individual 'maximizes out' π. There is a gain of increasing the survival probability π but also a cost in the form of reduced consumption. The individual invests in increasing the survival probability until the marginal gain from a further increase is equal to the marginal cost of the increase. This approach can be generalized so as to include within-household altruism, for example parents who invest so as to increase the survival probabilities of their children, and more general altruism. We will come back to these issues in later chapters. The reader is also referred to Jones-Lee (1991, 1992).

We have thus far considered models with a finite number of outcomes (in fact, two-state models). In some cases, it is natural to view the number of possible outcomes as infinitely large; for example, health status may be viewed as a continuous variable. Let us once again consider the simple indirect utility function $V(p,y,z)$ and assume that health is a continuous and stochastic variable. Let the triple (Ω, B, μ) be a probability space, where B is a so-called Borel algebra of sub-sets of the uncountable state space Ω, and μ is a probability measure defined on B; see Shiryayev (1984) and Stokey and Lucas (1989) for details. The probability measure gives the probability assigned to each possible state of the world. We assume here that health is bounded away from zero and bounded from above.

The expected utility of the individual can then be formulated in the following way:

$$E(V) = \int_{\Omega} V[p,y,z(\omega)]d\mu(\omega) \qquad (2.23)$$

where $\omega \in \Omega$. Instead of the probability measure, we will often use the distribution function. To arrive at this function let $\Omega = [a,b]$ and take $B = [a, z_\epsilon]$. Then we have $\mu(a, z_\epsilon) = F(z_\epsilon)$ for $z_\epsilon \in \Omega$, where $F(z_\epsilon)$ is a distribution function defined over the support $[a,b]$. Thus $F(z_\epsilon) = \text{prob}\{z \le z_\epsilon\}$ yields the probability that health (z) is no better than z_ϵ, i.e. is in the interval $[a, z_\epsilon]$, and $F(a) = 0$ and $F(b) = 1$.

The continuous-state model in (2.23) can be used to examine how to choose an optimal insurance. The first-order conditions for the optimal insurance in the continuous-state model represent a straightforward generalization of the conditions set out in (2.19), and are therefore stated in the appendix. Next, let us outline how to apply the continuous-state approach to the two-period maximization problem set out in (2.10). Assume that period 2 health is a stochastic variable, as viewed from today. Health status is however revealed at the beginning of period 2, implying that second-period consumption is chosen after uncertainty is revealed. Given this kind of uncertainty, and the assumption that the individual survives to the end of period 2, the maximization problem specified in (2.10) can be written as follows:

$$\max_{x_1, X_1, s} [u(x_1, z_1) + \int_\Omega v_2(p_2, y_2 + s, z_2(\omega))d\mu(\omega)] \tag{2.24}$$

subject to the first-period budget constraint $y_1 - s - p_1 x_1 - P_1 X_1 = 0$ and the health accumulation equation $z_2 = f(X_1) - \gamma z_1$. Of course, one must in addition specify how uncertainty enters into the 'production' of second-period health. We will, however, leave this issue to chapter 8, pp. 137–42, where the model is solved.

More complex intertemporal models

In some cases it may be of interest to consider continuous-time rather than discrete-time models. It would take us too far to go fully into the details of continuous-time models, but a simple continuous-time model with a health production function is outlined in this section. Initially, it is assumed that there is no uncertainty, but this assumption is relaxed later.

In order to develop a continuous-time model, we must assume that the individual has an instantaneous utility function, written as $u = u[x(t), h(t)]$, where $x(t)$ is consumption at date t, and $h(t)$ is interpreted as his or her *health capital* at date t. Health capital is produced by refraining from consuming goods and investing the resources in the health sector. It is assumed that $u(.)$ is twice continuously differentiable, strictly quasi-concave and increasing in its arguments.

The overall utility function of the individual is written as follows:

$$U = \int_0^T u[x(t), h(t)]e^{-\theta t}dt \tag{2.25}$$

where θ is the discount rate, and T is the length of life. Thus the individual is assumed to be concerned with the present value at time 0 of his or her future utility.

The accumulation of health follows the equation:

$$\dot{h} = \zeta(X) - \gamma h = f(X, h, \gamma) \tag{2.26}$$

where a dot denotes a time derivative, i.e. dh/dt, $\zeta(X)$ is a health production function, and γ is a depreciation factor. Thus, once again, we simplify matters by viewing health as any consumer durable. This problem can be handled at least partially by introducing time, t, as an argument in either the health production function or in the utility function. Then, ageing is introduced as a part of the individual's health profile; see (2.33) for such an extension.

The dynamic budget constraint of the individual is written as follows:

$$x(t) + X(t) + \dot{k} = w(t) + r(t)k(t) \qquad (2.26')$$

where k denotes real capital (assets) and r is the constant rate of interest. The left-hand side of the budget constraint is the sum of consumption, resources set aside for health investments, and the net accumulation of real capital (assets) at time t; there is thus a single homogeneous good whose price is normalized to unity. The right-hand side of the budget constraint consists of labour income, $w(t)$, and capital income at time t. It is assumed that the supply of labour is fixed (and normalized to 1 unit).

The maximization problem of the individual is assumed to be as follows:

$$\max_{x,X} U = \int_0^T u[x(t), h(t)]e^{-\theta t} dt \qquad (2.27)$$

subject to the dynamic budget constraint and the health accumulation equation:

$$\dot{k}(t) = w(t) + r(t)k(t) - x(t) - X(t) \qquad (2.27')$$

$$\dot{h}(t) = f[X(t), h(t), \gamma] \qquad (2.27'')$$

where, in order to simplify the presentation of the first-order conditions for a solution to this problem, we assume that the time horizon is infinite, i.e. $T = \infty$.

The (current value) Hamiltonian of this maximization problem can be written as follows:

$$H(x, X, h, \gamma, k, \mu_k, \mu_h) = u[x(t), h(t)] + \mu_k[w(t) + r(t)k(t) - x(t) \qquad (2.28)$$
$$- X(t)] + \mu_h[f[X(t), h(t), \gamma]]$$

where μ_k and μ_h are costate variables. Necessary conditions for an interior solution to this maximization problem are stated in the appendix to this chapter. Here we will just make a few comments on these conditions. Combining (A2.9i) and (A2.9ii), one finds that in optimum the marginal utility of consumption is equal to the marginal utility of health obtained by purchasing another unit of health goods. According to (A2.9iv), the individual will invest in health until the marginal WTP for health is equal to the discount rate *plus* the depreciation of health capital (assuming a steady state).

Assume finally that the length of life is uncertain, i.e. that T in (2.27) is stochastic. Let us assume that the death probability, denoted δ, is a constant, though in chapter 8 it will be viewed as an increasing function of age, i.e. the older one is, the more likely it is that one will die, but a decreasing function of the health capital.

Following Blanchard (1985), it is assumed that assets left by the deceased are distributed to the rest of the population by an inverted perfect insurance system; variations of Blanchard's insurance system seem to be used by virtually all authors within the field. The economy consists of a steady-state population, the size of which is normed to equal one. At each instant of time (interval of length ds), δ identical individuals are born. Of the cohort born s periods ago, there remain in the aggregate at time t, $\delta e^{-\delta(t-s)}$ individuals. This means that the total population at time t equals:

$$POP = \int_{-\infty}^{t} \delta e^{-\delta(t-s)} ds = 1. \tag{2.29}$$

At each instant of time, δ identical individuals also leave the population; each of these, on average, owns *per capita* assets of size $k(t)$, giving rise to *per capita* income of $\delta k(t)$. The individual obtains these benefits conditional on leaving his or her assets to the insurance system when s/he dies. In the aggregate, the law of large numbers makes profits in the insurance system equal to zero.

The individual therefore maximizes expected present value utility:[2]

$$\max_{[x, X]} E[u_0] = \int_{0}^{\infty} u[x(t), h(t)] e^{-(\theta + \delta)t} dt \tag{2.30}$$

subject to the dynamic budget constraint and the health accumulation equation:

$$\dot{k}(t) = w(t) + [r(t) + \delta]k(t) - x(t) - X(t) \tag{2.30'}$$

$$\dot{h}(t) = f[X(t), h(t), \gamma]. \tag{2.30''}$$

The left-hand side of the dynamic budget constraint is the net accumulation of assets at time t. The right-hand side consists of labour income, $w(t)$, and capital income at time t *less* the sum of consumption and resources set aside for health investments. Capital income consists of two components: profit income, $r(t)k(t)$, and income from the insurance system, $\delta k(t)$.

To assure that the individual does not violate the reasonable debt constraint, that debt does not increase faster than the interest rate, the following condition is imposed:

$$\lim_{t \to \infty} k(t) e^{-\int_0^t (r(s) + \delta) ds} = 0. \tag{2.31}$$

This condition is frequently referred to as a No-Ponzi game condition. The dynamic budget constraint in combination with (2.31) can be used to show, by integrating the budget constraint forwards, that the present value at time 0 of total consumption, $(x + X)$, equals the present value of wage plus capital income, where the discount factor at time t is equal to the sum of the interest rate r and the death intensity parameter δ:

$$\int_0^\infty [x(t) + X(t)]e^{-(\delta+r)t}dt = k(0) + \int_0^\infty [w(t)]e^{-(\delta+r)t}dt \qquad (2.32)$$

where, for the sake of simplicity, the rate of interest $r(t)$ is assumed to be constant over time. The maximization problem outlined here produces first-order conditions for an interior solution which are very similar to those obtained for the certainty case. The reason is the fact that the insurance system virtually eliminates uncertainty. The reader is referred to chapter 8, pp. 146–50 for a detailed analysis of a generalized version of the above model. See also Rosen (1988) who analyzes a similar model, though there is no health capital accumulation in his model.

Let us finally introduce an age-dependent utility function $u(\tau) = u[x(\tau), \tau]$, where the direct dependence on health capital is ignored. Integrating this function between zero and t yields the total present value utility of living for t years, and we assume that total present value utility is an increasing function of t, i.e. age. We speak of present value utility, since the individual's instantaneous utility function is time-dependent. This utility function thus captures any discounting of consumption at different points of time. The individual now maximizes:

$$\max_x E[u_0] = \int_0^\infty \left(\int_0^t u[x(\tau), \tau]d\tau \right) F_d(t)dt = \int_0^\infty u[x(t), t]e^{-\delta t}dt \quad (2.33)$$

subject to the expected life-time budget constraint (2.32) (or (2.30′) with $X(t) = 0$ for all t since health capital is ignored here and (2.31)). In (2.33) we have introduced $F_d(t)$ which is the probability density of living for exactly t years. The probability δdt of dying in a short interval $(t, t + dt)$ conditional on having survived until time t is given by the hazard $\delta dt = (F_d(t)/[1 - F(t)])dt$, where $F(t)$ is the cumulative distribution function (*cdf*) which yields the probability of dying before or at age t (and an exponential distribution of the age of death is assumed here as before). This relationship has been used in order to arrive at the equality in (2.33); see chapter 8, pp. 151–2 for further details. The reader is referred to Chang (1991) for a comparative statics analysis of a model very similar to the one given by (2.32)–(2.33).

Appendix

First-order conditions for an interior solution to the maximization problem in (2.1) in the main text are as follows:

$$\partial U(.)/\partial x_i = \lambda p_i \qquad \forall i$$

$$y = px$$

$$(A2.1)$$

where λ is the Lagrange multiplier associated with the budget constraint. Solving these conditions for x (and λ) yields the demand functions stated in (2.2).

The maximization problem on p. 14 is as follows:

$$\max_{[x,X]} U[x, f(X, z_0)]$$
$$\text{s.t. } y - px - PX = 0.$$

$$(A2.2)$$

First-order conditions for an interior solution to this optimization problem are:

$$\partial U(.)/\partial x_i = \lambda p_i \quad \forall i$$
$$\partial U(.)/\partial X_j = \lambda P_j \quad \forall j$$
$$y - px - PX = 0$$

$$(A2.3)$$

where λ denotes the Lagrange multiplier associated with the budget constraint in (A2.2). Solving these conditions yields the demand functions in (2.7).

The utility function used on p. 16 is:

$$U = U(x_{11}, \ldots, x_{nT}, z_1, \ldots, z_T)$$

$$(A2.4)$$

and the budget constraint is:

$$\Sigma_t [y_{nt} - \Sigma_i p_{nit} x_{it}] 1/(1+r)^{t-1} = y - \Sigma_t \Sigma_i p_{it} x_{it} = y - px = 0 \qquad (A2.4')$$

where the individual is assumed to leave no assets/debts to his or her heirs at the end of period T. First-order conditions for an interior solution to the problem of maximizing (A2.4) subject to (A2.4') are as follows:

$$\partial U(.)/\partial x_{it} = \lambda p_{it} \quad \forall i, t$$
$$y = px$$

$$(A2.5)$$

where λ is the Lagrange multiplier associated with the budget constraint (A2.4'). Conditions (A2.5) are straightforward generalizations of conditions (A2.1).

Turning to the two-period health production approach, the second-period problem is to maximize:

$$v(x_2, z_2)$$

$$(A2.6)$$

with respect to x_2 subject to:

$$y_{n2} + s(1+r) - p_{n2} x_2 = 0.$$

$$(A2.6')$$

Note that the sum of savings plus interest income is equal to $s(1+r)$. Dividing through (A2.6') by $(1+r)$ converts the expression to a present value. Solving this maximization problem yields demand functions of the form $x_2 = x_2(p_2, y_2 + s, z_2)$. In principle, the maximization problem stated in (2.10) in the main text yields demand functions of the form:

$$x_t = x_t(p, P_1, y, z_1) \tag{A2.7}$$
$$X_1 = X_1(p, P_1, y, z_1)$$
$$s = s(p, P_1, y, z_1)$$

where a subscript 1 refers to the first period and $t = 1, 2$.

The expected utility model in (2.23) can be used to derive the conditions for the choice of optimal insurance coverage in the following way. Denote the financial loss $L(\omega)$, and the fraction of the loss repaid by the insurance company $aL(\omega)$, provided the individual pays a premium equal to aK, where K is equal to the expected loss, i.e. $E[L(\omega)]$. Thus, $a = 1$ means full insurance coverage. The problem is to choose a so as to maximize:

$$E(V) = \int_\Omega V[p, y - L(\omega) - aK + aL(\omega), z] d\mu(\omega) \tag{A2.8}$$

The first-order conditions for an interior solution to this maximization problem are:

$$\int_\Omega V_y[p, y - L(\omega) - aK + aL(\omega), z](L(\omega) - K) d\mu(\omega) = 0 \tag{A2.8$'$}$$

These equations can be used to show that the optimal a is equal to one, given an actuarially fair insurance system.

The solution of the control problem defined by (2.27), with $h(0) = h_0$ and $k(0) = k_0$, where h_0 and k_0 are constants, must fulfil the following necessary conditions:

$$u_x(\cdot) - \mu_k = 0 \tag{A2.9i}$$

$$\mu_h f_X(\cdot) - \mu_k = 0 \tag{A2.9ii}$$

$$\dot{\mu}_k - \theta \mu_k = -\partial H / \partial k \tag{A2.9iii}$$

$$\dot{\mu}_h - \theta \mu_h = -\partial H / \partial h \tag{A2.9iv}$$

$$\dot{k} = w(t) + r(t)k(t) - x(t) - X(t) \tag{A2.9v}$$

$$\dot{h} = f(X, h, \gamma) \tag{A2.9vi}$$

where the costate variables μ_k and μ_h have the same meaning as in (2.28), and $\partial H / \partial h = u_h(.) - \mu_h \gamma$. There are also certain transversality conditions which must be satisfied; see Johansson and Löfgren (1994a) or Seierstad and Sydsæter (1987). A steady state is here taken to mean that the time derivatives of μ_k and μ_h are equal to zero.

3 Evaluating health changes in a certain world

In this chapter, money measures of the value of health changes are introduced, and their properties are examined. Throughout the chapter it is assumed that individuals do not face any uncertainty. This assumption will enable us to point out central properties of money measures, properties which carry over to the more complex risky world money measures which are introduced in chapter 4.

The chapter is structured as follows. The first section defines two money measures of the value of a change in health, the compensating variation (CV) and the equivalent variation (EV). The properties of these measures are investigated in the second section, while the third section presents a simple numerical example which hopefully illustrates the results of the previous discussion. The fourth section discusses how the calculation of intertemporal money measures can sometimes be simplified by using annual data. The two final sections define the conditions under which market prices can be used to evaluate health.

Two money measures of a change in health

Consider the individual in (2.3') (p. 16) who derives satisfaction from consuming n different private goods, and his or her health status in each of T periods. The individual's indirect utility function can be written as:

$$V = U[x(p, y, z), z] = V(p, y, z) \tag{3.1}$$

where the vector x is interpreted as $x(p, y, z) = [x_{11}(p, y, z), \ldots, x_{nT}(p, y, z)]$, i.e. as a vector of demand functions for private goods with the quantity demanded being a function of prices, income, and the health profile experienced, and z is a health profile vector such that the worst possible health state in period t ($t = 1, \ldots, T$) is $z_t = 0$ and full health is $z_t = 1$; initially it is assumed that $z_t > 0$ for all t. How the government finances its expenditures on health care is not explicitly considered here, but one possibility is to interpret y in (3.1) as after-tax income. Moreover, it is assumed that health status is exogenous to the individual, i.e. we ignore here

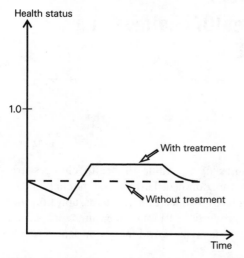

Figure 3.1 Illustration of how a treatment affects health

the possibility that the individual can 'produce' health. The indirect utility function in (3.1) is decreasing in prices, and increasing in income and the quality of health and is assumed to possess all other properties usually employed in microeconomics. See, for example, Varian (1992) for details.

Let us now introduce a change in health. For simplicity, this change is taken here to leave all prices as well as individual income unchanged. As is illustrated in figure 3.1, the considered project/treatment improves health in some periods and reduces health in others. This is however a quite general case since utility increases in some periods and decreases in others. The case illustrated in figure 3.1 is very demanding for any measure, for example a money measure, of the change in utility since we want the chosen measure to indicate whether or not the treatment increases utility.

The change in utility associated with the considered treatment is defined as follows:

$$\Delta V = V(p, y, z^1) - V(p, y, z^0) \tag{3.2}$$

where a superscript 0 (1) denotes initial (final) level values for the individual's health profile. Since the utility function is not observable, we need a money measure to evaluate the change in utility. Although a great number of measures have been proposed in the literature, attention is focused here on the concepts of compensating and equivalent variation. The reader interested in other, less frequently used, measures is referred to McKenzie (1983) and Ng (1979).

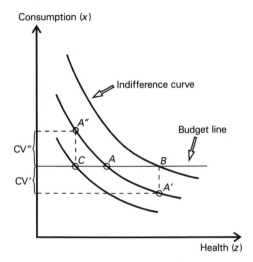

Figure 3.2 The CV associated with a change in health

Consider first the compensating variation (CV). This is an amount of money such that:[1]

$$V(p, y - \mathrm{CV}, z^1) = V(p, y, z^0). \tag{3.3}$$

The CV gives the maximum (once and for all) amount of money that can be taken from the individual while leaving him or her just as well off as s/he was before an improvement in health. In other words, CV is the willingness to pay (WTP) for an improvement in health. If health quality deteriorates, CV is the minimum amount of money that must be given to the individual to compensate him or her for the loss of health quality. CV thus measures the willingness to accept compensation (WTA) for a deterioration in health. This is illustrated for the (single-period) single private good-health 'good' case in figure 3.2.

Since health quality is assumed to be supplied free of charge, the budget line is horizontal. In the initial situation the individual is at point A. After an improvement in health the individual consumes the combination given by point B, attaining a higher level of utility than previously. Reducing the individual's income by an amount CV' will hold the individual at the initial level of utility. Combinations A' and A fall on the same indifference curve, the initial one. Similarly, a reduction in health given by point C requires a monetary compensation, equal to CV'' in figure 3.2, if the individual is to remain at his or her initial level of utility.

It should be stressed that CV in (3.3) is interpreted as a once and for all

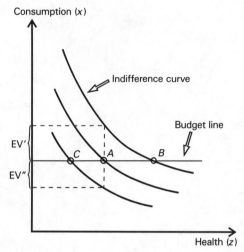

Figure 3.3 The EV associated with a change in health

payment/compensation. Due to the assumption that the individual has access to perfect capital markets, one can alternatively interpret CV as yearly payments cv_t such that $CV = \Sigma_t cv_t[1/(1+r)]^{t-1}$, where r is the discount rate, for simplicity kept constant. On pp. 41–2, we will discuss how to calculate money measures when the individual is unable to reallocate income and consumption over time.

Consider next the equivalent variation (EV). This is an amount of money such that:

$$V(p, y + \text{EV}, z^0) = V(p, y, z^1). \tag{3.4}$$

The EV is the minimum amount of money that must be given to the individual to make him or her as well off as s/he could have been after an improvement in health. If health deteriorates, EV is the maximum amount that the individual is willing to pay to prevent that deterioration. These definitions are illustrated in figure 3.3, where EV′ is the compensation needed to make the individual as well off as after an improvement in health from A to B, while EV″ is his or her WTP to prevent a deterioration in health from A to C. By comparing figures 3.2 and 3.3, the reader can verify that the CV of an improvement from A to B is equal to the EV of a deterioration from B to A. In other words, the CV associated with a particular improvement/deterioration is equal to the EV associated with the opposite change.

We have thus defined two money measures of a change in health. These measures are called income-compensated or Hicksian money measures since the individual pays or is compensated so as to remain throughout at the pre-specified level of satisfaction. Before we introduce uncompensated or Marshallian money measures of changes in health, we will explore some of the properties of CV and EV measures.

On the properties of compensated money measures

In general, the CV and EV measures impute different dollar values to a utility change. This is because the monetary valuation of a good depends on the utility level attained, as will be explained below. Both measures are, however, sign-preserving in the sense that they have the same sign as the underlying change in utility. Substitution of (3.3) and (3.4) respectively into (3.2) and using the intermediate value theorem reveals that:

$$\Delta V = V_y(p, y^a, z^1) \cdot \text{CV} \qquad\qquad (3.5)$$
$$\Delta V = V_y(p, y^b, z^0) \cdot \text{EV}$$

where $V_y(\cdot)$ is the individual's marginal utility of income, i.e. $\partial V(\cdot)/\partial y$, evaluated at some intermediate incomes $y^a \in (y, y - \text{CV})$ and $y^b \in (y, y + \text{EV})$, respectively, so as to preserve the equalities between left-hand side and right-hand side expressions in (3.5). Since the marginal utility of income is strictly positive for a non-satiated individual, the sign of CV (EV) must be the same as the sign of the change in utility caused by the change in the individual's health profile. This is true also for treatments, such as the one illustrated in figure 3.1, which improve health in some periods and reduce health in others. The marginal utility of income in (3.5) converts CV and EV from monetary units to units of utility, so that the left-hand side and right-hand side expressions in (3.5) refer to the same kind of units.

The two money measures are sign-preserving also in the more general case where, in addition to health, all relative prices and/or income change. This result can easily be verified by allowing p and y to change in (3.3) and (3.4), and deriving a new version of (3.5). In the first line of (3.5), prices and income, just like z, are evaluated at final levels, while they are evaluated at initial levels, just like z, in the second line of (3.5). The money measures are also *path-independent*, i.e. the order in which we change health, prices and income does not affect the magnitudes of CV and EV. We will come back to this issue in the appendix to this chapter.

If the underlying utility function is quasi-linear, see p. 41, so that the marginal utility of income is a positive constant, then the two money measures defined in (3.5) must obviously coincide. However, a quasi-linear utility function implies that all (additional) income is spent on a single commodity, i.e. demands for all other private goods are independent of income (above some minimum level). This is a questionable description of individual behaviour, to say the least. Suppose next that health is normal in the sense that the marginal WTP for the good increases with income. In this case EV > CV since EV is evaluated at the final utility level and CV at the initial utility level.[2]

This result has an important implication for applied research in the field. Let us assume that we have collected preference information by asking individuals how they value some change in health. If the money measure is interpreted as an equivalent variation and the good is normal, we know that the resulting amount of money would be larger than if individuals had been questioned about their CV.

Even though theory, as indicated above, tells us that CV and EV of the same change should differ in magnitude in general, empirical comparisons reveal unexpectedly large differences between WTP and WTA; see, for example, Rowe *et al.* (1980), Hammack and Brown (1974), Bishop and Heberlein (1979), Brookshire *et al.* (1980), Coursey *et al.* (1987) and Knetsch and Sinden (1984). No simple and completely convincing explanation of these large differences is available. However, an interesting idea put forward by Hanemann (1991) for environmental goods is that the substitution possibilities between environmental goods and other goods (money) play a crucial role. The more difficult it is to replace a loss of environmental goods with other goods, i.e. the steeper the indifference curves are to the left of the initial combination of private and environmental goods, the higher the compensation needed in order for the individual to accept the loss. In turn, this tends to create a large difference between the compensation or loss measure (WTA) and the willingness to pay (WTP) for more environmental goods. On the other hand, if there is a high degree of substitutability between environmental goods and ordinary market goods, then the compensation measure and WTP should be close in value. The same reasoning may be applied to public health care as well. In fact, a recent experiment with real payments/compensations by Shogren *et al.* (1994) reveals a convergence of WTP and WTA for a market good. However, for a non-market good (reduced health risk) with imperfect substitutes, they record a persistent difference between WTP and WTA. Several other possible explanations for the frequently observed large differences between WTP/WTA measures have also been suggested; the reader is referred to Gregory (1986) and Harless (1989) for a detailed discussion of these. To the best of my knowledge, there is no empirical evidence on the WTP/WTA issue in the case of health status except the study by Shogren *et al.* (1994).

The next question is whether our money measures can be infinitely large. With regard to an increase in z, the CV is a payment and is hence bounded by income. In the case of a decrease in z, the EV becomes the WTP measure and cannot exceed income. Apparently, however, nothing ensures that a compensation requirement falls short of income or even infinity. Suppose, though, that health is non-essential in the sense that $U(x,z) = U(x',0)$, i.e. any bundle including z can be matched by a bundle (x') excluding z. This is a necessary and sufficient condition for the health good to always have a finite consumer's surplus regardless of whether the surplus measure is the CV or the EV or some uncompensated money measure; see Willig (1978) for details. Geometrically, this is equivalent to all indifference surfaces intersecting the $z = 0$ hyperplane. Health and many environmental services such as air to breathe and water to drink are, however, ultimately essential, i.e. it does not make sense to compensate for the complete loss of these goods. Meaningful money measures can be defined for changes in the availability/quality of such goods and services provided that we do not pass critical levels. If the availability/quality of essential resources such as health is reduced too much, however, the monetary compensation needed in order to compensate for such reductions/losses may approach infinity.

Sometimes the investigator is interested in ranking several different treatments or health profiles. By introducing a third vector or health profile z^2 corresponding to utility level U^2, it is easy to show that the EV measure ranks any three (any number of) bundles in the same order as the underlying utility function. The EV measure uses z^0 as base bundle in comparing the bundles, i.e.:

$$V(p, y + EV^i, z^0) = V(p, y, z^i) \tag{3.6}$$

for treatment no. i (with $i = 1,2,\ldots$). Thus, in order to preserve the equality in (3.6) EV has to adjust, since all other left-hand side terms remain constant across health profiles. As a result, if treatment no. 2 (z^2) produces a higher utility than treatment no. 1 (z^1), $EV^2 > EV^1$. Proceeding in this way, the reader can use the EV measure to rank any number of projects/treatments correctly.

The CV measure, on the other hand, evaluates changes at final z values. Thus, we have:

$$V(p, y - CV^i, z^i) = V(p, y, z^0). \tag{3.7}$$

The problem in using the CV measure to rank several different projects is that both CV and z adjust in the left-hand side expression. This complication implies that CV^2 may exceed CV^1 although the individual's utility function ranks z^1 above z^2. This ranking failure can occur if $z_t^1 > z_t^2$ for some period(s) while $z_t^1 < z_t^2$ for some other period(s), i.e. if the two health profiles intersect. It can be shown, see Johansson (1987), that a quasi-linear utility function ensures that the CV measure ranks an arbitrary number of projects/treatments in the same order as the individual's own utility function.

It should be stressed that both money measures are suitable for binary comparisons, for example for a comparison of a particular treatment with no treatment at all. The ranking problem appears if we want to compare, i.e. rank, several different treatments. For the sake of completeness the following should also be noted. If there are two or more initial commodity bundles (health profiles) but only one final bundle (health profile), then it is easy to show that the bundles are ranked in the same order by both the CV measure and the individual's utility function. This is not necessarily true for the EV measure. For an empirical study facing this problem in using the EV measure the reader is referred to Johansson *et al.* (1988).

An example: using CV and EV

We have derived some general results concerning the properties of CV/EV measures. Some of these results may seem quite abstract and hard to understand. One can often get a fuller understanding of these results by working through simple examples. In this section we will therefore use a simple atemporal utility function to illustrate the CV/EV measures as well as some of the properties just discussed. We show how to define money measures, how the sign of CV/EV is related to the sign of a change in health and how our money measures can be used to rank two or more medical treatments.

A very common utility (and production) function in economics is the Cobb–Douglas function: $U = x^a z^{1-a}$, where a is a strictly positive parameter. The Cobb–Douglas function is linearly homogeneous, i.e. doubling all inputs doubles the utility (output), as is easily verified. Here we will take logarithms of the function in order to simplify the calculations: $u = \ln U = a \ln x + (1-a) \ln z$, where $z \in (0, \infty)$. This is an example of a monotonic transformation preserving the ranking, i.e. ordinal, properties of the utility function. Using the budget constraint $y = px$, it is easily verified that the indirect utility function can be written as follows:

$$V = a(\ln y - \ln p) + (1-a)\ln z. \tag{3.8}$$

Taking the partial derivatives with respect to p and y, the reader can easily verify that this function has the properties discussed in chapter 2, p. 11.

Suppose that we want to calculate the CV of a *ceteris paribus* change in z (health) and y (income) from z^0, y^0 to z^1, y^1. This is an amount of money such that:

$$a[\ln(y^1 - CV) - \ln p] + (1-a)\ln z^1 = a[\ln y^0 - \ln p] + (1-a)\ln z^0. \tag{3.9}$$

Thus CV keeps the individual at his initial level of utility. Consider next the EV of the *ceteris paribus* change in health and income. The EV is defined as follows:

$$a[\ln(y^0 + EV) - \ln p] + (1 - a)\ln z^0 = a[\ln y^1 - \ln p] + (1 - a)\ln z^1. (3.9')$$

The EV thus keeps the individual at his or her final level of utility. From (3.9) and (3.9') it should be obvious that CV and EV are increasing in z; the larger z^1 is, the larger are CV and EV for any given z^0. Moreover, both money measures have the same sign as the change in utility. To illustrate, if $z^1 \geq z^0$ (with $y^1 = y^0$) so that $\Delta V \geq 0$, then CV, EV ≥ 0. Also, if z^1 approaches $+\infty$, EV, which is a compensation whenever z^1 exceeds z^0, becomes infinitely large. Alternatively, if $z^1 < z^0$, CV is a compensation, implying that as z^1 approaches zero (from above), CV approaches $-\infty$. Thus, health (z) is an essential good according to the chosen utility function; utility is undefined if the individual dies. Substitution of (3.9') into (3.9), holding income constant, reveals after straightforward calculations that EV > CV, i.e. health is a 'normal' good. In order to check the ranking properties of the two money measures, the reader may care to work through the following example. Set $a = 0.5$, $y^0 = 100$, $p = 1$, and $z^0 = 1$, and assume that two different treatments are possible. The first treatment leaves y unchanged, i.e. $y^0 = y^1 = 100$, but increases z from $z^0 = 1$ to $z^1 = 2$. The second treatment reduces income (due to sick leave) from $y^0 = 100$ to $y^2 = 66.7$ and increases z from $z^0 = 1$ to $z^2 = 3$. This means that both treatments cause the same increase in utility (from $V \approx 2.3$ to $V \approx 2.65$). Show that $EV^1 = EV^2 \approx 100$, while $CV^1 \approx 50 \neq CV^2 \approx 33.4$. The reader can also use (3.9) and (3.9') to verify that the CV and the EV of a *ceteris paribus* change in income are equal to the change in income: for example, $y^1 = 110$ and $y^0 = 100$ implies that $CV = EV = 10$.

The reader may also care to check the properties of the following *quasi-linear* utility function: $U = ax + \ln z$, where a is a positive constant. Maximize this function subject to $y = px$, and examine the properties of the indirect utility function; alternatively substitute $x = y/p$, obtained from the budget constraint, into the direct utility function to obtain the indirect utility function. Show that $CV = EV$.

Overall versus instantaneous money measures

The WTP measures discussed above may be called overall or life-time measures. In terms of figure 3.1, the individual is asked to place a monetary value on the 'rest-of-life' shift in health profile. Suppose, however, that the WTP is instead calculated at each point in time or on an annual basis, as would probably be the procedure in an empirical study because of the obvious problems entailed in calculating an overall or life-time measure. Drawing on Blackorby et al. (1984), we should ask whether the present value of these instantaneous WTP amounts has the same sign as the overall utility change.

The life-time utility maximization problem assumes that the individual is free to borrow and lend any amount of money at the prevailing market rate of interest. The instantaneous or 'annual' indirect utility functions, on the other hand, assume that the individual is constrained by his or her instantaneous (or 'annual') income. The individual is thus prevented from reallocating consumption expenditures over time by borrowing and lending. In general, this means that the discounted value of the sum of instantaneous utility levels falls short of the maximum life-time utility level as defined by the function $V(p, y, z)$, assuming that the utility function is separable in time in order to ensure that instantaneous preferences (utility functions) exist.

As before, the overall CV is the maximum amount of present value income or wealth that the individual is willing to give up in order to secure a proposed change in health. Similarly, the instantaneous CV is the present value income in period t that can be taken from the individual while leaving him or her just as well off as before a proposed change in health in that period. It can be shown that:

$$CV \geq \Sigma_t cv_t [1/(1+r)]^{t-1} = \Sigma_t CV_t \qquad (3.10)$$

where cv_t is the *current value* CV for period t, r is the discount rate, kept constant for simplicity, and CV_t is the *present value* CV for period t. (3.10) indicates that the sum of discounted instantaneous CVs can, but need not, have the same sign as the overall measure CV. However, if $\Sigma CV_t \geq 0$, then it must be the case that $CV \geq 0$. In this case, the sum of discounted instantaneous CVs ranks the alternatives in the same order as the overall measure.

The present value criterion does not work when $\Sigma CV_t < 0$. Even if this sum is negative, the overall CV may be positive. In order to obtain a rule for project rejection, we must instead use the EV, i.e. the minimum amount which the individual would accept in lieu of the change from initial to final level values of health status. It can be shown that:

$$EV \leq \Sigma_t EV_t. \qquad (3.11)$$

Hence, if the sum of discounted instantaneous EVs is negative, then the overall equivalent variation EV must also be negative. This means that the sum of discounted instantaneous EVs can be used to check whether a proposed treatment should be rejected.

In short, if the sum of discounted CVs (EVs) is positive (negative), then life-time utility has increased (decreased). However, ambiguous results occur when the present value of the instantaneous CV is negative and the present value of the instantaneous EVs is positive. This is demonstrated by Blackorby *et al.* (1984). Nevertheless, in many cases the sum of discounted instantaneous money measures should be a useful concept.

Price ($)

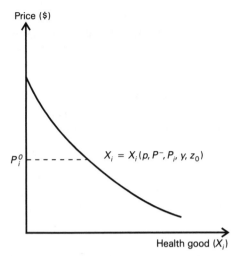

$$X_i = X_i(p, P^-, P_i, y, z_0)$$

Health good (X_i)

Figure 3.4 A demand curve for a health good

A health production function approach

The models used in the previous sections treat health as unpriced. In this section we reintroduce the simple health production function approach presented on p. 13. According to this approach, the individual purchases goods and services in the market and uses these goods to 'produce' health. This approach thus allows us to use market prices in an attempt to value changes in health.

On p. 14 we derived an indirect utility function for the case in which an individual produces his or her health. This indirect utility function, see (2.8), can be written as $V = V(p, P, y, z_0)$, where p is a vector of prices of consumption goods, P is a vector of prices of health goods, y is income, and z_0 is initial health status. The demand function for the ith health good is written as $X_i(p, P, y, z_0)$, as in (2.7). An illustration of the demand curve is found in figure 3.4, where P^- denotes all health goods prices except the price of the ith health good. The area to the left of the demand curve above the current market price, P_i^0 in figure 3.4, yields the uncompensated or Marshallian *consumer surplus*. The consumer surplus *plus* what is actually spent on the health good can be viewed as a measure of the consumer's valuation of the health good in question.

Thus, if the demand function is estimated, we are equipped with a tool which can possibly be used to evaluate changes in health. To illustrate this, if a new medical drug is introduced, the area to the left of the demand curve for the drug may provide some information about consumers' valuation of the drug. Or a new operation method for gastric ulcers may cause a shift in the demand curve for a particular drug, and this shift may be used to assess the new method. In what follows we will investigate the circumstances under which a health demand function is a useful tool in a valuation context.

For a small change in P_i, the consumer surplus is proportional to the underlying change in utility. To see this, differentiate the indirect utility function with respect to P_i and multiply through by dP_i to obtain:

$$dV = - V_y X_i(.)dP_i \qquad (3.12)$$

where V_y is the marginal utility of income. In this expression V_y is a constant since it is evaluated at a 'point'. Thus, for small changes in a price, the ordinary consumer surplus $dS = X_i dP_i$ is proportional to the change in utility. However, this is generally not true for a discrete change in the price since $V_y = V_y(p, P, y, z_0)$, i.e. V_y changes with a change in a price, in general.

Suppose now that income is adjusted so as to keep the utility in (3.12) unchanged. We then have the following result:

$$dV = - V_y X_i(.)dP_i + V_y dy = 0 \qquad (3.12')$$

where dy can be interpreted as the marginal compensating variation dCV (or as the marginal equivalent variation dEV). Thus for small changes in a price the three money measures coincide. Regardless of whether we calculate dS, dCV, or dEV, $X_i(.)$ and $V_y(.)$ are evaluated for the same vector of prices, income and health, explaining the fact that $dS = $ dCV $= $ dEV.

Let us next consider a discrete *ceteris paribus* change in the price of the ith health good from P_i^0 to P_i^1. Using the indirect utility function, the individual's CV of the price change is implicitly defined by the following equality:

$$V(p, P^-, P_i^1, y - \mathrm{CV}) = V(p, P^-, P_i^0, y) \qquad (3.13)$$

$$= V[x(p, P^-, P_i^0, y), f[X^-(p, P^-, P_i^0, y), X_i(p, P^-, P_i^0, y)]]$$

where $[p, P^-]$ is a vector of all prices except the ith health goods price, X^- is a vector of demands for all health goods except the ith good, $z = f[.]$ is health, and z_0 is ignored. In the second-line expression of (3.13), the demand functions are shown in order to highlight some of the points hinted at above and further discussed below. The CV in (3.13) yields the maximal WTP for a reduction in the price of the ith health good, and the minimum compensation needed in order to be as well off as before an increase in the price.

Expression (3.12') can be used to derive the compensated or Hicksian demand function for health good i. Note that income must be adjusted so as to maintain the individual throughout at his or her initial level of utility while the price is changed. This is most easily seen from (3.13), and (A3.1)–(A3.2) in the appendix to this chapter. It is well known that the ordinary and the compensated demand functions do not coincide, in general. A change in a price has both a substitution effect and an income effect on ordinary demand, while the income effect is neutralized in the case of compensated demand through an adjustment in income since the individual is held at a pre-specified level of utility; see (A3.3) in the appendix. The following result is derived in the appendix:

$$CV = \int_{P_i^0}^{P_i^1} X_i^c(p, P^-, P_i, V_0)dP_i \qquad (3.14)$$

where a superscript c refers to a compensated demand function, and V_0 is the initial level of utility, i.e. the level of utility attained when $P_i = P_i^0$. According to (3.14), the area to the left of a compensated demand curve between initial and final prices corresponds to the CV, as is illustrated in figure 3.5a. If the individual instead is held at the final level of utility, we would arrive at the EV as corresponding to the area to the left of a compensated demand curve defined for utility level V_1, i.e. the utility level attained when $P_i = P_i^1$; see figure 3.5b.

If (and only if) the utility function is quasi-linear then the three consumer surplus measures CV, EV and the ordinary consumer surplus coincide; see for example Johansson (1987) or work through the example on p. 41. In all other cases, the ordinary consumer surplus measure is unable to reflect CV or EV. However, if the health good in question is normal, i.e. $\partial X_i(.)/\partial y > 0$ so that demand increases with income, in the single price change case it holds that $CV < S < EV$, where S refers to the uncompensated consumer surplus. This result is most easily seen by inspecting figure 3.5b.

In the literature, one can find different ways of determining bounds for the difference between S on the one hand and CV and EV on the other; the classic reference is Willig (1976). For example, one approximation of the Willig formulae is that $(CV - S)/S \approx S\eta/2y$, where η is the individual's income elasticity, i.e. $(\partial X_i/\partial y)(y/X_i)$. Thus, if the income elasticity is small and S is small relative to income, S will be a good approximation of CV. The approach may seem simple to apply, but the problem is that it requires information about each and every consumer's income and income elasticity. If there are large variations in income and/or income elasticity of demand between consumers, the aggregate error may become quite large. The reader is referred to Johansson (1987, ch. 4) for a survey of different approximation techniques and their properties as well as a discussion of the circumstances in which one can deduce the properties of the individual's demand functions from market data (the theory of exact aggregation). Just

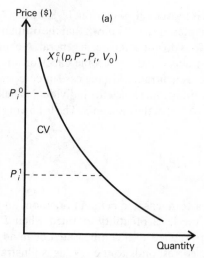

a The CV as an area to the left of a compensated demand curve

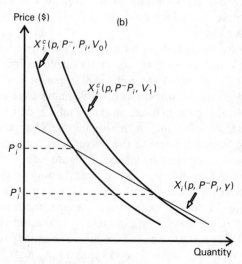

b Ordinary and compensated demand curves

Figure 3.5 Demand curves

et al. (1982) provide many useful approximation formulae and illustrate the magnitude of the error produced if S is used as an approximation of CV and EV, respectively.

In closing this section, it should be noted that market prices can be used to assess the value of a change in the price of drugs and other health goods and services.[3] The compensated money measures associated with changes in prices have all the properties derived in the previous sections. Note however that the ordinary money measure S is *path-dependent*, in general. This means that the magnitude, and even the sign of S, usually depend on the order in which prices are changed, i.e. the ordinary money measure cannot be used to evaluate multiple price changes. On the other hand, our compensated money measures do not suffer from this deficiency. (See the appendix for details.)

Using market data to evaluate changes in health

We have used market data to assess the value of a priced good. But can we use market data to value changes in health or even life itself? There are several problems in using market data to estimate the value of health. As explained above, the uncompensated consumer surplus measure does not express the consumer's WTP, in general. Although this problem can be overcome by estimating a compensated demand function, severe problems remain.

In order to illustrate the kind of problem encountered, let us assume that we want to assess the value of health using the market for a particular drug. The drug's compensated demand curve is taken to be the one depicted in figure 3.5a. We simply want to calculate the CV, i.e. the area to the left of the compensated demand curve in figure 3.5a above the market price which is taken to be P_i^1, treating all other prices and income as fixed. The CV is given by (3.13) with $P_i^0 = P_i^\infty$, where the superscript ∞ is taken to mean that the price approaches $+\infty$. This assumption ensures that we capture the entire area to the left of the demand curve above the market price.

Assume initially that health is an essential commodity. Moreover, by assumption, health cannot be produced without X_i, i.e. the considered drug is an essential input. Then our evaluation attempt breaks down since health approaches zero, i.e. the individual dies, as P_i approaches infinity. In other words, the right-hand side expression in (3.13) is undefined (or, say, zero) for $P_i^0 = P_i^\infty$. This simply says that we cannot place a meaningful value on the certain loss of a life.

Usually, a drug is not essential in the way assumed above. Rather, it can raise health above some reference level, but one does not lose one's life by refraining from taking the drug. Let us therefore assume that the health production function is $z = f(X_i, X^-) + z_0$, where X^- is a vector of all health goods except the ith good and z_0 is the reference level of health. The health good X_i is now said to be essential if it holds that $z = f(0, X^-) + z_0 = z_0$ for any $X^- \geqslant 0$. In this case, (3.13) and (3.14) work, i.e. we can safely let P_i^0 approach $+ \infty$. The magnitude of the CV is independent of any assumption that we may make about the initial level values of the prices of health goods other than the ith one. Recall that $z = z_0$ in the right-hand side of (3.13) for any prices P^- so long as $X_i = 0$, implying that it does not make sense to spend money on buying other health goods however low their prices may be. Thus in this case, we can capture the value of life above the reference level by examining the market for a single health good (for fixed levels of p and y). On the other hand, if X_i is non-essential in the sense that the individual can raise z above z_0 even if $X_i = 0$ – for example, there may be substitute drugs available – we cannot evaluate life (above the level z_0) by examining the market for X_i in isolation, i.e. by calculating CV in (3.13) or (3.14). The reason is that even if $X_i = 0$, the individual can attain a better health than z_0 by purchasing other health goods than the ith one. In this case, (3.13) and (3.14) yield only the willingness to pay for the ith health good, given a particular choice of p, P^- and y. We simply need an essential health good in order to evaluate life (above the level z_0).

A second example to consider is the way in which market data can be used to evaluate an unpriced treatment, say an operation method. Can we use the area to the left of the compensated demand curve for a drug used in the treatment, in order to calculate an individual's WTP (CV) for the operation method? In fact, given a set of assumptions, we can. The first assumption we need is that health can be 'produced' so as to increase above some base level z_0: $z = f(X, a) + z_0$, where a is is a shift variable capturing the operation. Secondly, the drug in question, say X_i, must be essential for the production of health. Thirdly, the operation method must be related to the drug in a particular way. For purely technical reasons, let us make the unrealistic assumption that a is a continuous variable. It must then hold that $\partial V(.)/\partial a$ approaches zero as P_i approaches $+ \infty$. In other words, if the drug is not available, the operation does no good, i.e. leaves utility unchanged.

Given these assumptions one can proceed as follows. Consider figure 3.6. The outer (inner) compensated demand curve for the drug is the one with (without) the operation. Calculate the area to the left of the demand curve with the operation and the demand curve without the operation, respectively, above the drug's market price P_i^1. The shaded area in figure 3.6 is the difference in consumer surplus, i.e. CV, between the cases with and without the operation. This difference is a monetary evaluation of the operation method. If the operation affects utility even in the absence of the drug, there

Price ($)

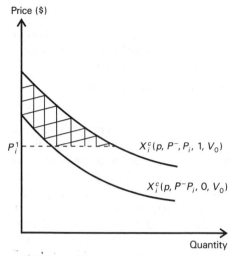

Figure 3.6 The CV when α changes from $\alpha = 0$ to $\alpha = 1$

remains a utility gain which is not captured by the method here. The assumption that $\partial V(.)/\partial \alpha$ approaches zero as P_i approaches $+\infty$ is thus central. Also note that we can use the approach outlined here to assess changes in the quality of a drug by interpreting α as a quality index. The outer curve in figure 3.6 then corresponds to the high quality (or small side effects) case and the inner curve corresponds to the low quality (or large side effects) case.

Another possibility is that an unpriced treatment, say an operation, is a perfect substitute for X_i so that $z = f(X^-, X_i + \alpha)$. If there is no cost for the patient associated with the operation, s/he will obviously prefer to be operated on. The marginal WTP for an operation is easily shown to be equal to the market price of X_i; recall that the two 'commodities' are perfect substitutes. The total WTP for a change, $\Delta \alpha$, in α, is equal to $P_i \Delta \alpha$. If X_i is used, or prescribed, in a fixed dose, the market value of this dose provides a proxy for the monetary value of the operation. This simple case illustrates the fact that substitutes can sometimes be used to estimate the value of an unpriced treatment. The reader interested in a detailed examination of the properties of household production functions, within an environmental economics perspective, is referred to Smith (1991).

Appendix

In order to arrive at (3.14) in the main text, let us start by stating the indirect utility function as follows:

$$V = V[p, P^-, P_i, y - \mathrm{CV}(P_i)] \tag{A3.1}$$

where $\mathrm{CV}(.)$ is equal to zero for $P_i = P_i^0$. If P_i is changed, $\mathrm{CV}(.)$ adjusts in such a way that the individual remains at the level of utility corresponding to $P_i = P_i^0$. Differentiating (A3.1) with respect to P_i yields:

$$\partial V / \partial P_i = - V_y X_i^c[p, P^-, P_i, y - \mathrm{CV}(P_i)] - V_y \partial \mathrm{CV}(P_i) / \partial P_i = 0 \tag{A3.2}$$

where $V_y = V_y[p, P^-, P_i, y - \mathrm{CV}(P_i)]$. Note that the demand function in (A3.2) is a Hicksian one since income, through the term $\mathrm{CV}(.)$, is adjusted throughout so as to keep the individual at his or her initial level of utility. Thus we could also write the demand function as $X_i^c[p, P^-, P_i, V_0]$, where V_0 refers to the initial level of utility. Rearranging and integrating (A3.2) between initial and final level values of P_i yields (3.14).

The relationship between an ordinary and a compensated demand function can be seen by noting that we have used the ordinary demand function to define the compensated demand function, i.e. $X_i^c = X_i[p, P^-, P_i, y - \mathrm{CV}(P_i)]$; note that $X_i^c = X_i$ for $\mathrm{CV} = 0$. Now, differentiating with respect to P_i yields:

$$\partial X_i^c(.) / \partial P_i = \partial X_i(.) / \partial P_i - [(\partial X_i(.) / \partial y)(\partial \mathrm{CV}(.) / \partial P_i)] \tag{A3.3}$$

where, using (3.12') with $dy = (\partial \mathrm{CV}(.) / \partial P_i) dP_i$, it can be shown that $(\partial \mathrm{CV}(.) / \partial P_i) = X_i(.)$. Thus the expression within brackets in (A3.3) is an income effect.

If several prices or health statuses in several periods are changed, we want our money measures to be independent of the order in which we change the prices, etc. If the ith price is changed before the jth price we should not obtain a money measure which is different from the one obtained if the jth price is changed before the ith price. The set of conditions that ensures that the order in which prices, etc. are changed does not affect the magnitude of a money measure is known as the *path-independency* conditions. To illustrate these conditions, an indirect utility function satisfies the path-independency conditions if the mixed derivatives are symmetric, i.e. $\partial^2 V(.) / \partial p_i \partial p_j = \partial^2 V(.) / \partial p_j \partial p_i$, etc., in a simply connected open set of space (for example, a convex set where any two points can be joined by a path in the set). These symmetry conditions must also hold for health in different periods. The path-independency conditions are assumed to hold for the indirect utility functions used in this book, unless otherwise explicitly stated. This means that our Hicksian or compensated money measures are path-independent. This is, however, generally not true for Marshallian or uncompensated money measures, as is shown in, for example, Chipman and Moore (1980) and Johansson (1987). The intuitive explanation is that the income elasticity of demand varies across goods, in general (income effects, however, are neutralized in the case of Hicksian demand functions; compare (A3.3)). Only a quasi-linear utility function ensures path-independency of ordinary money measures. This utility function ensures symmetric (zero) income effects across all goods except the numeraire good. In some cases, a homothetic utility function also works (for example, when only prices are changed; recall that the income elasticity is equal to unity for all goods, if the underlying utility function is homothetic).

4   Money measures in a risky world

The interpretation of a medical treatment or a health policy measure as having a certain impact on the individual's health profile is questionable, to say the least. Rather, the future health profile can be viewed as stochastic, and a treatment changes the probability that the individual will experience a particular health status. In this chapter risk is introduced and the money measures derived for the certainty case are generalized so as to cover changes in probability distributions. Throughout the chapter risk is considered, i.e. probabilities are assumed to be knowable. Note however that the words 'risk' and 'uncertainty' are used interchangeably here; this is stressed because uncertainty proper refers to a situation where we do not know the probability that a particular event will occur.

The chapter is structured as follows. The first section introduces two money measures of a shift in the health probability distribution and discusses their properties. In sharp contrast to the certainty case discussed in chapter 3, in a risky world there is in principle an infinite number of money measures keeping the individual at a pre-specified level of (expected) utility. This fact is used in the second section to derive a WTP locus, and to discuss the choice of money measure in a risky world. In the third section we discuss the circumstances under which it is meaningful to place a monetary value on changes in an individual's survival probability, and introduce the concept of the value of a statistical life. The fourth section introduces concepts such as endogenous risks and different forms of altruism, and discusses how to treat these concepts within a valuation context. The fifth section looks at the possibility of using expected income losses as a lower bound for the value of a life. The sixth and final section is devoted to intertemporal issues.

Introducing money measures in a risky world

This section introduces money measures to be used in a risky world. In order to highlight some basic properties of such measures the model will be kept as simple as possible. Consider an individual who consumes private goods and values his or her health. As in chapter 2, p. 18, s/he is assumed to

52

be an expected utility maximizer, and is equipped with well-behaved cardinal sub-utility functions $V = V(p, y, z_i)$, where p is a vector of fixed prices of consumption goods and services, y is a fixed income, and z_i is health in the ith state of the world. In order to simplify the exposition, we will consider a finite probability space, i.e. assume that z takes on values in a finite set. The different health states are ordered so that z_0 refers to the worst possible health state (death) and z_f refers to full health. There is a probability distribution assigning subjective probabilities $\pi_0, \ldots, \pi_f$ to the points $z_0, \ldots, z_f$, with $\pi_i \geq 0$ for $i = 0, \ldots, f$, and $\Sigma_i \pi_i = 1$. The analysis is here restricted to uncertainty with regard to z. Moreover, in this section the probability that the individual dies (π_0) is set equal to zero. We also proceed as if there is a single period, though these last three assumptions will be relaxed later on. The assumption that the individual is an expected utility maximizer will be abandoned in the analysis later in the chapter.

Expected utility of the individual is defined as follows:

$$E(V) = \Sigma_i \pi_i V(p, y, z_i) \tag{4.1}$$

where E is the expectations operator. Expected utility is simply a weighted average of the utility levels attained in different states of the world, using the probabilities π_i as weights.

A medical treatment, for example, can be viewed as causing a shift in the probability distribution. Hopefully, it reduces the probabilities of experiencing bad health states and increases the probabilities of attaining good ones. Denote the expected health level with treatment $E_1(z) = \Sigma_i \pi_i^1 z_i = z^1$ and the expected level without treatment $E_0(z) = \Sigma_i \pi_i^0 z_i = z^0$. Thus the treatment changes the probability of experiencing health state i from π_i^0 to π_i^1. The change in expected utility caused by the treatment is defined as follows:

$$\Delta E(V) = E_1[V(p, y, z)] - E_0[V(p, y, z)] = \Sigma_i \Delta \pi_i V(p, y, z_i) \tag{4.2}$$

where E_1 (E_0) denotes the expectations operator with (without) the treatment, $\Delta \pi_i$ denotes the change in the probability that state i occurs, and probabilities sum to unity both with and without the treatment, i.e. $\Sigma_i \Delta \pi_i = 0$. Note that the treatment may affect expected utility even if the means and variances of the two distributions coincide. They may still differ with respect to their skewness, implying that an individual may prefer the one that yields the smaller risk of experiencing very bad health outcomes. This is called downside risk aversion, and a risk averse person as well as a risk loving one may have downside risk aversion. (The second derivative characterizes risk aversion and risk loving, as was shown on p. 21, while the third derivative must be positive for a person having downside risk aversion; see Menezes et al., 1980, for details.)

In evaluating this shift in health, one possibility is to assess the change in expected health, i.e. to compare $E_1(z) = z^1$ and $E_0(z) = z^0$. This is parallel to the approach in chapter 3. We simply want to find money measures which equate utility with the treatment, i.e. $V(p, y, z^1)$, and without treatment, i.e. $V(p, y, z^0)$. The apparatus developed in chapter 3 can be used for this kind of evaluation, so the exercise is not repeated here. Instead we proceed by initially defining a state-independent CV, i.e. a payment/compensation which is independent of the health state that the individual actually experiences. This is an amount such that:

$$E_1[V(p, y - CV, z)] = E_0[V(p, y, z)] \qquad (4.3)$$

where CV denotes a uniform or state-independent amount of money such that the individual experiences the same level of expected utility with the treatment as he would do without the treatment. This 'contract', which specifies that the individual commits himself to paying/receiving the same amount of money regardless of what health he will experience, is here referred to as a *non-contingent CV*. It is similar to an insurance premium, which is also paid regardless of what state of the world one will experience later on. Compare also a charter trip. In general, one pays a price for the trip in advance, and this price is independent of, for example, what weather one will actually experience during the trip. For a simple numerical example further illustrating the meaning and interpretation of the CV measure, the reader is referred to the end of this section.

Alternatively, one can base the definition of the non-contingent money measure on the EV measure. The *non-contingent EV* is an amount such that:

$$E_0[V(p, y + EV, z)] = E_1[V(p, y, z)]. \qquad (4.3')$$

This contract specifies a uniform or state-independent amount of money such that the individual experiences the same level of expected utility without the treatment as he or she would do with the treatment. In other words, if the treatment increases expected utility then EV is a compensation, while if the treatment reduces expected utility it is a payment. Note, however, that the definitions of CV and EV are somewhat artificial in cases where treatments reduce expected utility. This is true because participation in medical treatments are voluntary, in sharp contrast to public safety programmes and environmental changes affecting human health, which are not.

In what follows, we will (arbitrarily) concentrate on the CV measure. Substitution of (4.3) into (4.2) yields:

$$\Delta E(V) = E_1[V(p, y, z)] - E_1[V(p, y - CV, z)]. \qquad (4.4)$$

The only difference between the two utility functions in (4.4) is that the latter has CV as an argument and the former does not. Thus in order for the equality in (4.4) to hold, CV must have the same sign as $\Delta E(V)$. In other words, if the treatment increases expected utility CV is positive, and if not CV is negative. The non-contingent CV is a sign-preserving measure of a change in expected utility; see the numerical illustration at the end of this section. The same is easily shown to be true also for the non-contingent EV. Note that the approach presented here covers as a special case a certain shift from one health state, say the jth one, to another health state, say the ith one; then $\pi_j^0 = 1$ and $\pi_i^1 = 1$. Then the non-contingent payments reduce to those defined in chapter 3. The reader should also note that CV (like EV) is a sign-preserving measure of the change in expected utility even if the treatment, in addition to health, changes income and all relative prices. This can be understood by interpreting the expectations operators in (4.4) as referring to multivariate probability distributions; π_i^1 is then the joint probability that the individual will experience prices i, income y_i and health z_i if s/he participates in the treatment. See the example provided below.

A state-independent payment scheme is not the only possible 'contract' in a risky world. We can, for example, instead let the individual pay (receive compensation) for the change in the probability that s/he will experience health state i. The state i CV is an amount such that:

$$\pi_i^1 V(p, y - \mathrm{CV}_i, z_i) = \pi_i^0 V(p, y, z_i) \qquad \forall i \tag{4.5}$$

for strictly positive probabilities. The *expected CV* is defined as $\mathrm{CV}^E = \Sigma_i \pi_i^1 \mathrm{CV}_i$, i.e. as a weighted average of the CV in each state of the world. The problem with the CV^E measure is that it does not reflect the sign of the underlying change in utility, in general. The reason for this problem is that the marginal utility of income, which is used to convert the expression from monetary units to units of utility, typically varies with health across states of the world;[1] for a numerical illustration, see below. However, if the individual's utility function is quasi-linear, see p. 41, the marginal utility of income is equal in all states of the world. This assumption ensures that the sign of CV^E reflects the sign of $\Delta E(V)$. We will come back to this issue below.

In order to illustrate numerically the money measures derived above, assume that the individual's expected utility is:

$$V^E = \Sigma_i \pi_i [\ln y_i + \ln z_i] \tag{4.1a}$$

where $i = 1, 2$, y_i is the fixed income in state i, π_i is the joint probability that the individual experiences income y_i and health z_i, and the sub-utility functions are identical to the utility function used on p. 40 except that a is here ignored. Set $\pi_i^0 = 0.5$ for all i, $y_1 = 100$, $y_2 = 70$, $z_1 = 1$, and $z_2 = 10$. Initial expected utility is therefore $V^{E0} \approx 5.58$. In the case under consideration, income is state-dependent. In order to illustrate the properties of our money measures, income is assumed to be low in the good-health state of the world, and high in the bad-health state.

Let us now consider a treatment which changes the probabilities of experiencing different states of the world, and initially ignore any costs associated with the treatment. Changing π_1 to 0.4 and π_2 to 0.6 yields the final expected utility $V^{E1} \approx 5.77$. Now, CV is a payment such that:

$$0.4[\ln(100-CV)+\ln(1)]+0.6[\ln(70-CV)+\ln(10)] = V^{E0} = 5.58$$
(4.3a)

i.e. $CV \approx 14$. That is, CV correctly indicates that the project/treatment increases expected utility. Suppose that the state-independent cost of the treatment is \$8 in terms of an income loss suffered during the treatment, costs of hospitalization, physician time, laboratory services, medical drugs, and so on; the reader is referred to chapter 7, pp. 126–7, for the multi-individual case in which others than the patient bear a part of the treatment cost. The individual's *gross* WTP for the treatment is still \$14, but his *net* WTP is \$6 (\$14 – \$8). If the cost of the treatment increases to more than \$14, the individual will not voluntarily undergo the treatment.

Our CV_i measures are obtained as follows:

$$0.4[\ln(100-CV_1)+\ln(1)]=0.5[\ln(100)+\ln(1)]$$
$$0.6[\ln(70-CV_2)+\ln(10)]=0.5[\ln(70)+\ln(10)]$$
(4.5a)

where the first line refers to state 1 and the second line to state 2; the probabilities that the individual will experience different states of the world are changed by the treatment (while any costs associated with the treatment are ignored here). It is easily verified that $CV_1 \approx -216.2$ and $CV_2 \approx 46.5$. Thus, the expected CV is equal to:

$$CV^E = -0.4 \cdot 216.2 + 0.6 \cdot 46.5 \approx -58.6.$$
(4.5b)

That is, though the considered project/treatment increases the individual's expected utility, CV^E indicates, wrongly, that his expected utility has fallen. The problem is that the compensated marginal utility of income, equal to $1/(y_i - CV_i)$ in state i, and used in transforming monetary units to units of utility, varies across states (and also depends on the magnitudes of the changes in y and z).

In closing this section, it should be emphasized that the non-contingent money measures, i.e. CV and EV, have the same properties as their certain world counterparts. For this reason the discussion in chapter 3 is not repeated here. It is simply noted that both the CV and the EV are still sign-preserving measures of a change in (expected) utility, that EV > CV for a 'normal' commodity, and that the two measures coincide for an infinitesimally small project, i.e. dCV = dEV; see the appendix to this chapter.

A WTP locus

In the previous section two forms of contracts were specified and one of these, the non-contingent CV (EV), turned out to have the desired sign-preserving property, i.e. to reflect the sign of the change in expected utility caused by a project. A non-contingent payment also has a nice property when undertaking a cost-benefit analysis: if it exceeds the (certain) costs, it will do so whatever state of the world is realized (since it is the same amount of money in all states of the world).

In this section we proceed by looking at other possible payment schemes or contracts. Generally speaking, and as shown by Graham (1981), the set of possible contracts is given by the following equality:

$$E_1[V(p,y-C,z)] = \Sigma_i \pi_i^1 V(p,y-C_i,z_i) = E_0[V(p,y,z)] \qquad (4.6)$$

where C_i is the amount that the individual pays/receives conditional on state i occurring. In principle, there is an infinite number of different contracts satisfying (4.6), including those considered in the previous section. To see this, suppose we start from a non-contingent contract, i.e. $C_i = CV$ for all i. Next, reduce the amount paid/received in state i, but increase the state j amount so as to preserve the equality in (4.6). Proceeding in this way, one can trace out a *WTP locus*, like the one illustrated in figure 4.1 for the two-states case. The locus is downward sloping since, in order for expected utility to remain constant, paying less in one state means paying more in the other, as is shown in the appendix; in the following we will speak of 'payment' instead of using the more clumsy expression 'payment/compensation'. In figure 4.1, the non-contingent CV is given by the intersection of the 45° line and the WTP locus; along the 45° line the individual pays the same amount in both states of the world. All other payment schemes along the locus in figure 4.1 are also such that the individual remains at his initial level of expected utility. Alternatively, one could define a locus based on the EV measure, but this variation is not performed here. For a generalization of (4.6) to the continuous-states case, the reader is referred to (A4.2) in the appendix.

There is a close correspondence between one of the money measures defined by the WTP locus in figure 4.1 and an insurance. In order to further illustrate this, let us assume that there is a large number of individuals, all facing the probability π_i^1 of experiencing state i for $i = 1,\ldots,f$, and that π_i^1 per cent of the individuals will actually experience state i with the treatment. This opens up the possibility of maximizing the expected payment from each individual. That is, maximize:

$$\max_C C^E = \Sigma_i \pi_i^1 C_i \qquad (4.7)$$

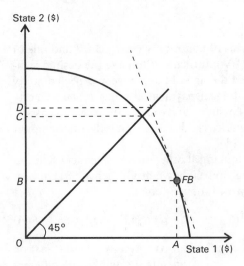

Figure 4.1 A WTP locus

where $C = [C_1, \ldots, C_f]$ is a vector specifying how much is to be paid in each state of the world, and C^E is the expected payment, subject to (4.6). It is easily verified that (an interior solution to) this approach allows the individual to even out his marginal utility of income across states of the world. This is parallel to the optimal insurance condition derived in chapter 2, p. 24.

For any amount C^E, (4.7) is like a budget constraint with π_i^1 serving as prices. This allows us to construct 'budget' lines. The dashed line through FB in figure 4.1 is one such budget line with the slope $-\pi_1^1/\pi_2^1$. Note that the farther away the line is situated from the origin, the higher C^E it represents. In fact, if the individual is to remain at his initial level of expected utility, i.e. remain along the WTP locus in figure 4.1, the dashed line yields payment combinations which maximize C^E. At the point of tangency the slope of the WTP locus is equal to the slope of the budget line, i.e. $-\pi_1^1/\pi_2^1$, which explains why the marginal utility of income must be equal across states at this 'fair bet' (FB) point; the reader is invited to use the second line in (A4.1) in the appendix to verify this result.

Thus by allowing the individual to pay the amount OA (OB) if s/he experiences state 1 (2), we can collect a *certain* amount equal to OD in figure 4.1. But note that this assumes that π_1^1 per cent of the individuals experience state 1 and π_2^1 per cent experience state 2, so that we know that in the aggregate $\pi_1^1 OA + \pi_2^1 OB$ can be converted into the certain amount OD per individual.

Alternatively, if the individual has access to perfect markets for contingent dollar claims, we can let him make a non-contingent payment equal to OD in figure 4.1 since s/he will use the market to even out the marginal utility of income across states of the world, i.e. attain the point FB in figure 4.1. In other words, he will use the fact that a state-independent income y can be redistributed across states according to $y = \Sigma_i \pi_i^1 y_i$. Maximizing expected utility subject to this budget constraint once again produces the result, assuming an interior solution, that the marginal utility of income is evened out across states (and paying a constant amount OD in each state of the world will not change this fact).

Thus in the case of insurable risk it is theoretically possible to collect a larger state-independent amount of money than the non-contingent payment OC in figure 4.1. The individual is willing to pay something extra for the possibility of evening out his marginal utility of income across states of the world. On the other hand, if there are no markets for contingent dollar claims, constructing complex contracts specifying how much to pay in different states is no easy or costless task. It also opens up the possibility of moral hazard, i.e. that individuals may get an incentive to adjust to or cheat the system. At the aggregate level there is another problem with contracts aimed at maximizing government revenues subject to everybody staying at their initial levels of expected utility. The problem is that the general equilibrium effects of any positive or negative excess of revenues over costs are not accounted for. See Graham (1992) for details.

In closing this section, it should be noted that we have examined just a few of all the possible contracts or payment schemes generated by our model. However, it is to be expected that many of these contracts will produce the same problem as the expected CV measure. That is, they need not have the same sign as the underlying change in expected utility. The reader who wants to use a particular contract is therefore recommended to examine its properties carefully.

Evaluating changes in mortality, and the value of a statistical life

In order to introduce money measures of the value of health changes in a risky world, we have thus far concentrated on changes in morbidity. The individual's survival probability has been set equal to one. In this section this assumption is relaxed, and the conditions under which one can meaningfully evaluate the loss of life are examined. The concept of the value of a statistical life is also introduced.

In chapter 2, p. 22, a set of assumptions on the value of life were introduced. These assumptions say that the individual prefers to stay alive even if this virtually means a zero income. Similarly, no income, however high, can compensate for the loss of one's life. These assumptions mean that

$V(p,0,z_1) > V(p,y,z_0)$, where z_1 means being alive, z_0 means being dead, and $y > 0$. Thus it is not possible to define a WTP such that the inequality is turned into an equality. Even if the individual pays his entire income, the inequality remains. This is reasonable, since it implies that we cannot place a meaningful value on the *certain* loss of a life.

This does not necessarily mean that the attempt to value life in terms of money is more or less doomed to failure. To see why, let us consider a treatment or project which increases the probability of death, π_0, but leaves it in the open interval $(0,1)$. Using (4.3), and the set of assumptions specified in (2.15), one finds that:

$$\sum_{i=1}^{f} \pi_i^1 V(p, y - \text{CV}, z_i) = \sum_{i=1}^{f} \pi_i^0 V(p, y, z_i) \tag{4.8}$$

since, by assumption, $V(p,y,z_0) = 0$. According to (4.8) there is a finite payment for a treatment that increases the individual's survival probability. The compensation needed in order for him or her to accept a measure which reduces his or her survival probability is also finite.[2] To illustrate, s/he may be willing to participate in a treatment which increases his or her 'quality of life' but is a bit risky in the sense that it increases the chance that s/he will die. If so, s/he will report a strictly positive and finite WTP, and will need a compensation in order to voluntarily refrain from the treatment.

The assumptions used in deriving the above result are not the only possible ones. Following Jones-Lee (1976), we shall change the assumptions slightly to:

$$V(p, y_1, z_1) \leq A$$
$$V(p, y_0, z_0) \leq B \tag{4.9}$$
$$\pi_1^0 V(p, y_1, z_1) + (1 - \pi_1^0) V(p, y_0, z_0) \gtreqless B$$

where for the sake of simplicity only two states are assumed to be possible, with a subscript 0 (1) referring to being dead (alive), and the positive and finite constants A and B are such that $A > B$. If the least upper bound of utility in state 0, i.e. B, falls short of initial expected utility as defined by the final line in (4.9), no finite sum will be sufficient to compensate the individual for the certainty of death, i.e. an event changing π_0 to $\pi_0^1 = 1$. In fact, Jones-Lee shows that there is a range of probabilities of death for which it will be impossible to compensate the individual. The intuition behind this result is simply that compensation cannot raise utility above B, which in turn falls short of the initial expected utility. Reversing the final line inequality makes compensation possible, even in the case of a certain death. The reader is also referred to Rosen (1988), who discusses the implications for the value of life of introducing a strictly positive subsistence consumption level.

We have thus far considered purely individual changes in survival probabilities, for example due to a medical treatment. In sharp contrast to such individual measures, many public safety and public health measures have the property that it is unknown in advance whose lives will be saved. Measures taken to improve the quality of a road or to increase the number of emergency vehicles in a region have this property. Suppose now that we have somehow calculated each affected individual's (marginal) non-contingent CV for such a measure. There are H affected individuals and the measure saves b lives, i.e. reduces the probability of death by b/H, where b/H is taken to be a small number. Then, and as is shown in the appendix to this chapter, the *value of statistical life* is equal to $\Sigma_h dCV^h/b$, where dCV^h is the marginal CV of individual h. In other words, the value of a statistical life is equal to the aggregate willingness to pay for a measure saving b lives divided by the number of lives saved (i.e. b). Alternatively, and as shown by (A4.4′) in the appendix, the value of statistical life is given by the mean, over the H affected individuals, of their marginal rates of substitution between income and risk.

In order to provide a simple numerical illustration, suppose that a programme reduces the number of people killed in traffic accidents from 7 per 100,000 trafficants to 5 per 100,000 trafficants. Suppose that the total number of trafficants is $H = 1,000,000$ so that the programme saves 20 lives, i.e. $b = 20$. If the total WTP, i.e. $\Sigma_h dCV^h$, is $30 million, then the value of statistical life is $1.5 million ($30 million/20).

We have used the marginal CV to illustrate the concept of the value of a statistical life. However, as was shown on p. 44, in evaluating marginal changes it holds that $dCV = dEV$. Thus we can use the EV measure as well in defining the value of a statistical life. This is further shown in the appendix.

To summarize, this section has demonstrated that we can put a monetary value on the value of changes in death risks. This should come as no surprise since people often seem to act as if they are prepared to accept a higher death risk in exchange for a benefit of one kind or another. This is not to say that we have proved that a monetary valuation of changes in death risks is meaningful. But we have at least indicated sets of assumptions that make such valuations of changes in (morbidity and) mortality a consistent exercise.

Endogenous risks and altruism

In many cases, an individual is able to affect the probability of experiencing a particular event. For example, he can buy fire alarms in order to reduce the risk of a fatal fire. In this section, we will discuss the implications of endogenous risk within a valuation context. Measures aimed at reducing risk often affect all members of a household, and not only the investing household member. For this reason, the treatment of altruism, both within the household and in a more general sense, is introduced in this section.

On p. 25 a simple but quite general endogenous risk model was introduced; the model generates as special cases the expected utility model and the prospect theory model, for example. The indirect utility function generated by this model is as follows:

$$V(p, P, y, a) = U[\pi_1(p, P, y, a), x(p, P, y, a)] \tag{4.10}$$

where π_1 is the survival probability, p is a vector of prices of consumption goods x, P is the price of the single health good (X), y is exogenous income, and a is an indicator of the quality of the health good.

The individual's WTP for a marginal increase in his or her survival probability is easily shown to be equal to the marginal cost of achieving the increase, assuming here an interior solution. This is so because s/he has already chosen the optimal level of π_1 subject to his or her budget constraint, implying that the marginal gain from a small increase in π_1 is equal to the marginal cost of achieving the increase in π_1:

$$[V_\pi(.)/V_y(.)]\partial\pi_1(.)/\partial X = P \tag{4.11}$$

where $V_\pi(.)$ is the marginal utility of risk reductions, i.e. $\partial U(.)/\partial \pi_1$. Market data can therefore sometimes be used to estimate the WTP for small risk reductions, as will be further illustrated in chapter 5, pp. 89–93.

Moreover, one can use the area to the left of the demand curve for the health good X to evaluate changes in its price or quality. Taking the partial derivative of the indirect utility function (4.10) with respect to P yields $-V_y X(p, P, y, a)$, i.e. minus the marginal utility of income times the demand for the good. In principle, one can now proceed as on pp. 44 and 45 and evaluate the monetary value of (small or large) changes in the price and/or quality of the health good. To illustrate, the non-contingent CV associated with a *ceteris paribus* change in P is implicitly defined by the equality:

$$V(p, P^1, y - \text{CV}, a) = V(p, P^0, y, a) \tag{4.12}$$

where $P^1 (P^0)$ is the final (initial) price of the health good. The change in P causes an adjustment in the survival probability since the individual will adjust purchases of the health good (and other goods) as the price P changes. (3.13) and (3.14) show how (4.12) can be used to calculate CV as an area to the left of a compensated demand curve for X between the initial and final level values of P, noting that life is an essential commodity so that we cannot completely recover the value of life by looking at an area to the left of a (compensated) demand curve. Similarly, a shift in the quality of X, for example an improved technology which raises a, can be assessed in the way suggested on pp. 48–9 – that is, by calculating the change in consumer surplus caused by the shift in α; see the shaded area in figure 3.6 (p. 49). Alternatively, and as further illustrated in chapters 5 and 6, one can ask people about their WTP for changes in P and α.

Some measures, for example installing a fire alarm in one's house, will affect the survival probabilities of all household members. Replace therefore the individual utility function by a well-behaved household welfare function:

$$u = [\pi_1(X), x] \qquad (4.13)$$

where $\pi_1(X) = [\pi_{11}(X), \ldots, \pi_{m_1}(X)]$ is a vector of the survival probabilities of the m different household members. According to this formulation, the health good X is a collective or public good at the household level. Investing in X will change the survival probabilities of all household members. The household will invest in (purchase) X until the sum of each household member's marginal utility of a risk reduction is equal to the marginal cost of the risk reduction; see the appendix to this chapter. The (household) indirect utility function will have prices and income as arguments, i.e. will appear identical to the one used above. This means that we can evaluate changes in P (and α) in the way proposed above.

The last case considered above illustrates *altruism* at the household level. The head(s) of the household care about the welfare of the other household members. One can also visualize cases in which people express altruism toward others than those in their own household. This may be the case for public good measures such as improved public safety. A person may be willing to contribute to such measures even if s/he will not himself be affected.

We will come back to the altruism issue in chapter 7, and discuss in detail the implications of altruism for the formulation of a WTP question in a valuation study. Here we will just note that it is quite complicated and tricky to undertake a valuation study when people have altruistic motives for contributing to a project. Note also that it is hardly possible to use market prices in order to evaluate safety measures (having or not having a public good property) in the presence of interhousehold altruism. Usually, the market does not cover such motives for WTP.

Changes in wealth and the value of health

The loss of expected (future) income is sometimes used as a lower bound of the value of life. In this section we will take a look at this argument and investigate the circumstances under which changes in expected income or wealth provide useful information within a valuation context.

In order to obtain a point of reference, consider the following simple expected utility model:

$$V^E = \Sigma_i \pi_i V(p, y_i, z_i) \tag{4.14}$$

where y_i is income in state i, and there is no possibility of transferring income between states. Assume, for simplicity, that $i = 1,2$, and change marginally the probability of experiencing state 1 using a non-contingent CV to keep expected utility constant. After straightforward calculations one obtains:

$$dCV = [(V(p, y_1, z_1) - V(p, y_2, z_2))/V_y^E] \, d\pi_1 \tag{4.15}$$

where V_y^E is the expected marginal utility of income. The difference in income between the two states does not show up in the expression. Next, undertake a linear approximation of the state 2 utility function around (p, y_1, z_1), and substitute the result into equation (4.15) to obtain:

$$dCV = [(V_{y_1}(p, y_1, z_1)(y_1 - y_2) + V_{z_1}(p, y_1, z_1)(z_1 - z_2))/V_y^E] d\pi_1 \tag{4.16}$$

where V_{y_1} is the marginal utility of income evaluated for state 1 prices, etc. and $V_{z_1}(.)$ is the marginal utility of health evaluated at state 1 prices, etc. We have thus broken down the change in utility caused by a marginal change in the probability of experiencing state 1 (and hence state 2). The first term covers the expected change in income while the second term covers the expected value of the change in health *per se*; we speak of expected values since we multiply by a change in a probability $(d\pi_1)$, i.e. $dy^E = y_1 d\pi_1 - y_2 d\pi_1$ is the change in expected income[3] since $d\pi_1 = -d\pi_2$. If both income and the health status are higher (or lower) in state 1 than in state 2, the change in expected income will provide a lower bound of the total monetary value, i.e. dCV or dEV, of the change in expected utility. It is however easy to visualize more complex changes, in particular when there are many states of the world, such that health and expected income change in opposite directions. In such cases, changes in expected income provide no guidance as to (or even the sign of) the overall monetary valuation of the change. This problem is parallel to the one faced in using the expected CV measure to evaluate health changes, explained on p. 55 above. In fact, the expected CV of *ceteris paribus* changes Δy_i in state-dependent income is easily shown to be equal to Δy^E, i.e. does not reflect risk aversion. (Hint: use the fact that $V(p, y_i + \Delta y_i - CV_i, z_i) = V(p, y_i, z_i)$ for all i.)

The circumstances in which expected income changes provide useful information can be further illuminated by undertaking a linear approximation of the utility functions in equation (4.2) around (p, y^E, z^E), where a superscript E refers to the expected value with the treatment. Thus it is now assumed that income is also state-dependent in (4.2). One obtains:

$$\Delta E(V) = \Sigma_i \Delta \pi_i V(p, y_i, z_i) = \Sigma_i \Delta \pi_i [y_i + (V_{zc} z_i / V_{yc})] V_{yc}$$
$$= [\Delta y^E + (V_{zc} \Delta z^E / V_{yc})] V_{yc} \tag{4.17}$$

where $V_{yc} = V_y(p, y^E, z^E)$ refers to the constant marginal utility of income, V_{zc} to the constant marginal utility of health, Δy^E (Δz^E) is the change in expected income (expected health), and the fact that $\Sigma_i \Delta \pi_i = 0$ has been used to eliminate $V(p, y^E, z^E), y^E$ and z^E. The linear approximation in (4.17) highlights the fact that health and income must change in the same direction in order that changes in expected income should make sense as a lower bound for the value of health changes. However, the kind of approximation undertaken in (4.17) provides some weak support for the idea of using expected income losses to evaluate changes in health or even the loss of a statistical life. Also note that CV, in sharp contrast to the change in expected income, is a sign-preserving measure of the change in expected utility. That is, $\Delta E(V) = V_y^E CV$, where the expected (compensated) marginal utility of income is evaluated somewhere between its initial and final level values in the way explained below (3.5) (p. 37).

It should be stressed that (4.17) can be viewed as including health state 0, i.e. the possibility that the individual dies. Given the assumptions employed on p. 60, it is possible to evaluate changes in the survival probability. Of course, we will still usually fail to evaluate a shift in probabilities such that π_0^1, i.e. the certainty of death.

The models used here to illustrate the relationship between changes in expected utility and changes in expected income are simple. For example, there is no endogenous supply of labour, the quality of which may depend on health. They are also single-period models. However, much would not be altered if we introduced more complex and general models. If the change in expected income is a poor welfare change indicator in a simple model, the probability that the expected income measure will perform better in a more complex model is small, to say the least. This is further illustrated in chapter 8, p. 145. The reader is also referred to Rosen (1988), who shows that introducing a strictly positive subsistence consumption level further weakens the possibility of using expected income changes as a lower bound for the value of a loss of a life.

Intertemporal models

In this section, money measures for intertemporal models are introduced. A few simple examples are given, and a few intertemporal models are outlined. The more detailed presentation of intertemporal models is, however, to be found in chapter 8.

The model used on pp. 52–3 can easily be generalized to the many-period case. Consider initially a simple two-period model. In period 1 the individual experiences one of f different health states (ruling out here the possibility that s/he dies in the first period). Introduce now a set of transition probabilities yielding the probabilities that s/he will end up in different states of the world conditional on experiencing a particular state in period 1. Then his or her expected utility can be written as follows:

$$V^E = \Sigma_i \pi_{11} V(p, y, z_{11}, z_{2i})_1 \pi_{2i} + \ldots + \Sigma_i \pi_{1f} V(p, y, z_{1f}, z_{2i})_f \pi_{2i} \qquad (4.18)$$

where all decisions are taken after uncertainty is revealed, p is a vector of present value prices, y is present value income, π_{1i} is the probability that s/he will experience state i in period 1 (with $i > 0$), z_{ti} denotes health state i in period t for $t = 1, 2$, $_i\pi_{2j}$ is the probability that s/he will experience health state j, $j = 0, \ldots, f$, in period 2 conditional on experiencing health state i in period 1, $\Sigma_j {}_i\pi_{2j} = 1$ for all i, and any state-dependence of income or prices is ignored.[4] Proceeding in the way suggested in (4.18), one can calculate expected utility for an arbitrary number of periods. A particularly neat assumption to employ in empirical contexts is that the transition probabilities have the Markov property. That is, the transition probabilities from period t to period $t + 1$ do not depend on what happened before period t. The reader interested in reading more about Markov chains is referred to Stokey and Lucas (1987).

Suppose that a medical treatment, for example, changes the transition probabilities. We can then calculate expected utility with and without treatment, see (4.2), and proceed as on pp. 54–5 to define different money measures of the change in expected utility. It is thus quite straightforward to generalize our basic risky world money measures so as to cover intertemporal phenomena. The main difference is that the notation becomes more complicated.

We now turn to a model where, in sharp contrast to the model outlined above, some decisions must be taken before uncertainty is resolved. This is the simple two-period model outlined in (2.24). The underlying production function is ignored here, but period 2 health is still random as viewed from period 1. Maximizing (2.24) with respect to x_1 and s, and solving for the demand functions yields an indirect expected utility function which can be written as follows:[5]

$$V^E = v_1(p, y, z_1^r, \phi) + \int_{z_2} v_2(p, y, z_1^r, z_{2e}, \phi) dF(z_{2e}, \phi, a) \qquad (4.19)$$

where p is a vector of present value prices of consumption goods in the two periods, y is present value income, z_1^r is the realized health status in period 1, ϕ, following Just *et al.* (1982), is interpreted as a vector containing the parameters or moments of z_2, such as the mean and the variance, characterizing the stochastic properties of the distribution function $F(.)$, defined over the support $z_2 = [a, b]$ as explained on p. 26 so that $F(z_{2\epsilon}, \phi, a) = \text{prob}\{z_2 \leq z_{2\epsilon}\}$, and a is a shift parameter. The reader is referred to chapter 8 for a derivation of (4.19).

In order to further illustrate the properties of this model, let us assume that:

$$z_2 = z^E + \beta \epsilon \tag{4.20}$$

where z^E is the expected health status in period 2, and β is interpreted as the standard deviation of z_2, a result which follows from the assumption that the stochastic variable ϵ, whose mean is equal to zero, has variance $\sigma^2 = 1$. Moreover it is assumed that $Pr\{\epsilon \geq -z^E/\beta\} = 1$ so as to ensure that z_2 does not take on negative values. According to (4.20), a spread-preserving increase in z_2 may be represented by an increase in the mean z^E and an increase in β may be used to represent a mean-preserving increase in the variability of z_2. In the present context, (4.20) can be interpreted as follows. A treatment, say, has an impact on the future health status experienced by an individual. The expected or average change is Δz^E. In the individual case, however, the impact of the treatment is stochastic so that the outcome may range between, say, $z_2 = a$ and $z_2 = b$, where $[a, b]$ is the support of the distribution function (with treatment). The change in β, if any, says how the spread or dispersion of the health state distribution is changed by the treatment.

Let a change from zero to unity in the shift parameter a, see (4.19), represent the considered treatment. The individual's non-contingent CV is implicitly defined by the equality:

$$v_1(p, y - \text{CV}, z_1^r, \phi_1) + \int_{z_2} v_2(p, y - \text{CV}, z_1^r, z_{2\epsilon}, \phi_1) dF(z_{2\epsilon}, \phi_1, 1) = V^{E_0} \tag{4.21}$$

where ϕ_1 denotes the mean, variance, and so on, with treatment, and V^{E_0} is the expected utility without treatment, i.e. (4.19) with $a = 0$. CV in (4.21) is the maximal uniform payment (positive or negative) which the individual is willing to make in exchange for the considered treatment. The treatment shifts the subjective probability distribution for future (period 2) health. For example, its mean or variance or skewness (or any or all of them) may be believed to change. The associated change in expected utility determines the individual's WTP for the treatment. If expected utility is increased (decreased) by the treatment, CV in (4.21) is positive (negative), i.e. CV is once again a sign-preserving measure of the change in expected utility. In chapter 8, p. 143 it is shown that CV is positive for a marginal increase in z^E, while an individual who is risk averse with respect to health risks needs a compensation to be prepared to participate in a treatment which causes a *ceteris paribus* small increase in β, i.e. a mean-preserving increase in the variability of health. Thus, it is not self-evident that CV is positive just because the expected outcome of a treatment is positive. The individual may also be sensitive to the riskiness of the treatment.

The model in (4.19) has been used to define a non-contingent CV. Of course, it can also be used to define other contracts $C(z_2)$ along the lines specified on pp. 57–8, but this exercise is not undertaken here.

Another approach which can be used in defining a money measure in an intertemporal setting was developed by Jones-Lee (1976). It is a continuous-time model in which the individual has a fixed initial wealth and faces a strictly positive probability of dying. The individual has a utility function $v(y, t)$ yielding utility as a function of initial wealth or income conditional on death at time t. The function is increasing in both arguments, i.e. the individual prefers more income to less and prefers to die later rather than sooner. As viewed from time 0, the probability that s/he will die at time t is $F_d(t, a)$, where $F_d(.)$ is a continuous probability density function; see (2.33). The non-contingent CV of a shift in the parameter a from zero to unity can be calculated as:

$$\int_0^T v(y - \text{CV}, t) F_d(t, 1) dt = \int_0^T v(y, t) F_d(t, 0) dt \tag{4.22}$$

where T is such that no one can survive beyond time T. According to (4.22), CV is the maximal WTP for a treatment, say, changing the probability density function for time of death. The change may include a change in the mean, i.e. in life expectancy, and other parameters of the distribution. Jones-Lee (1976) shows that CV is positive for a marginal increase in life expectancy, though Jones-Lee also points out that for technical reasons a *ceteris paribus* change in the mean of $F_d(t, a)$ is not possible, in general. The reader is referred to Jones-Lee (1976, pp. 103–9) for a detailed analysis. Here it is just noted that the kinds of money measure defined in this chapter can be used to assess virtually all kinds of projects/treatments affecting human health.

In the excellent paper by Rosen (1988), the reader can find a detailed analysis of how the valuation of risks varies over the life-cycle; Rosen's model is similar to the stochastic optimal control model discussed on pp. 29–30 and further explored in chapter 8. For example, Rosen shows that a person close to the end is willing to pay more to extend life than a person whose horizon is longer. On the other hand, older people tend to be willing to pay less than younger people to eliminate age-independent or current risk. Rosen also shows that the WTP for a reduction of a prospective risk is smaller than the WTP for a reduction of a current risk. Thus, old persons may be willing to pay more than younger ones for some risk reductions, because the risks are more immediate. In all these cases discounting of (future) risks plays a key role: the further away the risk/event is, the lower is its value today (*ceteris paribus*). See Rosen (1988) for details.

The reader is also referred to chapter 8 where we consider further intertemporal issues in a risky world. For example, the value of acquiring more information when the consequences of a measure, say a medical treatment, are possibly irreversible will be analyzed. Also, a model in which an individual can invest in health so as to improve his welfare as well as increase his survival probability is examined.

Appendix

In order to arrive at the slope of the WTP locus when there are two states of the world, differentiate (4.6) in the main text with respect to C_1 and let C_2 adjust so as to keep expected utility constant. One obtains:

$$\pi_1^1 V_{y_1}(.)dC_1 + \pi_2^1 V_{y_2}(.)dC_2 = 0$$
$$dC_2/dC_1 = -[\pi_1^1 V_{y_1}(.)]/[\pi_2^1 V_{y_2}(.)] \tag{A4.1}$$

where V_{yi} denotes the marginal utility of income in state i ($i = 1,2$), and the second line is obtained by rearranging the terms in the first line.

The continuous-state contract corresponding to the one in (4.6) is given by:

$$\int_\Omega V(p, y - C(z_\epsilon), z_\epsilon)dF(z_\epsilon; 1) = \int_\Omega V(p, y, z_\epsilon)dF(z_\epsilon; 0) \tag{A4.2}$$

where $F(z_\epsilon; a) = \text{prob}\{z \le z_\epsilon\}$ for $z_\epsilon \in \Omega$ is the distribution function with ($a = 1$) and without ($a = 0$) treatment, see (2.23), and the contract $C(z_\epsilon)$ specifies how much to pay in different states of the world. A non-contingent CV corresponds to $C(z_\epsilon) = \text{CV}$ for all levels of z_ϵ.

In order to arrive at the definition of the value of statistical life, assume a two-states world, and also that the expected utility of individual h can be written as follows:

$$V_{hE} = \pi_{h_1} V_h(p, y_h, z_1) \qquad \forall h \tag{A4.3}$$

where π_{h_1} is the survival probability of individual h, and the utility of not being alive, i.e. $V_h(p, y_h, z_0)$, is set equal to zero. Differentiating (A4.3) with respect to π_{h_1} and adjusting income so as to keep expected utility constant yields, after straightforward calculations:

$$dCV_h = V_h(p, y_h, z_1)d\pi_{h_1}/V_{hy}(.) = MRS_h d\pi_{h_1} \qquad \forall h \tag{A4.4}$$

where dCV_h is the marginal non-contingent CV, V_{hy} is the marginal utility of income if alive, and MRS_h denotes the marginal rate of substitution between income and risk. If $d\pi_{h_1} = b/H$ for all h, summing across individuals yields:

$$\Sigma_h dCV_h/b = \Sigma_h MRS_h/H \tag{A4.4'}$$

since $\Sigma_h dCV_h = \Sigma_h MRS_h d\pi_{h_1} = \Sigma_h MRS_h b/H$. The right-hand side expression in (A4.4') yields the average value of a marginal reduction in the probability of death. The left-hand side expression yields the aggregate WTP per life saved by the considered measure, i.e. what is known as the value of statistical life.

The reader is invited to differentiate (A4.3) with respect to π_{h_1} and calculate the associated change in expected utility. Next, adjust income through an amount dEV_h so as to obtain the same change in expected utility. The amount dEV_h represents the compensation the individual needs in order to be as well off as with an increase in the survival probability. Apparently, it must be the case that $dEV_h = dCV_h$. The value of statistical life in (A4.4') is thus the same regardless of whether we use the (marginal) CV or the EV measure.

The maximization problem behind the household indirect utility function discussed below (4.13) (p. 63) is:

$$\max_{x,X} u[\pi_{11}(X), \ldots, \pi_{m_1}(X), x]$$
$$\text{s.t.} \quad y - px - PX = 0. \tag{A4.5}$$

The first-order condition for an interior solution with respect to X is as follows:

$$\Sigma_h [\partial u(.)/\partial \pi_{h_1}][\partial \pi_{h_1}/\partial X] = \lambda P \tag{A4.6}$$

where $h = 1, \ldots, m$, and λ is the Lagrange multiplier associated with the budget constraint (in optimum equal to the marginal utility of income). Thus the sum across the household members of the marginal utilities obtained by marginally increasing X is equated to the price of the good times λ. The remaining first-order conditions for an interior solution are the usual ones. This explains why it is assumed that the indirect household utility function can be written as a well-behaved function of prices and income, i.e. as $V = V(p, P, y)$.

5   Evaluating health risks: practical methodologies

In the case of a commodity that is traded in the market, buyers and sellers reveal their preferences directly through their actions. Since health basically is a private good, one expects to be able to use market data to assess the value of health changes. However, in many countries, the government intervenes in the market or even runs the health care sector. Often, the price paid for a treatment is zero or fixed at an arbitrary level which is kept constant over long intervals of time. This makes it difficult to use econometrics to estimate demand curves. There is the further complication that risk plays a central role within the health field.

This raises the question of how to overcome the problem of preference revelation. Several different practical methods which can be used to measure the WTP for health services have been suggested in the literature. This chapter presents the three most frequently used and/or suggested methods: survey techniques, the human capital approach, and indirect methods using market data. The chapter also offers an overview of empirical studies using different methods to assess the value of health changes. The reader is also referred to chapter 9, where methods such as standard gambles, time trade-offs, risk–risk trade-offs and risk–dollar trade-offs are presented.

The contingent valuation method

The contingent valuation method (CVM) is the modern name for the survey method (since the answers to a valuation question are contingent upon the particular hypothetical market described to the respondents). The method was probably first used by Davis (1964), who used questionnaires to estimate the benefits of outdoor recreation. In their excellent book on the CVM, Mitchell and Carson (1989) list more than 100 US studies based on this technique, while in a more recent survey Green et al. (1990) list 26 UK studies. See also the survey of European studies in Navrud (1992). Since these lists were composed, a large number of new studies based on the CVM have been completed. For example, Carson et al. (1993) list around 1400 studies related to the method. The survey technique is thus widely used for the estimation of environmental benefits in particular, and there is a large body of knowledge on the method's advantages and disadvantages. In recent years, a number of studies using the CVM to assess health care have appeared. These studies will be reviewed in chapter 6.

Roughly speaking, the CVM collects preference information by asking individuals how much they are willing to pay for some change in the provision of a good, or for the minimum compensation individuals require if the change is not carried out. For example, the following questions may be asked of the respondent:

- (CV) Suppose that a particular measure/policy would improve your health from z^1 to z^2. What is the most you would be willing to pay for this improvement?
- (EV) Suppose the government refrains from undertaking the measure/policy. What is the minimum compensation you would need in order to be as well off as after an improvement in your health?

These concepts are illustrated graphically in figures 3.2 and 3.3 (pp. 35 and 36), where an increase in z moves the respondent from point A to point B.

In most empirical applications, the central valuation question is much more detailed than the above examples suggest. The following describes the procedure adopted in a Norwegian study aimed at determining the WTP for improved air quality in a heavily polluted industrial area; see Hylland and Strand (1983) for details. This is clearly a study where health plays a central role since a major problem with bad air quality is its impact on human health. The underlying policy measure, however, is not a private good like a medical treatment but has a public good property, like many public health measures. That is, the measure shifts the probability of experiencing a particular health state for everybody living in the area, regardless of whether they pay for the measure.

More than 1000 randomly chosen people out of 68,000 adults living in the area were interviewed. The interviews were based upon pictures depicting visibility ranges. Picture A shows the selected area on a day with heavy haze; roughly every tenth day is that hazy. Picture B depicts the same area on an average day. In order to make the interviewees familiar with the considered hypothetical change in the environment, they were asked to estimate the number of days per year which are as hazy as pictures A and B, respectively. Then the following question was asked:

It is impossible to eradicate all of the fog since part of it is caused by natural conditions. However a reduction in the discharge of industrial waste would undoubtedly lead to much cleaner air.

A reduction in the discharge of industrial waste may be financed by the company itself, by the local population, by society in general or by all three categories on a joint basis. In order to establish whether a further reduction in air pollution is desirable, it is essential to examine the effect of cleaner air on the welfare of the local population. One measure of this improvement in welfare is the maximum amount that an individual is willing to pay in order to receive a given improvement in visibility, provided that the local population and local companies are themselves required to meet a substantial share of the costs involved. In this study we are interested in finding out how individuals themselves evaluate the advantages of cleaner air.

Let us assume that it is possible to halve the number of days of type (*A*) and instead have a level of visibility approximating to type (*B*). It is further assumed that a proportion of the expenditure on the reduction of air pollution is financed jointly by means of a general income tax on all income-earners in the district. It is not easy to determine in advance the actual level of expenditure required by these improvement measures.

Would they themselves be prepared to pay ( ) per cent of their income towards such a project in the coming years if all of the other income-earners in the area were also prepared to do the same thing? It should be noted that a 1 per cent tax for an individual who earns 100,000 NEK per annum is equivalent to 1000 NEK per annum or 2.70 NEK per day. Similarly a 5 per cent tax is equivalent to 5000 NEK per annum or 13.70 NEK per day.

The respondent may either accept or reject the proposal to pay the suggested tax increase, say 1 per cent of annual income. If s/he refuses to pay that much, the bid is lowered; if s/he accepts, the bid is raised, say to 2 per cent. If the respondent still accepts, the bid is increased further, while if s/he refuses to pay 2 per cent, the bid is reduced to, say, 1.5 per cent. The highest tax increase accepted by the respondent is considered to be his or her bid (CV), the basic idea of this iterative bidding approach being that it is claimed to be much simpler for a respondent to come to a ('yes/no') decision when faced with a specified bid than to locate directly his or her maximal WTP for the considered change.

The central problem in a CVM study is to make the scenario sufficiently understandable, plausible and meaningful to respondents. The respondent must understand the characteristics of the good s/he is asked to value. In the Norwegian study referred to above, the investigators try to establish a baseline and clarify what change the respondent is paying for; the respondent is initially asked to estimate the number of days which are as hazy as pictures *A* and *B*, respectively. The respondent is then asked to pay for a specified change in visibility. Also, the mechanism for providing the good in a CVM must seem plausible in order to avoid scepticism that the good can or will be provided. It is both abstract and hardly convincing to ask the respondent to simply *imagine* that the good (say, a medical treatment or programme) will be provided.

There are a number of (other) pitfalls and problems in using the CVM. Table 5.1, which is taken from Mitchell and Carson (1989), briefly describes many of the principal biases that may appear in a CVM study. A few

Table 5.1. *Typology of potential response effect biases in contingent valuation studies*

1 Incentives to misrepresent responses

Biases in this class occur when a respondent misrepresents his or her willingness to pay (WTP).

A *Strategic bias*: where a respondent gives a WTP amount that differs from his or her true WTP amount (conditional on the perceived information) in an attempt to influence the provision of the good and/or the respondent's level of payment for the good.

B *Compliance bias*

i *Sponsor bias*: where a respondent gives a WTP amount that differs from his or her true WTP amount in an attempt to comply with the presumed expectations of the sponsor (or assumed sponsor).

ii *Interviewer bias*: where a respondent gives a WTP amount that differs from his or her true WTP amount in an attempt to either please or gain status in the eyes of a particular interviewer.

2 Implied value cues

These biases occur when elements of the contingent market are treated by respondents as providing information about the 'correct' value for the good.

A *Starting point bias*: where the elicitation method or payment vehicle directly or indirectly introduces a potential WTP amount that influences the WTP amount given by a respondent. This bias may be accentuated by a tendency to yea-saving.

B *Range bias*: where the elicitation method presents a range of potential WTP amounts that influences a respondent's WTP amount.

C *Relational bias*: where the description of the good presents information about its relationship to other public or private commodities that influences a respondent's WTP amount.

D *Importance bias*: where the act of being interviewed or some feature of the instrument suggests to the respondent that one or more levels of the amenity has value.

3 Scenario misspecification

Biases in this category occur when a respondent does not respond to the correct contingent scenario. Except in A, in the outline that follows it is presumed that the *intended* scenario is correct and that the errors occur because the respondent does not understand the scenario as the researcher intends it to be understood.

A *Theoretical misspecification bias*: where the scenario specified by the researcher is incorrect in terms of economic theory or the major policy elements.

B *Amenity misspecification bias*: where the perceived good being valued differs from the intended good.

  i *Symbolic*: where a respondent values a symbolic entity instead of the researcher's intended good.

  ii *Part-whole*: where a respondent values a larger or a smaller entity than the researcher's intended good.

    a *Geographical part-whole*: where a respondent values a good whose spatial attributes are larger or smaller than the spatial attributes of the researcher's intended good.

    b *Benefit part-whole*: where respondent includes a broader or a narrower range of benefits in valuing a good than intended by the researcher.

    c *Policy package part-whole*: where a respondent values a broader or narrower policy package than the one intended by the researcher.

  iii *Metric*: where a respondent values the amenity on a different (and usually less precise) metric scale than the one intended by the researcher.

  iv *Probability of provision*: where a respondent values a good whose probability of provision differs from that intended by the researcher.

C *Context misspecification bias*: where the perceived context of the market differs from the intended context.

  i *Payment vehicle*: where the payment vehicle is either misperceived or is itself valued in a way not intended by the researcher.

  ii *Property right*: where the property right perceived for the good differs from that intended by the researcher.

  iii *Method of provision*: where the intended method of provision is either misperceived or is itself valued in a way not intended by the researcher.

  iv *Budget constraint*: where the perceived budget constraint differs from the budget constraint the researcher intended to invoke.

  v *Elicitation question*: where the perceived elicitation question fails to convey a request for a firm commitment to pay the highest amount the respondent will realistically pay before preferring to do without the amenity. (In the discrete-choice framework, the commitment is to pay the specified amount.)

  vi *Instrument context*: where the intended context or reference frame conveyed by the preliminary non-scenario material differs from that perceived by the respondent.

  vii *Question order*: where a sequence of questions, which should not have an effect, does have an effect on a respondent's WTP amount.

Source: Mitchell and Carson (1989, pp. 236–7).

remarks regarding the table will be made, but the reader interested in details is recommended to read Mitchell and Carson's 463-page examination of the CVM. In chapter 6 we will also elaborate upon some of the steps in a CVM study.

The most well known problem is the free rider problem. This may be expressed as follows: If consumers have to pay according to their stated WTP, they may try to conceal their true WTP in order to qualify for a lower price. On the other hand, if respondents believe that the price or the tax charged is unaffected by their response, they may have an incentive to overstate their WTP in order to secure a large supply of the (public) good. However, the available evidence from a number of empirical studies and experiments seems to indicate that strategic bias is a minor problem in CVM studies. It can occur if the valuation question is sufficiently 'biased' but should not pose a great problem for a skilled investigator.

Other biases due to *incentives to misrepresent responses* may occur if the respondent reacts positively or negatively to the fact that a particular institution is sponsoring the study. For example, suppose we are evaluating a new medical drug produced by the X company. Respondents may report different WTPs depending on whether they are informed that the study is sponsored by the X company; for example, a respondent may suspect that the aim of the study is to increase the company's profits. Similarly, a respondent may avoid reporting his or her true WTP in order to please the interviewer, i.e. s/he may feel a pressure to give the 'right' answer when responding to an in-person or telephone interviewer.

It is difficult to locate one's maximum WTP for a proposed project. In order to simplify the task, a respondent may try to use some pieces of information provided by the researcher as cues to the project's 'correct value'. One then speaks of *implied value cues*. An obvious example is provided by information in a questionnaire about the *per capita* cost of the project. A respondent may feel that this amount of money is what s/he should pay, and hence not report his or her 'true' WTP. Similarly, the respondent may interpret a starting bid as providing some information about the project's benefits. Thus, a starting bid can influence the respondent's answer to a valuation question. In fact, many studies, including the Norwegian one cited above, report a positive relationship between the size of the starting bid and the maximum WTP. Using a payment card with a large number of amounts may induce the respondent to use the range of these amounts as a frame of reference in estimating his or her own WTP. Other features of the survey, such as the order in which questions are asked or information provided about the cost of related/competing goods or projects, may also provide information which is interpreted as clues to the true value of the project.

A respondent may not fully understand the scenario specified by the researcher. *Scenario misspecification* occurs when the respondent incorrectly perceives one or more aspects of the contingent market and the good to be valued. For example, it is well known that even small changes in wording can cause large differences in responses. This is similar to opinion polls about voting behaviour. Due to differences in the wording of the referendum question, different investigators often come to different conclusions. Also, the respondent may view the proposed project as being symbolic of a larger policy package, and report his or her WTP for this larger package. When asked to value improved air quality in a small area, the respondent may view this as symbolic for improved national air quality unless the valuation question appropriately clarifies what is to be valued. This is related to the so-called 'embedding effect' of Kahneman and Knetsch (1992a, 1992b): they claim that a particular good (a medical treatment) is assigned a lower value if the WTP for the good is inferred from the WTP for a more inclusive good (a broad medical programme) rather than if the good is valued on its own. In fact, this is the outcome economic theory would lead us to expect; see the example on p. 95. The reader is referred to Carson and Mitchell (1994a, 1994b), Kahneman and Knetsch (1992a, 1992b) and Smith (1992) for discussions of the embedding problem.

Similarly, it may be difficult to value sub-components of a policy package. To illustrate, even if you know your WTP for a charter trip to the Bahamas, it may be difficult to specify the WTP for the weather, the WTP for the hotel, and so on; it is the package, not a number of sub-components, that you buy.

There are also a number of possible context misspecification biases. For example, the respondent may misperceive the payment vehicle. If the respondent is assumed to pay a fee for a treatment, s/he may feel that 'I am already paying for this through my tax payments' and hence report a low/ zero WTP. Distributional considerations can also affect the respondent's reactions to a particular payment vehicle. A respondent is probably willing to pay more if s/he feels that the payment vehicle is 'fair' than if s/he feels it to be unfair. The respondent can even refuse to pay if s/he feels that somebody else, say the industry, should pay. This can easily happen in situations where it is possible to identify a party who the respondent can blame for the problem under investigation (say, some pollution problem caused by industrial activities). It is therefore important that the investigator explains why a particular WTP question is asked; compare the question cited above.

Contingent valuations provide hypothetical answers to hypothetical questions. In particular, the respondent reports his hypothetical WTP, i.e. there are no real payments. This fact may induce the respondent to overstate his or her WTP. It may also be difficult to appreciate that reporting a WTP of $50 means that other expenses must be reduced by $50 since no real payment is made. Thus the respondent may overlook his or her budget constraint. This is probably one of the most serious drawbacks of the CVM. It is extremely important to use whatever tricks one can think of to emphasize to respondents that they should think as if they are making real payments. In an in-person or telephone interview, the interviewer may discuss with the respondent what expenses s/he plans to reduce in order to be able to pay a particular amount of money for the project under investigation. It is also important to emphasize for the respondent that there are many other projects or commodities which s/he may want to sponsor or buy. Otherwise, the respondent may ignore the fact that such projects or commodities exist. In particular, s/he may devote his or her entire 'health budget' to the medical project under investigation.

The reader should also note the following. If we evaluate the WTP for a proposed priced treatment or drug, it is rational for the respondent to overstate his or her WTP. This will increase the likelihood that the treatment or drug is introduced, by which the respondent receives an option to try the commodity. The actual decision whether or not to buy the commodity occurs once it is on the market. It is important to be aware of this two-stage decision problem, although the present author has no easy solution to suggest.

It should be noted that investigators are of course aware of these and other problems associated with the questionnaire technique. Moreover, it could be argued that many of the 'biases' associated with the CVM are quite natural. For example, there is no reason to believe that people are indifferent to the choice of payment vehicle, i.e. who pays and how. After all, we know that many people are concerned about distributional issues, implying that they may view the payment vehicle as a part of the policy package. Similarly, it is quite natural that the stated WTP for a project is conditional on the amount and quality of the information provided. This should be no more surprising than the fact that advertising may affect the WTP for a Mercedes Benz. It should be emphasized that this is not to say that the problems in using the method are minor. On the contrary, methods based on hypothetical behaviour, regardless of whether we use them to estimate WTP or qalys or hyes, must be controversial. The basic problem lies in the fact that we cannot know for sure that individuals would behave in the same way in a real situation as they do in an interview or in an experiment. Still, it is important to emphasize that the reader should not blame the method for any potential problem. Rather one must try to distinguish between problems which are due to economists' inability to fully understand/model human behaviour, those problems which arise in virtually all applied studies (e.g. econometric problems), and those problems which are specific to the CVM.

For a recent discussion of many of the issues and problems in using the survey technique to estimate money measures (or qalys or hyes), the reader is once again referred to Mitchell and Carson (1989); see also the set of articles on the CVM in the *Journal of Economic Perspectives* (Fall 1994). Critical assessments of the method can be found in, for example, Cummings and Harrison (1992), Desvousges *et al.* (1992), Hausman (1993) and in the 1994 (Fall) issue of the *Journal of Economic Perspectives*. The reader is also referred to the evaluation of the CVM by Arrow *et al.* (1993). This evaluation followed attempts to use the CVM to evaluate the Exxon Valdez oil spill off the coast of Alaska in 1987. (This evaluation has induced the responsible agency, NOAA, 1994, to issue guidelines for the design of CVM studies of large oil spills.) It should be noted that the debate induced by the Exxon Valdez evaluations (and the standards proposed by NOAA) centre around the possibility of meaningfully measuring passive-use values, and the problems debated are basically those considered previously in this section and whether these problems are so serious that they invalidate the whole approach. Passive-use values are primarily due to *public good* properties or *externalities* of a project such as existence values and intergenerational and intragenerational altruism. On the other hand, *health is primarily a private good*, though altruistic concerns are sometimes involved. This fact probably means that the problems in using the CVM are somewhat smaller, or at least different, when the method is applied to health care than when it is applied to large environmental changes or other public good projects. Still, altruism causes a problem when one aggregates individual WTPs. An extensive investigation of the implications for cost-benefit analysis of different formulations of the valuation question in a CVM when respondents are altruistic is provided in chapter 7, pp. 127–34.

In closing, the following should be noted. The reader who finds the CVM (or the market-based methods described later) too unrealistic may find it tempting to abandon money measures and turn to other measures such as qalys or hyes. Unfortunately, s/he will face the same problems as those faced in using the CVM since qalys and hyes are also derived from hypothetical answers to hypothetical questions. There is simply no easy solution to the valuation problem. This will be further explained in chapter 9.

Closed-ended techniques

The valuation techniques in which a respondent is asked for his or her maximal WTP for a particular change are often referred to as 'open-ended' or 'continuous' techniques. Another approach, the 'closed-ended' or

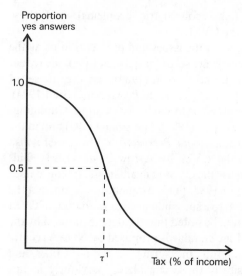

Figure 5.1 A bid curve

'discrete' (or binary) approach, confronts each respondent with a single bid or tax increase, which s/he has to accept or reject.[1] The important point, however, is that different sub-samples are confronted with different bids. To illustrate, in the study by Hylland and Strand (1983) referred to on pp. 72–73, a respondent in sub-sample 1 is asked if s/he is willing to pay 1 per cent of his or her income, a respondent in sub-sample 2 is confronted with a bid corresponding to 2 per cent of his or her income, and so on. The resulting relationship between the proportion of the total sample (or the population from which the sample is drawn) that accepts a particular tax increase in exchange for better air quality may be of the form depicted in figure 5.1. Almost 100 per cent are prepared to accept a small tax in order to obtain the specified improvement in air quality, but the higher the tax, the lower the proportion of the respondents prepared to vote 'yes'. Using figure 5.1, one can locate the median voter, i.e. the voter who accepts a tax, τ^1 in figure 5.1, such that 50 per cent of the voters would accept a higher tax and 50 per cent would be prepared to accept only a lower tax in exchange for the considered improvement in air quality. In other words, there is a 50:50 chance that the tax τ^1 would be accepted in a majority-voting referendum. The results can thus be interpreted in terms of a *median voter*.

Though the above example relates to the value of improved air quality, the technique is equally applicable to medical treatments. Then each sub-sample of respondents/patients is confronted with a single price of the treatment which has to be accepted or rejected. The price is however varied across different sub-samples. Note that an insurance works like a 'yes/no' question. You either agree or decline to pay the specified insurance premium. This opens up the possibility of using insurance data to indirectly estimate money measures of the value of health risks; compare the study by Cameron and Trivedi (1991).

We now turn to the question of how to use 'yes/no' data to arrive at a WTP measure. The typical formulation of the underlying choice problem, as first presented by Hanemann (1984), who was drawing on McFadden's (1973) random utility model, ignores risk faced by the respondent. A slightly modified version incorporating risk is therefore used here. The individual's indirect utility function is assumed to be of the form $V = V(\pi, y)$, where π is the exogenous survival probability, and y is income; compare (4.10). This function is chosen simply in order to minimize notational clutter, but the analysis will of course also work for, say, the model used on p. 53. Suppose the individual is offered a measure which changes the survival probability from π^0 to π^1 in exchange for a payment of $\$A$. The proposal is accepted if:

$$\Delta V = v(\pi^1, y - A) - v(\pi^0, y) + \eta > 0 \tag{5.1}$$

where η is a random variable whose expected value is equal to zero. The particular assumption behind this formulation is that the individual knows his or her utility function with certainty, but from the point of view of the investigator it contains some unobservable elements. In other words, on average the investigator is right, i.e. $V = v(\pi, y)$ since the expected value of η is zero, but in the individual case the investigator is wrong due to unobservable and seemingly stochastic variations, in tastes for instance. These latter components generate the stochastic structure of the model.

Hanemann (1984) shows that the stochastic nature of the model means that a cumulative distribution function (*cdf*) can be used to calculate the average or expected WTP; see also Cameron (1988). Usually a *cdf* is defined as a function $F(A) = \text{prob}\{\text{WTP} \leq A\}$ yielding the probability that the respondent is willing to pay no more than $\$A$, i.e. vote 'no' to paying $\$A$ (or is indifferent). Thus the downward sloping curve in figure 5.1 is equal to $G(A) = 1 - F(A)$ since it yields the probability that the respondent is willing to pay $\$A$ or more. Now the average or expected WTP can be written as:

$$\text{CV} = \int_0^b G(A)dA - \int_a^0 [1 - G(A)]dA \tag{5.2}$$

where $a \leq 0$ and $b > 0$ are the lower and upper limits of integration, respectively, $F(b) = 1$, and $F(a) = 0$; see the appendix to this chapter and chapter 6, pp. 105–6 for a derivation of this expression. For an interpretation of (5.2) in terms of a market demand curve, the reader is referred to pp. 83–6 below.

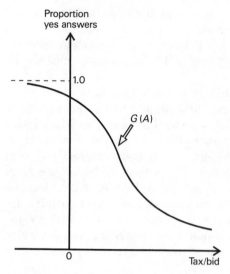

Figure 5.2 A bid curve when the probability of a negative WTP is strictly positive

If $a=0$, as in figure 5.1, CV is equal to the area below the curve. To many investigators evaluating changes in health, it may seem natural to assume that $a=0$, i.e. to rule out the possibility of a negative WTP. However, it is important that an investigator using discrete response data does not mechanically ignore the second term in (5.2), when calculating the average WTP. In order to see this, consider the logistic distribution, which is often used in discrete response data experiments:

$$G(A)=1/(1+e^{-\Delta v}) \qquad (5.3)$$

with $\Delta v=v_\pi\Delta\pi-v_yA$, i.e. a linear approximation of the utility change in (5.1). The distribution in (5.3) has the property that $G(-\infty)=1$ while $G(+\infty)=0$, implying that (5.2) must be integrated between $a=-\infty$ and $b=+\infty$ to obtain CV (which on pp. 105–6 is shown to be equal to v_π/v_y). In contrast to figure 5.1, where the curve intersects the 'y axis' at the point where the probability of a 'yes' is equal to unity, the curve will now intersect the axis below that point. This is shown in figure 5.2. A part of the distribution is hence to be found in the north-west quadrant, i.e. corresponding to a negative WTP. The average or expected WTP, CV, is equal to the area below the curve in the north-east quadrant (the first term in (5.2)) *less* the area between the dotted line and the curve in the north-west quadrant (the second term in (5.2)). An example in Johansson *et al.* (1989), based on actual data, produced CV = \$220 while setting $a=0$ yielded a 'mean' equal to \$430, i.e. a considerable difference which may have far-reaching consequences for the outcome of a cost-benefit analysis.

On the other hand, suppose that $\Delta v = v_\pi \Delta \pi - \ln A$, which is similar to the example discussed by Hanemann (1984). Negative bids are then ruled out so that (5.2) should be integrated between zero and $+\infty$.[2] There are also other possibilities open to the investigator who wants to rule out negative bids, as shown in Kriström (1990a), for example. The important point to make here, however, is that there seems to be a considerable uncertainty about the 'shape' of the tails of the distribution obtained in empirical studies, and the assumptions made in this respect seem to have a considerable impact on the magnitude of the estimated mean WTP. The example referred to above confirms this. In fact, there is no guarantee that the integral in (5.2) converges in an empirical application. For example, Bishop and Heberlein (1979) face this 'infinitely high mean WTP problem'; see (6.12) for the technical reason for this problem. The conclusion that emerges is that the investigator must invest a lot of time in designing the bid vector, and possibly use a pilot study to test its properties. A finite 'mean' WTP can always be achieved by some cunning truncation, e.g. by ruling out negative bids and limiting b to income, but this is a completely arbitrary procedure, which casts doubt on the results of a study; see chapter 6, pp. 110–12 for a further discussion of the 'tail' issue.

The econometric steps which are necessary in order to be able to estimate an average WTP from 'yes/no' data will not be discussed here. A detailed examination is found on pp. 106–13. The reader is also referred to pp. 113–14, where we have collected a number of formulae for the computation of the average WTP in applied studies. We now turn to a discrete choice approach which is probably easier to understand and handle than the one presented above when estimating the average WTP for a policy measure.

A useful interpretation of WTP measures

This section, which is much inspired by Suen (1990) and Mäler (1974), presents an interpretation of WTP measures, including measures based on binary responses, in terms of a market demand curve. Hopefully, this interpretation is useful as a complement to the interpretations supplied in most other textbooks, and outlined in the previous section.

Let us once again consider the individual whose indirect utility function is stated in equation (5.1). The individual is asked about his or her WTP for a proposed increase in his or her survival probability. The maximal WTP is implicitly defined by the following equation:

$$V(\pi^1, y - CV) = V(\pi^0, y) \tag{5.4}$$

where $V(.)$ is the indirect utility function, and CV is the non-contingent CV.

Suppose there is a continuum of individuals with different valuations of the proposed project or treatment, i.e. a change in the survival probability. In order to simplify the interpretation, without any loss of generality, the number of individuals is normalized to one. The valuation of the project is described by a continuous distribution function $F(p) = \text{prob}\{CV \leq p\}$, where p is the bid ('market price'). Thus $F(p)$ yields the number of individuals who are willing to pay no more than $\$p$ for the treatment, i.e. the specified change in the survival probability. Since an individual either 'purchases' the treatment or not, aggregate or market demand for the treatment is given by:

$$D(p) = 1 - F(p) \tag{5.5}$$

where $D(p)$ is the aggregate demand curve, i.e. it yields the number of individuals who are willing to pay at least $\$p$ for the treatment. The aggregate consumer surplus can be interpreted as the area to the left of a demand curve above p^0, as is illustrated in figure 5.3a, where p^0 can be interpreted as the price or the average cost of the treatment. Thus integrating (5.5) between p^0 and the highest possible p value yields the aggregate consumer surplus.[3] The area under the demand curve can be interpreted as aggregate or total WTP for the proposed treatment. The fat horizontal part of the demand curve in figure 5.3a illustrates the case in which a fraction of individuals report a zero WTP for a treatment, possibly because they find that the pain of the measure exceeds its positive impact on the survival probability, or because they do not suffer from the medical problem under investigation.

It need not be the case that everyone is willing to pay a non-negative sum of money for the project, as is illustrated in figure 5.3b. If the project provides a pure and unpriced public safety measure which everyone is forced to consume, the total WTP is given by area $CV' - CV''$ in figure 5.3b. In this case, some individuals need a compensation to voluntarily accept the project. In terms of (5.2), area CV'' corresponds to the integral from a to 0. On the other hand, if the project provides a priced private service, say a medical treatment, the consumer surplus is equal to the area to the left of the demand curve above the market price for the treatment, i.e. CV in figure 5.3a, provided participation in the treatment is voluntary. Note that we have normalized the number of individuals to one, i.e. CV is the average consumer surplus. The aggregate or total CV is obtained by multiplying CV by the number of individuals.

If an open-ended bid question is used in a study, one can simply plot the individual maximum bids to obtain the market demand curve, as in figure 5.3a. Still, it may be of interest to use regression techniques in order to

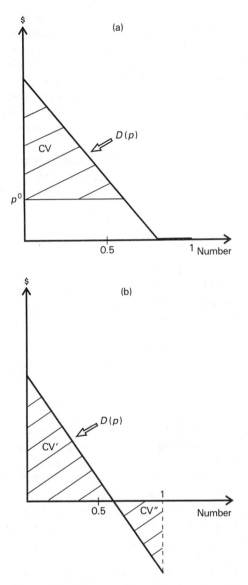

Figure 5.3 Aggregate demand curves for a 'discrete' project

examine what factors determine the location of the curve. If the study uses a closed-ended valuation question, one must estimate the function $F(p)$ in (5.5). One of the most commonly used functions in such studies is the logistic one; see p. 82 above. In any case, once the function is estimated, the consumer surplus is calculated in the way explained above. This shows that it is not necessary to start from a utility function and make complicated derivations in order to arrive at an expression to estimate. The market demand curve approach described here seems simpler and more intuitively appealing.

In closing, it should be noted that the compensated demand curve defined by (5.5) and the ordinary demand curve coincide. This is due to the assumption that you either participate or you do not. In other words, you purchase one unit of the good or you purchase none.

CVM studies of health risks

The first attempt to use the CVM in order to value risk reductions was probably that of Acton (1973), who investigated the WTP for mobile coronary care units which would decrease the risk of dying after a heart attack. Jones-Lee (1976) carried out an early study of the value of airline safety. Both these early studies were explorative in nature and used very small samples. Two later and much larger studies investigating the value of risk reductions are those of Jones-Lee *et al.* (1985) and Smith and Desvousges (1987).

Jones-Lee *et al.* (1985) used the CVM to investigate the value of reductions in the risk of traffic deaths in the UK. A random sample of 1150 individuals was used, and 1103 interviews were carried out (i.e. a non-response of about 5 per cent). A follow-up study was also carried out of a sample of 210 individuals from the original sample, to test the reliability and stability of the answers. The results show a value of a statistical life of about £1.5 million (1982 prices) with only the WTP for own risk reduction included, and about £2 million when the WTP for reductions in other people's risks is included. The authors also note that the results as a whole conform to the theoretical predictions, and that individuals seem to be able to understand changes in probabilities.

Smith and Desvousges (1987) used the CVM to value risk changes from hazardous waste. A representative sample of 720 households in Boston was used in the study and 609 interviews were carried out with these households (i.e. a non-response of about 15 per cent). The risk of dying from exposure was divided into two parts: the risk of exposure, and the risk of dying given that one is exposed. The sample was divided into eight different sub-samples confronted with different risk reductions. The variation in WTP between the different sub-samples was small. Contrary to the theoretical predictions, the WTP for a small risk reduction was found to decrease with the level of the risk, the 'baseline risk'. However, within each sub-sample the hypothesis of equal marginal WTP over a range of risk levels could not be rejected. The regression analysis also indicated that individuals exaggerate small risks. Moreover, the WTP for a marginal risk reduction was greater than the WTP to avoid an identical marginal risk increase. The results were thus contrary to most theoretical predictions, which contrasts with the results and conclusions of the study by Jones-Lee *et al.* (1985). The fact that the risk was divided into two components (exposure and mortality risk if exposed) may, however, have led to problems for the individuals to interpret the actual risk reductions. In comparing the results from Smith and Desvousges (1987) and Jones-Lee *et al.* (1985) it also appears that the results are consistent within samples, i.e. the WTP increases with the risk reduction within a sample, but not between samples. (The latter was not studied by Jones-Lee *et al.*, 1985.) This fact may indicate that individuals have difficulties when asked to distinguish between risk reductions involving small probabilities, unless they are given some kind of reference point, as for example when the WTP is elicited for several risk reductions within a sample. In contrast to Smith and Desvousges (1987), Horowitz and Carson (1993) in a recent study find strong support for the hypothesis that individuals do prefer to reduce risks for which the baseline risk is higher.

The studies by Jones-Lee *et al.* (1985) and Smith and Desvousges (1987) concerned mortality risks, but studies of morbidity risks are also starting to appear in the literature (Berger *et al.*, 1987; Evans and Viscusi, 1991, for example). There are also experiments with risk–risk trade-offs instead of WTP (Viscusi *et al.*, 1991; Krupnick and Cropper, 1992; Dolan *et al.*, 1993). This means that instead of investigating how much income people are prepared to give up in order to secure a risk reduction, the trade-off between a morbidity risk and a mortality risk is investigated. Individuals may for instance be indifferent between their initial situation and a project that reduces the risk of chronic bronchitis from $100/100,000$ to $90/100,000$ and increases the risk of car accident fatalities from $10/100,000$ to $11/100,000$. In this case the car accident-death equivalent of chronic bronchitis is 0.1. The WTP per statistical life saved from car accident fatalities can then be used to compute the WTP per statistical case of chronic bronchitis prevented, to be used in a cost-benefit analysis; see chapter 9 for details. It should be noted that if the WTP approach is just as valid and reliable as the risk–risk approach, then it is more straightforward to directly elicit the WTP for the reduction in the morbidity risk. A comparison of the validity and reliability of these approaches to valuing reduced morbidity is an important issue for future research. For a further presentation of the risk–risk method the reader is referred to chapter 9.

A typical feature of many public safety programmes is that they yield a benefits stream far in the future; a programme aimed at the reduction of pollutants causing cancer provides a good example. This raises the question of how people discount lives saved at different points in time. In an empirical study of people's discounting of future lives saved versus lives saved today, Cropper *et al.* (1992) found that discount rates are much higher for short horizons than for long horizons. Respondents were more willing to give up lives today if the programme saved 100 lives in a distant future than if the programme saved 100 lives 10 years from now, but the discount rate decreases with time. Thus respondents attach a lower priority to lives saved in the future than to lives saved today. (The study was a small-scale study based on brief telephone interviews.) It seems to be an important task for health economists to examine in more detail how people discount lives saved today versus lives saved in the future.

There are also studies appearing in which learning processes are examined. For example, Viscusi and Magat (1992) examine individual responses to ambiguous risk information. They assume a model of expected utility that incorporates a Bayesian learning process. The model receives some empirical support in that individuals weight the information that they are given, and they place a greater weight on the scientific evidence that is more recent and which should be more credible. The reader is referred to Viscusi and Magat (1992) for further details as well as references.

The CVM has so far mainly been used to evaluate environmental health risks, but studies are also starting to appear in the health care field. In chapter 6, we will present the results of these studies in some detail.

The human capital approach

The human capital (HC) approach views the value of an individual as being equal to the value of his or her contribution to total production, and assumes that this value can be measured as his or her earnings. This means that the value of preventing someone's statistical death or injury is equal to the gain in the present value of his or her future earnings.

Suppose that a medical treatment changes both health and income. The circumstances in which expected income changes provide useful information can be illuminated by undertaking a linear approximation of utility functions of the form $V(p,y,z)$, where both income y and health z are assumed to be stochastic, around (p,y^E,z^E), where a superscript E refers to the expected value with the treatment. One obtains:

$$\Delta E(V) = \Sigma_i \Delta \pi_i V(p,y_i,z_i) = \Sigma_i \Delta \pi_i [y_i + (V_z z_i / V_{yc})] V_{yc}$$
$$= [\Delta y^E + (V_{zc} \Delta z^E / V_{yc})] V_{yc} \tag{5.6}$$

where $\Delta E(V)$ is the change in expected utility caused by the treatment, $\Delta \pi_i$ refers to the change the treatment causes in the probability that the individual earns income y_i and experiences health status z_i, V_{yc} refers to the marginal utility of income evaluated at (p, y^E, z^E), V_{zc} is the marginal utility of health evaluated at (p, y^E, z^E), and $\Delta y^E (\Delta z^E)$ is the change in expected income (expected health) due to the treatment. The linear approximation in (5.6) highlights the fact that health and income must change in the same direction in order that changes in expected income should make sense as a *lower bound* for the value of health changes. However, the kind of approximation undertaken in (5.6) provides some weak support for the idea of using expected income losses to evaluate changes in health or even the loss of a statistical life.

Still, valuations, such as cost-of-illness studies, based on changes in expected incomes have some disturbing consequences; see, for example, Lindgren (1981) for details on the cost-of-illness approach. For example, the statistical life of retired people has no value. Similarly, the implication of discounting future earnings is that the statistical life of children is likely to be worth less than that of adults in or near their best period of earnings. People whose value for production is not reflected by wage payments are also difficult to handle within the HC framework; housewives may serve as a good example. Moreover, the approach does not take into account the indirect damage due to death and injuries, e.g. pain and suffering, either of persons directly affected or of relatives and friends. These and other shortcomings have led to attempts to adjust estimates obtained by the HC approach, for example by evaluating housewives' production in terms of wages of domestic servants, and by including allowances which aim at capturing economic losses due to pain and suffering.

Such attempts do not, however, solve what is usually viewed as the most important drawback of the HC approach. It is simply not consistent with the individualistic foundation of welfare economics, since it does not take people's own preferences on changes in health risks into account. This can be seen from the final term within parentheses in (5.6). For this reason, the HC method will not be considered further here. The reader is also referred to Schelling (1968) and Rosen (1988) for assessments of the human capital approach.

Market-based estimation methods

There is a class of methods which exploits people's behaviour in markets where goods related to health risks are traded. These methods are often referred to as indirect methods since the preference revelation is indirect via a market, in contrast to the CVM which aims at a direct preference revelation.

The basic idea can be illustrated using the endogenous risk model given in (4.10). The indirect utility function of an individual is written as follows:

$$V(p, P, y) = U[\pi_1(p, P, y), x(p, P, y)] \tag{5.7}$$

where p is a vector of prices of consumption goods x, P is the price of a health good X used in increasing the survival probability π_1, and y is the fixed income. The first-order condition for interior utility maximization with respect to X is easily shown to be equal to:

$$[(U_\pi(.)/V_y(.)]\partial\pi/\partial X = P \tag{5.8}$$

where $U_\pi = \partial U/\partial\pi_1$, and V_y is the marginal utility of income. The expression within brackets in (5.8) can be interpreted as the marginal WTP for a risk reduction. Through the survival production function, a change in the use of the health good X is converted into a marginal WTP which can be calculated if we know the market price P of the good in question. This illustrates the fact that market prices can sometimes be used to evaluate health risks, a point made emphatically by, for example, Courant and Porter (1981). Note, however, that if some individuals refrain from purchasing the good X, then its market price does not provide a lower bound for the valuation of a small risk reduction. The reader is also referred to the discussion following (8.13) (p. 145), which further illuminates the problems one faces in using market prices to assess health risks.

A further example is provided by wage differentials in the labour market due to differences in health risks between different jobs. To illustrate the idea in the simplest possible way, let us rewrite (5.7) slightly as:

$$V[\pi_1, p, y + w(\pi_1)] \tag{5.9}$$

where the health good X is ignored. Instead, the individual can accept a lower survival probability in exchange for a higher wage w, i.e. w is viewed as decreasing in the survival probability so that, *ceteris paribus*, more risky jobs are better paid than less risky ones. Thus the individual chooses π_1 so as to equate V_π/V_y, the marginal WTP for risk reductions on the job, and the wage increase obtained by accepting a slightly higher risk in the job:

$$V_\pi(.)/V_y(.) = \partial w(.)/\partial\pi_1 \tag{5.10}$$

where we can interpret the wage offer function $w(.)$ as being determined by employers. (5.10) indicates the possibility of using labour market data to access the valuation of changes in mortality risks.

Let us now turn to empirical studies. To study individuals' averting behaviour is intuitively appealing, since this is really a case where individuals buy themselves a risk reduction for money. For example, Åkerman *et al.* (1991) examined households living in houses with indoor radiation due to radon decay products. Given information on radiation levels and the health risks, households decide whether or not they should take measures against the radiation. This decision obviously involves a consideration of how much they are willing to pay for a radiation reduction. Using data on measures undertaken, costs and radiation levels, Åkerman *et al.* estimate a WTP and the implied value of statistical life. Other examples of averting behaviour are purchases of smoke detectors, see Dardis (1980), and the use of seatbelts, Blomquist (1979); see also the review in Folland *et al.* (1993). It is important to note that averting behaviour implies that health risks faced by the individuals are endogenous, as was also illustrated at the beginning of this section. Crocker *et al.* (1991) analyze the consequences of endogenous risk for economic valuation, and draw attention to the fact that individuals may differ in their ability to reduce risk. This is not reflected in the notion of the value of a statistical life. It has also been argued that self-protection expenditures can be interpreted as a lower bound to the value of risk reduction. Shogren and Crocker (1991) show that this claim is not necessarily true. For example, some individuals may refrain completely from buying self-protection, implying that their marginal valuation of the risk reduction falls short of the market price or cost of the risk reduction in question. See also the discussion below (8.13) (p. 145).

There are a number of studies using house markets to examine health risks. These studies are based on the hypothesis that house characteristics yielding differences in health risks across houses should be reflected in property value differentials. Examples are provided by air pollution, for example the study by Portney (1981), Kohlhase's (1991) study of exposure to hazardous waste, and a study of radon radiation by Söderqvist (1991).

The most common indirect method, however, is to study wage differentials on the labour market. In principle, wage differentials are explained as the outcome of firms' different offers of wages depending on what health risks are involved, and workers' different preferences for safety, given firms' and workers' institutional environment; see Rosen (1986) and Viscusi (1993). To put it simply, it is costly for firms to reduce the health risks that jobs involve, which implies a trade-off between wages and risk reduction costs; if a firm has undertaken risk reduction measures, the maximum wage it is willing to offer will be lower than otherwise. Workers differ in their views on safety, implying that their indifference curves for trade-offs between health risks and wages also differ. As a consequence one obtains a series of tangency points between the (aggregated) offer curve of firms' and workers' indifference curves. The idea is to estimate this locus of tangency points, which is sometimes called the hedonic wage function. In essence, one uses regression analysis, where wages/earnings are regressed on worker and job characteristics including risk levels. The partial derivative of the estimated hedonic wage function with respect to the risk characteristic is interpreted as the risk premium for a given level of risk (and given values of other characteristics). Given the risk premium, one can infer the value of a statistical life.

An article by Kniesner and Leeth (1991) may serve as an example of a recent wage differential study. The authors use data from the labour markets in Australia, Japan and the United States, respectively. It should be noted that they follow the normal track and use cross-industry data. An alternative, first employed by French and Kendall (1992), is to concentrate on data on a single industry. Use of data from different countries implies that Kniesner and Leeth can examine the effects of differences in institutional environments on wage differentials. In order to illustrate the econometrics involved, let us examine their estimation of a hedonic wage function for the manufacturing industry of the United States. The authors begin by noting that an estimated hedonic wage function is sufficient for their purposes; they do not need to digress into the complicated issue of estimating underlying offer functions and indifference curves; see Epple (1987). They then choose a semilogarithmic form of the hedonic wage function, apparently because of its popularity in econometric studies and not its fitness for available data. The dependent variable of the hedonic wage function is defined as average weekly earnings of full-time manufacturing workers. This variable is regressed on fatality rate, injury rate, benefits from workers' compensation system measured as the maximum weekly death benefit to the surviving spouse, a dummy variable for the existence of a maximum limit of total spouse benefit, race, sex, marital status, age, education, union membership, region, the industry's new hire rate and its separation rate. This choice of variables illustrates some important issues.

First, there is always the risk that some characteristics causing differences in worker productivity are not included as independent variables (or are unobservable). Hwang *et al.* (1992) have analyzed this issue within a simulation framework and conclude that 'point estimates reported in existing studies are likely to seriously underestimate the true compensating wage differentials they are intending to measure. For example, … if (i) wages constitute 65 per cent of total compensation, (ii) differences in tastes account for 20 per cent of total wage variation, and (iii) unobserved productivity variance equals 40 per cent of total productivity variance, then workers' true valuations of life will be 10 times greater than valuations calculated from the estimated wage differentials.' The difficulty of observing all relevant data is a general problem in empirical research, but the results of Hwang *et al.* emphasize the high degree of attention it deserves. Viscusi (1992) also touches upon this issue when noting that any omission of job characteristics positively correlated with job health risks would result in an overestimate of the health risk premium. Secondly, note that Kniesner and Leeth take into account the workers' compensation system. They find that this system has a considerable influence on the estimates of wage differentials. In early wage differential studies the presence of compensation systems was not always considered. Thirdly, it can be questioned whether workers really have information on the health risks of the jobs they are applying for. It has been argued that mobility among workers gives them risk experience from different firms so that they eventually learn the true risks. Hire and separation rates may therefore be of relevance for hedonic wage functions. Kniesner and Leeth, who do include these rates as independent variables, note that wage allowances for hazardous jobs may be formalized due to government or union action. Such action clearly causes wage differentials, but the problem of workers' actual perception of job risks remains. This latter problem is directly related to the general issue of objective versus subjective risks, an issue which is not discussed further here.

Kniesner and Leeth estimate hedonic wage functions for four levels of aggregation (individuals, states, regions and nation, respectively) in order to study what turned out to be the large effect of aggregation on the significance and magnitude of coefficient estimates. They also present estimates of the compensating wage differentials for death risks for Australia (2.5 per cent), Japan (zero) and the United States (1 per cent). In closing, the reader who is interested in reading more about hedonic methods is referred to Palmquist (1991) and Viscusi (1992); see also the simultaneous equation studies by Biddle and Zarkin (1988) and Garen (1988).

The value of a statistical life

Comparisons between studies and methods are usually carried out in terms of the value per statistical life. It is however important to bear in mind that the value per statistical life can be expected to vary with the type of risk (e.g. voluntary versus involuntary), the initial risk level, the size of the risk change, age and income. For example, the discussions in chapters 4 and 8, pp. 68–9 and 148–50 clearly indicate that there may be an age-dependency in the valuation of current as well as future risk changes. Similarly, some studies, see p. 87, indicate that the magnitude of the baseline risk influences the WTP for a risk reduction. There is thus no reason to believe that different studies should come up with one and the same number for the value of a statistical life. Still, it is of interest to compare different estimates in order to check if different methods produce similar estimates of one and the same risk change and if there are systematic differences in the valuation of different risk changes.

A number of reviews of the value per statistical life in the literature have been carried out; see, for example, Fisher *et al.* (1989), Miller (1990), and Viscusi (1992). In the most recent survey by Viscusi (1992) the value per statistical life varies between $0.6 million and $16.2 million in the surveyed labour market analyses of wage–risk trade-offs, between $0.07 million and $4.0 million in the studies of consumer markets, and between $0.1 million and $15.6 million in the CVM studies (in December 1990 dollars). Viscusi (1992, p. 73) notes that for labour market studies of wage–risk trade-offs 'most of the reasonable estimates of the value of life are clustered in the $3 to $7 million range'. He also notes that this estimate conforms quite well with the results of the large-scale CVM studies, whereas the results of the studies of consumer markets are well below this estimate. A similar conclusion is reached by Fisher *et al.* (1989), who note that the newer CVM and wage–risk studies yield similar results with respect to the value per statistical life. Fisher *et al.* (1989, p. 96) conclude that 'The most defensible empirical results indicate a range for the value-per-statistical-life estimates of $1.6 million to $8.5 million (in 1986 dollars)'. Both Fisher *et al.* (1989) and Viscusi (1992) conclude that the estimates from the studies of consumer markets are biased downwards due to the assumptions made in these studies and the problems of isolating the income–risk trade-off from confounding factors.

Miller (1990) in his review identifies 65 studies of the value per statistical life, and eliminates 18 of those as unreliable. He then adjusts the value of the remaining 47 studies according to, for instance, risk perception. After the adjustments he finds a mean value per statistical life of $2.2 million, with $2.2 million for the labour market studies of wage–risk trade-offs and $2.5 million for the CVM studies (in 1988 dollars). However, the adjustments and elimination in Miller's studies are to a large extent arbitrary and the review therefore exaggerates the similarity of results across different methods and studies.

The different methods discussed here are all associated with important advantages and disadvantages. The major problem of the indirect methods is to isolate the risk–income trade-off from confounding factors and to take into account the institutional restrictions of the observed markets. The area of application is also limited to those risks that are traded in markets, whereas the need for information about the value of health changes is greatest in the areas where no markets exist. The CVM overcomes these problems of the indirect methods, but its major disadvantage is of course that little is still known about the extent to which answers to hypothetical questions mimic actual behaviour. Most studies based on actual behaviour on markets have been based on objective rather than subjective risks, which will bias the results to the extent that these risks diverge. In principle it should, however, be possible to adjust the results for this factor to the extent that it is possible to measure the subjective risk levels. Although the CV methods usually ask the respondents to value a specified risk reduction, little is known about how such risk information is processed and to what extent the risk reductions are taken at face value or weighted by some prior belief.

An important issue identified on p. 63 is altruism, i.e. when people are concerned about other people's welfare or safety. Indirect methods based on market behaviour probably do not capture altruistic values. It is however far from self-evident that this implies that indirect methods underestimate the value of health changes; see the discussion in chapter 7, pp. 127–30. The issue of altruism has to a large extent been neglected in empirical studies, with the noteworthy exceptions of Jones-Lee *et al.* (1985), who found that the value per statistical life increased by about a third if altruism (probably paternalistic or safety-oriented) is included, and Viscusi, Magat and Forrest (1988). A further investigation into the role of altruism when assessing the value of health changes is important for future research.

A final issue to consider is how to aggregate results from different studies. In order to illustrate the basic problem, let us assume that an individual's WTP for medical programme no. 1 is $\$A$, for programme no. 2 is $\$B$ and for programme no. 3 is $\$C$. These numbers may have been obtained from different empirical studies. In any case, one cannot sum these amounts and interpret the resulting sum (i.e. $A + B + C$) as the individual's total WTP for the three programmes, unless each programme is very (infinitesimally) small. To illustrate, suppose that my WTP for a Mercedes Benz is \$50,000 and my WTP for a Volvo is \$10,000. This does *not* mean that my total WTP for cars is (at least) \$60,000. Returning to our medical programmes, either we must ask the individual about his or her WTP for programme nos. $1 + 2 + 3$, or we ask about his or her WTP for (say) programme no. 1, then ask about his or her WTP for programme no. 2, *given* what s/he has already paid for programme no. 1, and then ask about his or her WTP for programme no. 3, *given* what s/he has paid for programmes nos. 1 and 2. These two approaches should, at least theoretically, produce the same *aggregate* amount of money. On the other hand, due to substitution effects, the (conditional) WTP for an individual programme is *not*, in general, independent of the order in which the questions are asked; see, for example, Johansson (1993) for details. In any case, one must be careful if, in arriving at an estimate of the aggregate WTP for a set of treatments, data is collected from a number of sources.

Appendix

The average WTP measure stated in (5.2) in the main text is defined as follows:

$$
\begin{aligned}
CV &= \int_a^b A F_d(A) dA = -\int_a^b F(A) dA + F(b)b - F(a)a \\
&= \int_0^b [1 - F(A)] dA - \int_a^0 F(A) dA \\
&= \int_0^b G(A) dA - \int_a^0 [1 - G(A)] dA
\end{aligned}
\tag{A5.1}
$$

where $F_d(A)$ is the probability density function, $F'(A) = F_d(A)$ with a prime denoting a derivative, $F(a) = 0$, and $F(b) = 1$. The first-line equality is obtained by integration by parts.

6 Contingent valuation studies of health care

In chapter 5, we introduced methods which can be used to assess the value of changes in health risks. This chapter concentrates on one of these methods, the contingent valuation method (CVM). As is obvious from chapter 5, the method is widely used to assess changes in health risks due to changes in environmental parameters such as air quality and water quality. In this chapter, however, we concentrate on applications within the health care field.

The first section of the chapter indicates what medical treatments and diseases have been evaluated using the CVM. A few studies are given a slightly fuller presentation. The following two sections of the chapter are devoted to a Swedish study of high blood pressure (hypertension). The purpose is to give the reader an idea of the different steps in a study using the closed-ended valuation technique. The chapter closes with a few useful formulae for the computation of the average WTP in empirical studies.

Empirical studies of the WTP for health care: a brief review

In this section we will present a number of the available empirical studies regarding people's WTP for different kinds of medical treatments. After a brief consideration of the kinds of health care which have been examined by various authors, the results of some key studies will be presented.

Donaldson (1993) presents a brief review of empirical studies of the WTP for health care. His review includes the following (and a few other) studies. Acton (1973) asked 93 people about their WTP for a programme that reduces heart attack mortality and saves a certain number of lives in their community. Appel et al. (1990) asked 100 outpatients about their WTP to reduce the risk resulting from the injection of contrast media in a radiographic diagnostic procedure. Berwick and Weinstein (1985) interviewed 62 women receiving prenatal care during normal pregnancies. They were asked about their WTP for information derived from ultrasound tests under different assumptions on how the information could be used. Culbertson et al. (1988) asked 317 patients attending six different pharmacy practices about their WTP for pharmaceutical information. Donaldson (1990) interviewed 119 relatives of elderly people in long-term care. A bidding procedure was used to find out how much they thought the government should pay for national health service care in hospital and in nursing homes and if they were willing to accept the resulting increase in taxes resulting from their answers. Easthaugh (1991) examined haemoglobin solutions to reduce the risk of disease transmissions via blood/blood products. He asked 20 regional blood bank managers and 50 health services administration students about their WTP for such risk reductions given a certain probability that the respondent would be the patient. Einarson *et al.* (1988) asked 27 patients at a community pharmacy about their WTP for a serum cholesterol test. The actual price was $10 and the patients were asked both before and after taking the test. Gafni and Feder (1987) asked 13 women in a kibbutz about their WTP for visiting a private clinic in order to obtain contraceptives, these women were unhappy with their public clinic. Grimes (1988) asked 100 women who had a negative cervical smear result about their monetary valuation for the test. Thompson (1986) interviewed 247 persons with rheumatoid arthritis. They were asked how much of their family's regular income they were willing to give up in exchange for a complete cure for arthritis. Thompson *et al.* (1982, 1984) reports similar studies with subjects with osteoarthritis or rheumatoid arthritis.

We now turn to a short review in Johannesson *et al.* (1992) of a number of Swedish CVM studies of the WTP for drug treatment. These applications fall into three different medical areas: angina pectoris, i.e. vascular spasms; hypertension, i.e. high blood pressure; and hypercholesterolaemia, i.e. high cholesterol levels. Here we will summarize the two latter applications. The reader interested in the angina pectoris study is referred to Jönsson *et al.* (1988).

Hypertension

Two Swedish applications of the CVM have been carried out by Johannesson, Jönsson and Borgquist (1991) and Johannesson *et al.* (1991) in the hypertension field. The first study estimated the WTP for anti-hypertensive drug therapy. The population consisted of 481 patients at a primary health care centre. The patient population was divided into two sub-samples. Sub-sample 1 received an open-ended WTP question in which they were asked to state their maximum WTP for their current treatment for hypertension. Sub-sample 2 received a binary ('yes/no') valuation question in which they were asked to accept or reject a specified increase in annual user fees (bids) for their current treatment; the bids varied between 100 SEK and 10,000 SEK in 15 sub-samples ($1 \approx 8$ SEK). This design allows the authors to compare open-ended and binary valuation questions.

In total, 322 patients (67 per cent) returned the mail questionnaire. There was a large difference in item non-response between the open-ended and the binary valuation questions. The average WTP using the open-ended question was 390 SEK per year. It was concluded that the question did not work well. The item non-response rate was high (59 per cent), due to protest answers and difficulties in answering the question. There were also problems with implied value cues, since it was stated in the valuation question that the respondents at the moment paid approximately 350 SEK each per year in user fees. In the open-ended question about one-third of the respondents stated a WTP 350 SEK.

Logistic regression analysis and a non-parametric approach were used to estimate the parameters which are used to calculate mean and median WTP from the binary responses.[1] The reason for using two different approaches is that the mean and the median are known to be sensitive to the assumption about the distribution of people's WTP; see pp. 110–12 below for details. In the calculation of mean WTP it was assumed that maximum WTP is equal to the maximum bid of 10,000 SEK in the study. In order to check what this truncation means for the magnitude of the mean, a calculation with a maximum WTP of 15,000 SEK was also carried out.

According to the logistic model, the median WTP is 2900 SEK. The average or mean WTP is 4500 SEK if the maximum WTP in the population is assumed to be 10,000 SEK, and 5500 SEK if the maximum WTP is assumed to be 15,000 SEK. The median using the non-parametric approach is 2400 SEK. The means are 4200 SEK and 5100 SEK, respectively, using the aforementioned two assumptions about maximum WTP. The logistic model and the non-parametric approach thus produce similar results. Since there was too little information about WTP above the highest bid (10,000 SEK), the calculation of mean WTP is highly uncertain, and should be interpreted with caution.

In the reported study, the binary valuation question performed better than the open-ended valuation one, at least with respect to non-responses. Binary valuation questions according to which the respondent 'votes' 'yes' or 'no' are easier to answer and minimize incentives for strategic behaviour. The valuation decision also resembles a market situation for the respondent. On the market the respondent chooses between buying and not buying at a specified price (the price being an exogenous variable). The study indicates that it is possible to use the CVM in the health care field, but further studies are needed to test the reliability and validity of the method.

The second Swedish application of the CVM in the hypertension field is with regard to non-pharmacological treatment of hypertension; see Johannesson et al. (1991). In this study a non-pharmacological treatment (NPT) programme and conventional drug treatment of hypertension were compared in a cost-benefit analysis.

The NPT programme involved 400 patients and was carried out at 8 health centres from 1984 to 1986. It consisted of monthly visits by a nurse, doctor visits every 6 months, measuring blood pressure at home, dietary advice, relaxation therapy, physical activity, etc. The patients were also followed for 2 additional years after the study to assess whether the programme still worked and whether future treatment costs were affected. The NPT programme was compared with the treatment that the patients would have received without the programme (conventional drug treatment). Since no control group was used it was assumed that the patients without the programme would have received the same care as in the 2 years before the trial.

The WTP in excess of the actual payment was assessed with two open-ended survey questions during the 48-month follow-up visit. The patients were first asked whether they would participate in the NPT programme if it was free of charge, if the charge was 200 SEK, if the charge was 400 SEK, if the charge was 600 SEK, and if the charge was 800 SEK. In the second question they were given the following amounts to choose among (SEK): 100, 200, 300, 400, 500, 600, 700, 800, 900, 1000, and more than 1000. The response rate was very high on both WTP questions: 99 per cent and 97 per cent, respectively. This fact shows that an open-ended valuation question does not necessarily cause problems in the form of protest answers and difficulties in answering the question.

The mean for the first question is 358 SEK and the mean for the second question is 390 SEK. The difference between the means is not statistically significant, and in the cost-benefit analysis the mean of the two questions was used (374 SEK). The cost of the NPT programme is approximately 5300 SEK higher than for conventional drug treatment during the 2 years of the programme. The benefits are about 3200 SEK, divided into an increased actual payment of about 1460 SEK, additional WTP of about 370 SEK, and reduced treatment costs of about 1380 SEK in the 2 years after the programme. Thus the NPT programme results in a loss of about 2100 SEK for the period studied. It is, however, possible that a longer follow-up period for the programme would show future cost savings of such a magnitude that the programme would in fact be socially profitable.

The results of the WTP questions should be interpreted cautiously since the reliability and validity of the approach are largely unknown. The possibility of bias due to the specification of the question scenarios cannot be excluded. For example, there is a possibility of bias due to implied value cues, since it was stated in the question that the cost of the programme is 800 SEK. The possibility that the results were affected by the range of values to choose from cannot be excluded either. The main conclusion with regard to the answers to the WTP questions is therefore that they indicate a positive

WTP for the NPT programme but that the size of the WTP is highly uncertain.

High cholesterol levels

Johannesson (1992) reports a CVM study of treatment for high cholesterol levels. The study was carried out at a primary health care centre in Sweden. 142 persons with high lipid levels registered at the health care centre were sent a postal questionnaire (mean total cholesterol level was 7.30 mmol/L). The questionnaire included questions regarding WTP, willingness to give up time, and maximum acceptable risk. The idea was to test how these types of question function when applied to health care. Regarding the willingness to give up time, leisure time rather than money was the measuring stick. Possibly, respondents find it less value-laden to sacrifice time rather than pay for a medical treatment. The major disadvantage with a leisure time question is that the opportunity cost of leisure time must somehow be decided in order to use the measure in cost-benefit analysis; see, however, the analysis in Brent (1991). In the maximum acceptable risk question the maximum mortality risk which an individual is prepared to accept in order to eliminate high cholesterol levels was investigated. The standard gamble method, see chapter 9, pp. 154–5, was used to investigate the maximum acceptable risk in the same way as Thompson (1986) did with his study of rheumatoid arthritis.

The respondents were asked about their WTP, willingness to give up time, and maximum acceptable risk for a reduction of their lipid levels to normal, which means that the potential gains from treatment were investigated. If lipid therapy does not reduce lipid levels to normal or if it is associated with side effects, the actual benefit will be lower. Each question consisted of 6 response alternatives (bids) and the respondents were asked to answer 'yes/no' to each alternative. The bids in the WTP question were 50, 100, 250, 500, 750, and 1000 SEK per month. The bids in the willingness to give up time question were 0.5, 1, 2, 4, 7, and 12 hours of leisure time per week. The bids in the maximum acceptable risk question were 0, 0.0001, 0.001, 0.01, 0.05, and 0.1 immediate mortality risk. The questionnaire also included three questions about how the questions were perceived by the respondents. The respondents were asked whether the questions were difficult to answer, unpleasant to answer, or unrealistic.

The response rate from the postal questionnaire was 66 per cent. The item non-response rate was 2 per cent for the WTP question, 1 per cent for the willingness to give up time question, and 4 per cent for the maximum acceptable risk question. Median WTP is 350 SEK and mean WTP varies between 416 SEK and 520 SEK per month depending on the assumption made about the highest WTP in the sample.[2] Median willingness to give up time is 5.6 hours and the mean is 6.4–7.7 hours per week. Median maximum acceptable risk is 0.001 and the mean is 0.013–0.014.

The correlation coefficient is 0.64 between the WTP and the willingness to give up time question, 0.16 between the WTP and the maximum acceptable risk, and 0.08 between the willingness to give up time and the maximum acceptable risk. The low correlation of the WTP and maximum acceptable risk is in accordance with the results of Thompson (1986), who found that subjects seem to focus on different aspects of their disease in answering maximum acceptable risk and WTP questions. The percentage of the respondents that perceive the questions as difficult varies between 18 and 37. Between 2 per cent and 12 per cent of the respondents found the questions unpleasant to answer, and between 5 per cent and 15 per cent found the questions unrealistic. The percentage figure is highest in the case of the maximum acceptable risk question in all cases.

The high response rate, given the fact that the study used a postal questionnaire, and the results regarding the perception of the questions indicate that the valuation questions posed by the study were acceptable to the respondents. The proportion of the respondents who found the maximum acceptable risk question difficult, unpleasant or unrealistic was much higher than for the WTP and willingness to give up time questions. The maximum risk question may thus be less suitable than the WTP and willingness to give up time questions. This indication is emphasized by the low correlation between maximum acceptable risk and the other measures. Johannesson (1992) concludes that further research should focus on the reliability and validity of these methods, and include systematic comparisons of different elicitation techniques. The study also indicates that (even open-ended) WTP questions are at least as acceptable to respondents as questions regarding willingness to give up time or maximum acceptable risk.

A study of high blood pressure

This and the next section, which draw on Johannesson, Johansson, Kriström and Gerdtham (1993), present a Swedish study with patients having problems with high blood pressure (hypertension). High blood pressure increases the risk of having a stroke and also causes other risks and health problems.

A postal questionnaire was used in order to estimate the WTP for antihypertensive therapy. The questionnaire was mailed to 525 patients treated for hypertension at a primary health care centre in Sweden at the beginning of 1991. The patients were asked to hand in the questionnaire during their next visit to the health centre. The patient population was randomly divided into 15 sub-samples in which the monthly price for the treatment varied from 50 SEK to 1500 SEK. The patients were asked whether they would continue their current treatment at the specified price. Instead of using the usual 'yes/no' response alternatives the respondents were allowed to choose between five different responses: yes, definitely; yes, probably; no, probably not; no, definitely not; don't know. This design allows the investigators to check if there are systematic differences between certain and uncertain respondents. The question was as follows:

This question concerns how you value your treatment for high blood pressure in economic terms. Assume that you would have to pay a greater share of the treatment cost than today, and that the fees for both medicine and physician visits were raised.

Would you choose to continue your current treatment for high blood pressure if your fees for the treatment were 500* SEK per month?

☐ Yes, definitely
☐ Yes, probably
☐ No, probably not
☐ No, definitely not
☐ Don't know

* The bid varies from 50 SEK to 1500 SEK in 15 sub-samples.

Data were also collected about the perceived health with and without treatment by using a visual-analogue-scale (VAS) where the respondents were asked to indicate their perceived health status with and without treatment between worst possible health state (0 cm) and best possible health state (15 cm). Data about the following socio-economic background variables were also collected in the questionnaire: taxable household income, education, age, sex, and household size.

Of the 525 questionnaires despatched 335 were returned, i.e. the response rate was about 64 per cent. This is similar to the response rate in other Swedish CVM studies using the same approach; see, for example, Johannesson, Jönsson and Borgquist (1991) and Kriström (1990a). The item non-response rate was about 5 per cent on the WTP question. About 16 per cent of the replies to the WTP question were 'don't know'. This means that 260 persons answered 'yes/no' to the WTP question. The bulk of the non-response was on the health status (VAS) question. The item non-response rate was 18 per cent on this question. In table 6.1 the mean and standard deviations of the variables for the different answers to the WTP question are shown.

The following model was used to calculate WTP from the binary responses in the study. The (von Neumann–Morgenstern) individual is

Table 6.1. *Characteristics of the different answers to the WTP question, mean values. Standard deviations are shown within parentheses*

Variable	Sex[a]	Age	Income[b]	Educ.[c]	Househ. size	ΔVAS[d]	A
Yes, def.	0.43	58.0	20,660	1.52	2.07	5.42	239
	(0.52)	(11.6)	(10,990)	(0.79)	(1.06)	(4.44)	(244)
Yes, prob.	0.53	57.8	19,241	1.32	2.33	5.08	372
	(0.52)	(11.2)	(9629)	(0.65)	(1.26)	(3.74)	(335)
No, prob.	0.56	60.0	18,183	1.25	2.08	4.55	612
	(0.50)	(10.6)	(9498)	(0.59)	(0.87)	(3.24)	(437)
No, def.	0.53	64.1	15,159	1.47	1.79	3.65	1000
	(0.51)	(10.8)	(7539)	(0.84)	(0.71)	(3.23)	(437)
Don't know	0.29	61.7	16,513	1.13	2.07	5.86	600
	(0.46)	(12.3)	(8039)	(0.47)	(0.92)	(3.82)	(507)
Total	0.46	59.6	18,704	1.33	2.12	5.08	467
	(0.51)	(11.5)	(9904)	(0.68)	(1.05)	(3.86)	(434)

Notes:
[a] Coded 1 for male and 0 for female.
[b] Taxable household income per month.
[c] Coded 1 for primary education, 2 for secondary education, and 3 for university or other higher education.
[d] The difference in the visual-analogue scale (VAS) value with and without treatment.

assumed to value health, denoted z, and a composite good which serves as the numeraire. The smooth indirect utility function of the individual is written as $V(y, z_i)$, where y is (for the sake of simplicity state-independent) disposable income, and z_i is health in state i. There are $f + 1$ health states and the subjective probability that state i will occur is denoted by π_i for $i = 0, \ldots, f$. In order to simplify the analysis, it is assumed that utility is non-negative for all possible health states (including death), and that the analysis is restricted to uncertainty with regard to z. From the point of view of the investigator, the individual's expected utility is assumed to be:

$$V^E = \Sigma_i \pi_i v(y, z_i) + \epsilon \qquad (6.1)$$

where ϵ is a random disturbance term whose expected value is zero. According to (6.1), the individual is assumed to know his or her utility function, but it contains some components which are unobservable to the investigator. The latter components generate the stochastic structure of the model (needed in the statistical analysis). Note, however, that whereas on average the investigator is 'right' since the expected value of ϵ is zero, in the individual case the investigator may be wrong due to unobservable and stochastic variations in, for example, tastes.

In what follows, it is shown how the model can be used to derive an expression which can be estimated on the empirical data set. The individual is asked if he would be willing to pay $\$A$ for a treatment which changes the probability distribution in (6.1). The offer is accepted if:

$$\Sigma_i \pi_i^1 v(y - A, z_i) + \epsilon^1 \geq \Sigma_i \pi_i^0 v(y, z_i) + \epsilon^0 \tag{6.2}$$

where π_i^1 is the probability of experiencing health state z_i with the treatment, π_i^0 is the corresponding probability without treatment, and ϵ^1 and ϵ^0 are identically and independently distributed random variables with zero means. According to (6.2), the offer is accepted if utility with a treatment costing $\$A$ is expected to be at least as high as utility without treatment.

Linearly approximating $v(y - A, z_i)$ around (y, z_i) one obtains:

$$v(y - A, z_i) = v(y, z_i) - v_{yi} A \qquad \forall i \tag{6.3}$$

where $v_{yi} = \partial v(y, z_i)/\partial y$ is the marginal utility of income in state i. Substitution of (6.3) into (6.2) yields:

$$\Sigma_i \Delta \pi_i v(y, z_i) - v_y^E A + \epsilon^1 \geq \epsilon_0 \tag{6.4}$$

where $\Delta \pi_i = \pi_i^1 - \pi_i^0$, and $v_y^E = \Sigma_i \pi_i^1 v_{yi}$ is the expected (with treatment) marginal utility of income.

Suppose A is chosen so that (6.4) is turned into an equality. Then the uniform or state-independent WTP for the proposed treatment can be written as follows:

$$A = \left[\Sigma_i \Delta \pi_i v(y, z_i)/v_y^E \right] - \eta/v_y^E \tag{6.5}$$

where $\eta = \epsilon^0 - \epsilon^1$. Since $E(\eta) = 0$ the bid A in (6.5) can be considered as a random variable with mean:

$$E[A] = A^* = \left[\Sigma_i \Delta \pi_i v(y, z_i)/v_y^E \right]. \tag{6.6}$$

The average WTP A^* can be interpreted as an EV if treatment (no treatment) is considered to be the initial (final) situation. In order to estimate A^*, Johannesson, Johansson, Kriström and Gerdtham (1993) assumed a logistic distribution function. Then the probability Π that the individual will accept paying $\$A$ for a treatment is given by:

$$\Pi = G(A) = 1/[1 + e^{-\Delta v^E}] \tag{6.7}$$

where $\Delta v^E = \left[\Sigma_i \Delta \pi_i v(y, z_i) \right] - v_y^E A = \alpha - \beta^- A$. Thus by estimating the following equation:

$$\ln[\Pi/(1-\Pi)] = \alpha + \beta A \qquad (6.8)$$

where $\ln[.]$ is the natural logarithm of the odds ratio and $\beta = -\beta^-$, the mean A^* can be calculated as:

$$A^* = -\alpha/\beta = \alpha/\beta^-. \qquad (6.9)$$

This last result can be arrived at by choosing A in such a way that $\Delta v^E = \alpha - \beta^- A = 0$. Alternatively, the reader can use (6.7) and proceed as in (5.2).

The specification in (6.8) rules out (unobservable) variations in the marginal utility of income across various individuals. It is, however, possible to let the marginal utility of income vary among individuals in a model of this type, although such an approach leads to a more complicated specification than the one used by Johannesson, Johansson, Kriström and Gerdtham (1993). The reader is referred to Pudney (1989, p. 108) for details.

The results

The theoretical model presented in the previous section and underlying the empirical analysis in Johannesson, Johansson, Kriström and Gerdtham (1993) is extremely simple. They choose to use a simple model in order to be able to estimate an expression which is compatible with (expected) utility maximization. Hanemann (1984) demonstrates the danger in estimating *ad hoc* expressions: there may simply not be a utility function generating the model estimated. For example, Hanemann shows that replacing A in (6.8) by the logarithm of A yields an expression which cannot be derived from any known utility function. Moreover, the data set used by Johannesson, Johansson, Kriström and Gerdtham (1993) is such that they cannot meaningfully include risk attitudes, explaining the theoretical simplification implicit in (6.8), for example, an expression which implies constant risk attitudes across individuals. These are the main reasons for estimating a very simple model. There is also the minor aspect that it is extremely difficult to calculate an average WTP measure from a complicated non-linear regression equation. However, Johannesson, Johansson, Kriström and Gerdtham (1993) also estimates the mean WTP with a non-parametric method. This exercise is undertaken in order to test whether the mean WTP is sensitive to the restrictions imposed in the simple theoretical model.

The logistic function is initially run with A as single explanatory variable. This is in agreement with the simple theoretical model derived above. The change in perceived health status caused by the treatment, i.e. a measurement of $\Sigma_i \pi_i^1 z_i - \Sigma_i \pi_i^0 z_i$, is then added as an explanatory variable (measured as the difference in the VAS value with and without treatment). In the last step the different socio-economic variables are added to the model. All explanatory variables except A are measured as deviations from their mean, implying that the estimated mean A is still equal to α/β. Johannesson, Johansson, Kriström and Gerdtham (1993) also use three different sets of data: the full sample of 'yes/no' answers, a sample that only includes the responses of those who definitely were willing or not willing to pay the suggested sum of money ('certain' respondents), and a sample that includes only the probable 'yes/no' responses ('uncertain' respondents). The two sub-samples are used to test the hypothesis that there is a behavioural difference between those delivering certain responses to the 'yes/no' question and those delivering uncertain ones.

In table 6.2 the statistical analysis is shown for the full sample; see also the appendix to this chapter. The logistic regressions were estimated by maximum likelihood methods. About 16 per cent of the answers to the WTP question were 'don't know' answers. This means that 260 persons answered 'yes/no' to the WTP question. These 260 observations were used to estimate an equation, Eq_1 in table 6.2, with A as the single explanatory variable. A data set consisting of the 210 persons who answered all the questions in the questionnaire was used to estimate a set of equations, Eq_2–Eq_4 in table 6.2, in order to statistically compare the different equations.

In the first model (Eq_1), only A is used as an explanatory variable. Both α and β are highly significant, with expected signs. The mean WTP is about 770 SEK per month: $-\alpha/\beta = 1.93/0.0025 = 772$. In the second regression (Eq_2) the same equation is run for the sample with 210 observations. The mean WTP in this sample is about 860 SEK. In the third regression (Eq_3), the measure of the perceived change in health status (ΔVAS) is included. The health status variable has the expected sign and is significant at the 10 per cent level. Mean WTP changes only slightly. In the last model (Eq_4), the socio-economic variables are included. The health status change variable is now significant at the 5 per cent level, but none of the socio-economic variables is significant. The reader is also referred to the appendix, where the statistical tests, such as goodness of fit measures, are briefly explained.

The same four regressions were also run for the sample with definite 'yes/no' responses and probable 'yes/no' responses, respectively. The results of these regressions are not shown here. However, restricting the analysis to 'certain' respondents improves the results from a statistical point of view. Moreover, the health status variable is now significant on the 5 per cent level in both regressions, i.e. Eq_3 and Eq_4. The mean WTP as estimated from these equations is similar to the mean for the full sample. It is interesting to compare these results with the results of the sample with 'uncertain'

Table 6.2. *Coefficients of the logistic regressions for full sample; t-ratios are shown within parentheses*

Regressor variable	Equation			
	Eq_1	Eq_2	Eq_3	Eq_4
Intercept	1.93^a	1.97^a	2.00^a	2.06^a
	(8.21)	(7.49)	(7.50)	(7.44)
A	-0.0025^a	-0.0023^a	-0.0024^a	-0.0024^a
	(-6.45)	(-5.48)	(-5.50)	
ΔVAS			0.083^c	0.12^b
			(1.83)	(2.42)
Sex				0.12
				(0.34)
Age				-0.021
				(-1.13)
Income				0.000016
				(0.75)
Education				0.12
				(0.44)
Household size				0.086
				(0.43)
n	260	210	210	210
Log-likelihood	-136.55	-108.98	-107.21	-104.05
Goodness of fit				
Individual pred.	75.38%	76.67%	77.62%	79.52%
LRI	0.16	0.15	0.16	0.18
Slope restrictions				
Eq_j vs Eq_0, LR test	$52.57(1)^a$	$36.89(1)^a$	$40.43(2)^a$	$46.75(7)^a$
Eq_j vs Eq_2, LR test	—	—	3.54(1)	9.86(6)
Eq_4 vs Eq_3, LR test	—	—	—	6.32(5)
Functional form				
Box–Cox, lambda $A = 1$				
LR test	$6.58(1)^b$	2.70(1)	3.44(1)	$4.64(1)^c$
WTP:				
Mean	772	857	833	858
Std	115	98	99	100

Notes:
n = number of respondents, Individual pred. = individual prediction,
LRI = likelihood ratio index, LR test = likelihood ratio test.
[a,b,c] Significant at 1%, 5% and 10% levels (two-sided t-test).

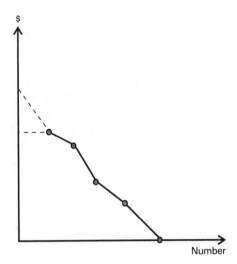

Figure 6.1 Using an 'Ayer' curve to calculate mean WTP

respondents. In the latter models the fit of the equations is lower but A is still highly significant. The mean as calculated from the equations for the 'uncertain' respondents is similar to the mean for the 'certain' respondents.

The mean WTP is also calculated with a non-parametric method developed by Kriström (1990a, 1990b). In this method the proportion of yes answers at each bid level is used to construct a survival function (an 'Ayer' curve) with respect to the bid (A) that is integrated to arrive at the mean WTP. This approach is illustrated in figure 6.1, where the number of respondents is normalized to unity. For each bid, the proportion of yes answers is available. These proportions are illustrated by filled circles in figure 6.1. Connecting these points by straight lines produces a curve. In order to arrive at the average WTP, one simply calculates the area below this curve. If the proportion of acceptance is not 0 per cent at the highest bid level the upper limit for the WTP needs to be decided in order to calculate the mean WTP; this problem is illustrated by the two dashed lines in figure 6.1. In the study under discussion the proportion of acceptance is 24 per cent at the highest bid level (1500 SEK). The mean was calculated with 1500, 2000 and 2500 SEK, respectively, as the highest WTP. The mean according to this method is 735 SEK, 795 SEK, and 855 SEK, respectively, using the three assumptions just mentioned regarding the highest WTP. This is similar to the mean WTP of 772 SEK in Eq_1 in table 6.2.

It should be noted that the seemingly simple approach illustrated in figure 6.1 has a nice theoretical property. By standard arguments, see Kriström (1990a, 1990b), it can be shown that the maximum likelihood estimate of the probability for a yes answer is the proportion of observed yes answers at each bid level. In other words, as the sample size is increased, the proportion of yes answers converges to the true probability of a yes answer.

In order for the above calculations of mean WTP to be representative of all respondents, the mean WTP of the respondents answering 'don't know' has to be the same as for those answering 'yes/no'. A possible interpretation of 'don't know' is that the respondents are indifferent to the proposed bid. If this is the case the mean WTP of these indifferent respondents is about 600 SEK in the study. This causes a slight decrease in the mean WTP for all respondents compared to the mean in table 6.2. An alternative and more conservative approach is as follows. Only those respondents who are certain that they are willing to pay a certain amount are considered to be 'true' buyers. All others, including those who don't know, are unlikely to buy the commodity/project in a real situation, i.e. they are treated as voting 'no' to the project. This approach will produce a considerably lower average WTP than the approach used by Johannesson, Johansson, Kriström and Gerdtham (1993).

The log-linear specification $\alpha + \beta A$ is often preferred to the linear one since it rules out a negative WTP. It is however a bit problematic to use a log-linear model in the Hanemann-inspired approach outlined in (6.1)–(6.9). The specification $\alpha + \beta \ln A$ cannot be derived from an explicit utility function. Thus the log-linear model is not compatible with utility maximization. Alternatively, the log-linear model (or any other specification which one may want to estimate) can be viewed as representing an aggregate demand curve for the treatment, i.e. it is compatible with the approach outlined in chapter 5, pp. 83–6; see (6.12) (p. 114) for a formula which can be used to compute the mean WTP in the case of a log-linear specification. Also note that the problem (if it is a problem) with a strictly positive probability for a negative WTP in the linear model can be overcome by assuming that the distribution function is mixed, i.e. consisting of (for example) a logistic one on R^+ and having an atom at zero. This restricts WTP to being non-negative and allows the probability of finding people with zero WTP to be greater than nil; compare figure 5.3a (p. 85). If this assumption is employed in the calculations, mean WTP increases from 772 SEK to 826 SEK in Eq_1 in table 6.2; see (6.11) for the formulae used in calculating the mean.

Ideally the bid vector should be designed in such a way that it covers the whole distribution of WTP. This will reduce the uncertainty in the estimation of mean WTP. If the whole distribution is not covered by the bid vector the mean WTP is open to manipulation by selecting the 'right' upper limit of integration (and the 'left' lower limit as discussed above). In

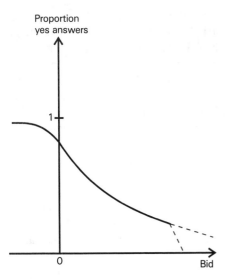

Figure 6.2 Illustration of the distribution of 'yes answers' in a 'yes/no' study

particular, the average WTP may become infinitely large (the integral diverges) unless the distribution is truncated. This is true both for the non-parametric method and in a log-linear regression model. In the regression models presented in table 6.2 the estimates of α and β may be biased if the whole WTP distribution is not covered by the bid vector. Quite a few authors who have failed to collect sufficient information on the right-hand side tail of the distribution have faced these kinds of problem. This fact emphasizes the importance of carrying out a pilot study or using some bid design algorithm to determine the optimal bid vector.

The 'tail' problem is further illustrated in figure 6.2. The first question the investigator must decide upon is if a negative WTP is theoretically possible or not. The distribution in figure 6.2 implies that negative bids are possible. The valuation question should ideally cover negative bids (compensation) if some respondents can be expected to report a negative WTP. For example, an introductory question can be used to separate those with a positive WTP from those with a negative WTP. The positive/negative bid question is then asked.[3] If there are reasons to believe that some respondents have a zero WTP, a follow-up question or the introductory question inquires whether the respondent is willing to pay anything at all for the considered treatment. Note, however, that in calculating the mean WTP one must ignore negative bids (compensation claims) if participation in the 'project' under investigation is voluntary. This is typically the case for medical measures but not for public safety measures affecting everyone.

Thus for medical treatments, the central issue is to find out how large a proportion of the population has a strictly positive WTP. After all, it is their WTP which is to be used in a cost-benefit analysis of the treatment.

The right-hand side tail problem has turned out to be difficult to handle in empirical applications. Given a maximum bid such that some respondents accept to pay the bid in question, one must make an assumption on the missing part of the distribution. As is obvious from the two dashed parts of the distribution function in figure 6.2, the assumption on the shape of the tail can have a dramatic impact on the estimated mean WTP. Recall that the mean WTP is equal to the area under the curve in figure 6.2 for $A \geq 0$ (*less* the area above the curve and below unity for $A < 0$ if it is a public safety measure). A pilot study can give valuable information on the tails. This information can then be used to design the bid vector to be used in the main study. Alternatively, recent theories for the optimal design of bid vectors can be employed. Algorithms can be found in Nyquist (1992) and Sitter (1992), for example.

There are essentially three ways to test the validity of the CVM. First, one can compare the results of the method with those of indirect methods of measuring WTP. In the health care field the indirect methods are, however, seldom applicable. Comparisons are thus precluded, unless a particular treatment is priced in the market so that price variations can be used to estimate a demand function for the treatment. Secondly, one can use simulated market experiments in which hypothetical payments are compared with actual payments. This approach to the testing of validity may be difficult to carry out in practice. For example, there is an ethical problem when patients have to pay different amounts of money for the same treatment. Thirdly, one can assess whether the hypothesized theoretical relationships are supported by the data. This third type of validity test was carried out in the study summarized here, by estimating the theoretically derived regression equations.

The estimated equations are in accordance with the theoretical predictions. The bid (A) is highly significant in all equations, showing that an increased price reduces the demand for anti-hypertensive treatment. The perceived change in the expected health status (ΔVAS) is significant on the 10 per cent level in all equations, indicating as expected that an increased difference in health status between the treatment and no treatment cases increases WTP. The results thus support the validity of the CVM using binary responses.

Experiments with real payments provide a further possibility to test the working of the CVM. Setting aside the practical and any ethical problems, such an experiment can be designed as follows. Let us assume that there is a new treatment for a particular illness. Patients are randomly assigned to, say, six different groups. Five of these groups get the new treatment provided they pay a certain amount of money, but this fee or price is varied between the groups; those belonging to group 1 get the treatment if they pay $100, those in group 2 get the treatment if they are prepared to pay $200, and so on. This produces 'points' on an aggregate demand curve, i.e. we can calculate the proportion that is willing to pay $100, the proportion that is willing to pay $200, and so on. Those belonging to the the sixth group do not make any real payment but are asked about their (hypothetical) WTP for the treatment, i.e. they participate in a conventional CVM. One sub-group may be asked if they are willing to pay $100, another sub-group if they are willing to pay $200, and so on. It is then possible to check if the CVM produces the same demand curve as the experiment with real payments.

Useful formulae for the computation of the mean WTP

It is often quite complicated to derive formulae for the average WTP from 'yes/no' data. A few useful formulae are stated in this section.

Suppose that we estimate (6.8), i.e. $\ln[\Pi/(1-\Pi)] = \alpha + \beta A$, in order to obtain estimates of α and β. Then the mean, here interpreted as a CV, is equal to:

$$CV = -\alpha/\beta. \tag{6.10}$$

The total WTP is obtained by multiplying CV by the total number of individuals in the population.

An investigator may want to include other independent variables than A. One can then calculate CV using the mean values of these other independent variables, an approach which often turns out to be very complicated. However, Johansson and Kriström (1992) show that (asymptotically) CV remains unchanged if other independent variables than A are included. That is, as a rule of thumb, if you want to calculate CV, estimate $\alpha + \beta A$ and use (6.10) to calculate CV.

If we estimate $\alpha + \beta A$ but want to calculate CV on the assumption that WTP is non-negative, and the probability of a zero WTP is strictly positive, the mean is equal to:

$$CV = \int_0^\infty [1/(1 + e^{-(\alpha + \beta A)})]dA = -(1/\beta)\ln[1 + e^\alpha] \tag{6.11}$$

a result which is obtained by using the first term on the right-hand side of (5.2) (p. 81). Thus, if $\alpha = 1$ and $\beta = -1.5$, then $CV \approx (1/1.5)\ln(3.718) \approx 0.876$. In a regression, one can also accommodate the fact that a proportion of the respondents report a zero WTP, which will affect the estimates of α and β. The reader is referred to Hanemann and Kriström (1994) for such an algorithm.

If we estimate $\alpha + \beta\ln(A)$, the mean is equal to:

$$CV = -e^{\alpha/\beta} \frac{\pi/\beta}{\sin(-\pi/\beta)} \tag{6.12}$$

where $\pi = 3.141592$, and $0 > 1/\beta > -1$ in order for the integral to converge; see Hanemann (1984) for details. (Hint: An angle of 90° has radian measure $\pi/2$. If $\beta = -1.5$, $-\pi/\beta$ corresponds to 120° so that $\sin(-\pi/\beta)$ is equal to about 0.866; and if $\alpha = 1$, then $CV \approx -(1.95)(-2.09)/0.866 \approx 4.7$.) (6.12) illustrates that the formulae for the calculation of the mean WTP can become quite complicated. In the estimation of involved regressions in solving for the mean WTP, it may be useful to use computer programmes, such as Derive: A Mathematical Assistant (Soft Warehouse Inc., Honolulu, 1988).

Appendix

In table 6.2, two goodness-of-fit measures are reported: individual prediction and the likelihood ratio index (LRI); see Amemiya (1981). Individual prediction is the percentage of binary responses correctly predicted by the equation. $LRI = 1 - (L(\text{general})/L(\text{restricted}))$, where $L(\text{general})$ is the maximum likelihood value of the log-likelihood function, and $L(\text{restricted})$ is the maximum likelihood value of this function under the constraint that $\beta = 0$. LRI is between 0 and 1, and a better fit gives a value closer to 1. The likelihood ratio test (LR test) is used to compare the models with one another and with the hypothesis that the independent variables are unrelated to the probability of acceptance (Eq_j versus Eq_0). The test statistic for this asymptotic test is $-2[L(\text{general}) - L(\text{restricted})] \sim \chi^2$. A Box–Cox-inspired likelihood ratio test is used to test for functional form. Four alternative lambda (λ) transformations of the A variable are used (the additional variables are untransformed): $\lambda = 0, -1, 0.5, -0.5$. The Box–Cox transformation of A is specified as $(A^\lambda - 1)/\lambda$ for $\lambda \neq 0$ and $\ln A$ for $\lambda = 0$. Different values of λ lead to different transformations of A. In the Eq_j models in table 6.2 A is estimated with $\lambda = 1$, which is the null hypothesis. The likelihood ratio test is used to compare the null hypothesis ($\lambda = 1$) with the best transformation of A.

According to the likelihood ratio test there is no significant difference between Eq_2 and Eq_3 or Eq_4. The analysis of functional form shows that the linear specification used cannot be rejected in Eq_2 or Eq_3. In Eq_1 and Eq_4, however, the linear form is rejected on the 5 per cent and 10 per cent level, respectively, in favour of a log-linear specification, i.e. $\alpha - \beta\ln A$.

7   Aggregation

Thus far we have mainly been concerned with the definition and measurement of money measures at the individual level. In a few cases, average WTP measures, such as the WTP *per capita*, have been used. There is of course nothing wrong with such averages *per se*, but the central question is what, if any, useful information the decision-maker can extract from the average WTP for a proposed measure. After all, behind an average, there are typically both those who gain and those who lose. It is sometimes claimed that a positive aggregate CV or EV, which is equivalent to a positive average WTP, means that those who gain from a project can, at least hypothetically, compensate those who lose from it. If true, this claim would mean that a distributional analysis of a project's consequences is more or less superfluous. However, more than 20 years ago, Boadway (1974) proved this claim to be false. Thus, the aggregation issue is still of central importance in project evaluations.

In this chapter we will take a look at the aggregation problem and examine the conditions under which the sum of WTPs for a measure indicates whether a proposed project is socially profitable. The chapter should also be useful for those working with other output measures such as qalys and hyes; there are always some basic ethical assumptions behind an aggregation procedure, and the investigator should clarify these assumptions to the decision-maker and other users of the investigation.

The chapter is structured as follows. The first section introduces the concept of a social welfare function, and briefly discusses its properties. The second section uses the function to assess a project, say a proposed new medical treatment, and our money measures are used in an attempt to estimate the unobservable change in social welfare. A few different methods which can be used to highlight a project's distributional consequences are indicated in the third section. It is then shown how our money measures can be disaggregated so as to reveal the components of a project, say a medical treatment, such as income losses, direct costs, the value of the change in health, etc. The two final sections address the important issue of how to treat altruism in a cost-benefit analysis. In particular, we discuss how to

115

formulate the valuation question in a CVM study so that it will be useful in a cost-benefit analysis when people are altruists.

The social welfare function

A complete and consistent ranking of social states ('projects') is called a social welfare ordering, and is much like the individual's preference ordering. If the social welfare ordering is continuous, it can be translated into a *social welfare function*. This is simply a function of the utility levels of all individuals such that a higher value of the function is preferred to a lower one. Such a function is often called a Bergsonian welfare function, after Abram Bergson, who first used it. Alternatively it is called a Bergson–Samuelson social welfare function.

Let us start with the certain world case. In such a case, the social welfare function can be written as follows:

$$W = W[V_1(p, y_1, z_1), \ldots, V_H(p, y_H, z_H)] \tag{7.1}$$

where p is a vector of prices of consumption goods, y_h is income of individual h for $h = 1, \ldots, H$, and z_h is his or her health. *A priori* there is not much we can say about the form a social welfare function takes. The form depends on who is 'behind' the function: it may express the views of Parliament or of the reader, for example. In the literature, however, a social welfare function is generally assumed to have four convenient properties. First, it is assumed to satisfy *welfarism*, which means that social welfare depends only on the utility levels of individuals, just as in (7.1). Secondly, social welfare is assumed to be increasing with each individual's utility level, *ceteris paribus*. The function is thus assumed to satisfy the (strong) *Pareto criterion*, since a *ceteris paribus* increase in the utility of any individual increases social welfare. Moreover, if one individual is made worse off, then another individual must be made better off to maintain the same level of social welfare. Thirdly, the *intensity* of this trade-off is usually assumed to depend on the degree of inequality in society. Social indifference curves are therefore convex to the origin. Fourthly, it is often assumed that it does not matter who enjoys a high or low level of utility. This principle is known as *anonymity*. The reader who is interested in a critical assessment of this conventional approach to normative economics is referred to Sugden (1993).

If utility functions are ordinal (see chapter 2, p. 18 for a discussion of the meaning of the concepts of ordinality and cardinality), then Arrow's *impossibility theorem* states that the only possible and consistent social welfare function is a dictatorship. That is, the social welfare function must coincide with the ordinal utility function of some individual regardless of the preferences of the others. We thus need further assumptions in order to be able to use the concept of the social welfare function. These further assumptions relate to the measurability (degree of cardinality) and comparability of utility. The strongest assumption is full measurability. In this case the individual is equipped with a unique utility function. This assumption (plus welfarism and the Pareto principle) permit the general Bergson–Samuelson social welfare function (7.1) to rank social states consistently. Intermediate or partial measurability and comparability assumptions restrict the set of possible social welfare functions in comparison to the full measurability case. For example, utility functions may be cardinal in the sense that we allow affine transformations: $u_h = a_h + b_h U_h$, where a_h and b_h are constants (with $b_h > 0$) and the subscript refers to individual h. Comparability may be partial in the sense that we assume that $b_h = b$ for all individuals but a_h can differ across individuals; full comparability thus means that $a_h = a$ and $b_h = b$ for all individuals. For a fine discussion of this issue the reader is referred to Boadway and Bruce (1984).

Figure 7.1 illustrates three different and commonly employed social welfare functions (assuming here sufficient degrees of measurability and comparability of individual utilities; see Boadway and Bruce (1984, ch. 5) for details). It is sometimes argued that society's welfare is equal to the sum of the utilities of different individuals. In this case the social welfare function can be written as follows:

$$W = \Sigma_h V_h(.).\tag{7.1'}$$

This view is called *utilitarianism*, and was first introduced by Jeremy Bentham in the eighteenth century. In a utilitarian society, the social welfare indifference curves are negatively sloped straight lines, as is illustrated in figure 7.1a. That is, society is willing to give up one unit of individual 1's utility for a gain of one unit of individual 2's utility. This holds regardless of the degree of inequality in society; society is completely indifferent to the degree of inequality between individuals. Note that W^i for $i = 1,2$ in figure 7.1 denotes social welfare level i and $W^2 > W^1$.

Another view of inequality is expressed by the indifference curves in figure 7.1b. Society should be willing to accept a decrease in the utility of the poor only if there is a much larger increase in the utility of the rich. Accordingly, society's indifference curves are strictly convex.

A more extreme position, associated with John Rawls (1972), is to argue that the welfare of society depends only on the utility of the poorest or worst-off individual:

$$W = \min\{V_1, \ldots, V_H\}.\tag{7.1''}$$

In this case, society's indifference curves can be viewed as L-shaped. As is illustrated by the dotted vertical line in figure 7.1c, society is better off if the welfare of the poorest individual, individual 2 in figure 7.1, is improved.

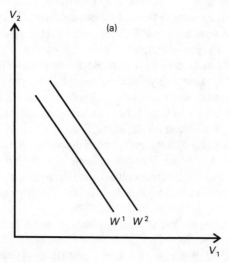

a Utilitarian

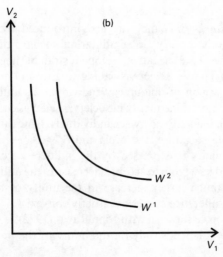

b Strictly convex

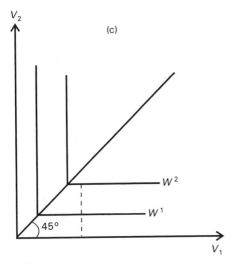

c Rawlsian

Figure 7.1 Social indifference curves

Starting from the dotted line and moving horizontally to the right, it can be seen that society gains nothing from improving the welfare of the richer individual 1.

Project evaluations

We have given a short presentation of the concept of the social welfare function, and illustrated some of its properties. The social welfare function, as defined in the previous section, can be used to assess the social profitability of any project in a certain world. In principle, one checks if the project moves society to a higher or a lower social welfare indifference curve.

Since risk plays a central role in the case of health, it is necessary to work with a social welfare function which captures risk. Basically, one can then look at social welfare *ex ante* or *ex post*. The former approach means that one views social welfare as a function of the expected levels of utility attained by different individuals; we will, at least initially, base the analysis on the concept of expected utility. The *ex post* approach means that one first calculates social welfare conditional on everybody experiencing the same state of the world. Then the resulting level of social welfare is weighted by the probability that this state of the world occurs, and one sums such weighted amounts across all possible states of the world to arrive at social welfare.

It can be shown that the social welfare function must be utilitarian in order to rank states in the same order *ex ante* and *ex post*, i.e. for the *ex ante* welfare optimum to coincide with the *ex post* one. We will not undertake this exercise here but refer the reader to Milne and Shefrin (1987), for example, for a detailed investigation. We will simply assume that the social welfare function is utilitarian, or rather generalized utilitarian since constant but differing weights can be attributed to different individuals, for example depending on their age.[1] Moreover, the analysis is based on the *ex ante* social welfare function, and individuals are assumed to be expected utility maximizers; see p. 18 for a discussion of the particular cardinality assumption employed in an expected utility analysis. Before proceeding, it should be mentioned that the *ex ante–ex post* problem seems to parallel the time-inconsistency problem familiar from modern macroeconomics. That is, a policy (path) which is optimal as viewed from today may turn out to be profitable to change at a later point in time, for example, because some costs which are variable as viewed from today are sunk or fixed at a later date. We will come back to this issue in chapter 8.

Turning to the analysis, expected utility of individual h is written as follows:

$$E[V^h] = V_{he} = \Sigma_i \pi_{hi} V_h(p, y_{hi}, z_{hi}) \qquad \forall h \qquad (7.2)$$

where a subscript hi refers to the hth individual experiencing state i; for example, π_{hi} is the probability that individual h will experience state i. This is basically the same model as the one employed in chapter 4, pp. 52–5, though here we explicitly allow for a state-dependent income. The possibility of health state zero, i.e. death, is also allowed. The corresponding level of utility is set equal to zero, i.e. we employ the basic set of assumptions introduced on p. 22.

Social welfare is a weighted average of the expected utility levels of the H different individuals in society. The social welfare function is therefore as follows:

$$W = \Sigma_h W_h V_{he} = \Sigma_h W_h [\Sigma_i \pi_{hi} V_h(p, y_{hi}, z_{hi})] \qquad (7.3)$$

where W_h is the constant welfare weight that society attributes to individual h, and V_{he} is his or her expected utility. In terms of figure 7.1a, the social welfare indifference curves are straight lines whose slope is determined by the welfare weights W_h for $h = 1, 2$.

Consider now a project, say a new treatment, which changes the probabilities of experiencing different states of the world from π_{hi0} to π_{hi1}, where a subscript 1 (0) means with (without) the project. We want to find out if this project increases social welfare or not. This is achieved by calculating social welfare with and without the project, respectively. The change in social welfare is:

$$\Delta W = \Sigma_h W_h \Delta V_{he} = \Sigma_h W_h[\Sigma_i \Delta \pi_{hi} V_h(p, y_{hi}, z_{hi})]$$
$$= \Sigma_h W_h[E_{h1}[V_h(p, y, z)] - E_{h0}[V_h(p, y, z)]] \tag{7.4}$$

where E_{hj} denotes the expectations operator of individual h with ($j = 1$) and without ($j = 0$) the project, and when the expectations operator is used we ignore the subscripts of y and z in order to avoid unnecessary clutter. This is simply an aggregated version of (4.2) (p. 53). If the project is purely private, the change in probabilities of experiencing different states of the world will be equal to zero for all individuals except the one participating in the treatment. Other projects may affect π_i of many or even all individuals in society. Moreover, the project may affect the expected disposable incomes of different individuals. This is true even if the project is a medical treatment of individual h since, for example, the health care system may be such that the cost of the treatment is spread across all income-earning individuals in society. This fact will be elaborated upon below, pp. 126–7.

The change in social welfare in (7.4) is unobservable. There is no way of directly observing the sign and magnitude of ΔW. In order to attempt to indirectly capture the sign of the change in social welfare we use two of our money measures. Define the non-contingent CV and EV, respectively, of individual h:

$$E_{h1}[V_h(p, y - \mathrm{CV}, z)] = E_{h0}[V_h(p, y, z)] \qquad \forall h$$
$$E_{h0}[V_h(p, y + \mathrm{EV}, z)] = E_{h1}[V_h(p, y, z)] \qquad \forall h. \tag{7.5}$$

The non-contingent CV keeps the individual at his initial level of expected utility, while the non-contingent EV keeps him at his final or with-project level of expected utility.

Substitution of the first line in (7.5) into the social welfare change expression (7.4) yields:

$$\Delta W = \Sigma_h W_h[E_{h1}[V_h(p, y, z)] - E_{h1}[V_h(p, y - \mathrm{CV}_h, z)]] = \Sigma_h W_h v_{hye} \mathrm{CV}_h \tag{7.6}$$

where v_{hye} denotes the expected marginal utility of income of individual h evaluated for some intermediate incomes $y_{hia} \in (y_{hi}, y_{hi} - \mathrm{CV}_h)$ as in (3.5) (p. 37); alternatively, one can express the change as a line integral, as is done on p. 131. The product of the welfare weight imputed to individual h and his or her expected marginal utility of income is here called the *marginal social utility of income*. The reader should note that the only difference between the two terms within bold brackets in (7.6) is that CV_h appears in the second but not in the first term; the terms have the same probabilities (captured by E_{h1}), prices and health states. This explains the fact that the right-hand side expression only contains each individual's CV weighted by the marginal social utility of income assigned to that individual.

Our money measure provides us with part of the information needed in a social *cost-benefit analysis* of the project. What is needed in addition is essentially an ethical rule for the weighting of gains and losses accruing to different (groups of) individuals in society. In other words, in order to arrive at the project's social profitability, one must somehow decide on the magnitude of the marginal social utility of income to be assigned to each affected individual. There is no objective or neutral way of establishing the magnitude of the social marginal utility to be attributed to a particular individual; it must reflect a view on what is a 'good' or 'fair' society. It should be stressed that this fundamental problem is inescapable in the sense that a decision-maker (or you and I) must somehow weight gains and losses in order to arrive at a decision (a view on the project). This is an inevitable feature of any decision mechanism, not only those based on attempts to place 'price tags' on the different components of a project.

In order to provide a simple numerical illustration of the dangers involved, let us consider a two-individual society and assume that $W_1 = 1$, $W_2 = 2$, $v_{1ye} = 1$, and $v_{2ye} = 1.5$ in (7.6). In other words, consider the case where society attributes a higher welfare weight to (the poor) individual 2, and where individual 2's expected marginal utility of income exceeds the expected marginal utility of income of individual 1. Thus under these assumptions, the marginal social utility of income of individual 2 is three times as high as that of individual 1. Further, assume that the project is associated with the non-contingent compensating variations $CV_1 = 10$ and $CV_2 = -5$. Thus, the sum of CVs is positive, indicating that the project is socially profitable. On the other hand, it is clear that $\Delta W = 1 \cdot 10 - 3 \cdot 5 = -5$, i.e. the project, due to its large adverse effects on individual 2, actually reduces social welfare. This example highlights the fact that it is dangerous to draw far-reaching conclusions about a project's desirability from the unweighted sum of money measures.

There is however a special case in which one can sum the WTP across individuals. Suppose that the government redistributes incomes across individuals so as to maximize social welfare. To illustrate the main point in the simplest possible way, take the sum of expected incomes to be fixed, and let the government maximize the social welfare function (7.3) subject to $Y = \Sigma_h E_h[y_h]$. The first-order condition for an interior solution with respect to y_{hi} is as follows:

$$\partial W / \partial y_{hi} = \pi_{hi} W_h V_{hyi} - \pi_{hi} \lambda = 0 \qquad \forall h, i \qquad (7.7)$$

i.e. $W_h V_{hyi} = \lambda$ for all h, i, where λ is the Lagrange multiplier associated with the constraint $Y = \Sigma_h E_h[y_h]$, and V_{hyi} is the marginal utility of income of individual h in state i. Thus, given the assumptions made, the government will redistribute incomes so as to even out the social marginal utility of income across individuals and states.

This means that if one evaluates a reasonably small project close to a social welfare optimum, it holds that:

$$dW = \lambda \Sigma_h dCV_h, \tag{7.6'}$$

i.e. the sum across individuals of non-contingent CVs is proportional to the change in social welfare. In this case, one need not worry about the project's distributional consequences, implying that monetary amounts can safely be summed across individuals. If the sum is positive, the project increases social welfare, and vice versa, since the sum of dCV_h is proportional to the change in social welfare caused by the project under consideration. Also note that if a project saves a small number b of lives in a large population of H individuals, one can interpret $\Sigma_h dCV_h / b$ as the *value of statistical life*. This provides further justification for the procedure used in chapter 4, p. 61.

In the general case, however, and as shown above, there is no guarantee that the sum of monetary amounts (and hence the value of a statistical life) has the same sign as the change in social welfare; for a formal proof of this, the reader is referred to Blackorby and Donaldson (1986). Before discussing some possible ways to handle this complication in empirical studies, it is necessary to assess the considered project using the EV measure. Substitution of the second line in (7.5) into (7.4) yields:

$$\Delta W = \Sigma_h W_h [E_{h0}[V_h(p, y + EV_h, z)] - E_{h0}[V_h(p, y, z)]] = \Sigma_h W_h v_{hye} EV_h \tag{7.6''}$$

where the intermediate value theorem has been used to arrive at the 'intermediate' expected marginal utilities of income in the right-hand side expression of (7.6''). Since individuals in the case of EVs stay at their final levels of expected utility, v_{hye} in (7.6'') generally differ from the corresponding ones in (7.6) where individuals are held at initial levels of expected utility; see also chapter 3, p. 37. If v_{hye} differ between the expressions it must be the case that $CV_h \neq EV_h$ in order for (7.6) and (7.6'') to produce the same change in social welfare ΔW.

Since CV_h and EV_h differ, their sums across all individuals will also differ (unless all individuals have quasi-linear utility functions). Thus one may end up in a situation where the sum of CVs is positive while the sum of EVs is negative, or vice versa. Thus one measure says that the project is socially profitable and the other measure says that the project is socially unprofitable. Even if both aggregate measures have the same sign, this does not ensure that the change in social welfare has the same sign. Each CV_h and EV_h is weighted by the marginal social utility of income attributed to individual h, implying that the sign of these weighted amounts, i.e. ΔW, may differ from the sign of the aggregated monetary amounts. This was illustrated above (for the CV measure) by means of a simple example.

The only case in which one really can be sure that one's monetary measures provide the correct information is when welfare distribution is optimal and the project is so small that it leaves the marginal social utilities of income unchanged. It then holds that:

$$dW = \lambda \Sigma_h dEV_h = \lambda \Sigma_h dCV_h. \tag{7.6'''}$$

This result can be interpreted as follows. For a small project, a medical treatment say, $dCV_h = dEV_h$ for all h, as is easily verified. If the project is evaluated close to a social welfare optimum, the marginal social utility of income must be equal across all individuals (and equal to λ, as was shown above). In turn, this means that regardless of whether we base the evaluation on the CV or the EV measure, the sum across the individuals of their monetary valuations of the project is proportional to the unobservable change in social welfare dW. Thus, the sum of dCV or dEV across the individuals provides us with a sign-preserving measure of the change in social welfare; if the sum is positive, the treatment increases social welfare while if the sum is negative it reduces social welfare.

Pragmatic views on the aggregation problem

If the distribution in society is optimal, or society has at its disposal means for unlimited and costless redistributions, then monetary gains and losses can be summed across individuals. This is perhaps an acceptable assumption (value judgement) to employ in evaluations of projects which primarily affect just a single individual or a few individuals or have a small impact on the probabilities of experiencing different states of the world. In all other cases a weighting procedure is required. Since the weights are not directly observable, one faces a formidable problem in assessing the social profitability of a project which affects more than a single person. Unless one simply gives up, some indirect and rough approach must be used to obtain information about the weights needed in the aggregation procedure. In what follows a number of possible approaches are suggested. The reader is also referred to Stoker (1993) who discusses different empirical approaches to the problem of aggregation over individuals.

In some cases it may be possible to estimate a social welfare function for a particular country. In fact, such attempts have been undertaken. Danzig *et al.* (1989) and Yunker (1989), for example, have estimated social welfare functions for the US economy.

Alternatively, one may choose a particular social welfare function in order to show how different distributional considerations affect the outcome of a social cost-benefit analysis. To illustrate, consider the social welfare function:

$$W = [\Sigma_h W_h (V_{he})^{1-\sigma}]/(1-\sigma). \tag{7.8}$$

If $\sigma = 0$ and the weights $W_h = 1$ for all h, (7.8) reduces to the simple utilitarian social welfare function. As $\sigma \to 1$ with $W_h = 1$, (7.8) reduces to the Bernoulli–Nash (Cobb–Douglas) social welfare function, while as $\sigma \to \infty$ the limiting case is the Rawlsian social welfare function; see Boadway and Bruce (1984) for details.[2] In this way, one can also use the monetary measures to show the decision-maker how different distributional assumptions affect the sign of the cost-benefit analysis.

Mäler (1985) has suggested that the choice of compensated money measures should in some cases be influenced by distributional considerations. Suppose that *initially*, i.e. before a reasonably small project is undertaken, society is indifferent to small changes in income distribution. Then the EV measure, which is based on *initial* incomes, etc. is the relevant measure. On the other hand, if we believe that income distribution *with* the project is such that small changes in income distribution would not affect social welfare, then the cost-benefit analysis of the project should be based on the CV measure; this measure is defined in terms of *final* levels of incomes, etc. See Mäler (1985) for details.

Yet another possibility is simply to calculate the unweighted sum of gains and losses and supplement this figure with a distributional analysis where gains and losses are allocated to different groups, e.g. high income earners, low income earners, young people, elderly people, people suffering from severe illness, etc.

The final approach suggested here is to discuss the outcome of a cost-benefit analysis in terms of compensation criteria. In a certain world, it is sometimes claimed that if the sum of CV_h is positive, then gainers from the project can, at least hypothetically, compensate those who lose from the project. If the sum of EV_h is positive, the losers are claimed to be unable to 'bribe' those who would gain from it to not undertake the project. The two compensation criteria referred to here are known as the Kaldor criterion and the Hicks criterion, respectively; see Hicks (1939) and Kaldor (1939). Unfortunately, it has been shown that one cannot, in general, interpret a positive sum of CVs or EVs as meaning that a compensation test is passed. This so-called Boadway paradox, see Boadway (1974), is basically due to the fact that the vector of prices and the compensated incomes used in defining CV and EV measures do not correspond to a general equilibrium. The reader is referred to Boadway and Bruce (1984) for a detailed examination of this issue. Also note that compensation is hypothetical, implying that some will actually gain while others will lose from the typical project. Thus compensation tests do not provide a way of avoiding the distributional issue.

An illustration: how to assess a treatment

We have defined the change in welfare corresponding to an arbitrary project which affects the probabilities of experiencing different states of the world. Let us now use our tools to evaluate a particular project. Consider an individual who is offered a particular medical treatment. The treatment shifts the probabilities of experiencing different health states. Implicitly this also shifts expected income. In exchange for the treatment, the individual has to bear some direct costs, may be on sick leave for a period of time, and may have to pay a share of the treatment cost. Denote these direct costs dP. Part of the cost for the treatment is covered by the government. This means that all tax payers are affected by the treatment, if undertaken: taxes paid by individual h in state i change by $d\tau_{hi}$.

We want to find out how the treatment affects social welfare. Differentiating the social welfare function (7.3), assuming that individual 1 is considered for the treatment, one arrives at the following awkward-looking expression:

$$dW = W_1 \Sigma_i [V_1(p, y_{N1i}, z_i) d\pi_{1i} - V_{1yi} \pi_{1i}(d\tau_{1i} + dP)]$$
$$- \Sigma_{h \neq 1} W_h \Sigma_i V_{hyi} \pi_{hi} d\tau_{hi} = \Sigma_h W_h V_{hye} dCV_h \tag{7.9}$$

where $y_{N1i} = y_{1i} - \tau_{1i} - P$ is disposable income of individual 1 in state i, and V_{hyi} is the marginal utility of income of individual h in state i. The expression can however be given an intuitively appealing interpretation. The first term within brackets yields the change in utility of individual 1 due to changed probabilities that s/he will experience different states of the world by participating in the treatment. This term captures the impact of the treatment on his or her expected utility of changes in health as well as disposable income. Recall the linear approximation undertaken in (4.17) (p. 65), where the term was approximated by a change in expected health and a change in expected income. The second term within brackets captures the change in tax payments for the individual due to the treatment plus his or her direct out-of-pocket costs dP for the treatment. Other individuals are affected through their tax payments and any change in tax payments by the treated individual. This is captured by the first expression in the second line of (7.9).

In order to further illustrate the interpretation of (7.9), let us assume that we are close to a social welfare optimum. Using (7.7), one arrives at the following simplified version of (7.9):

$$dW/\lambda = [\Sigma_i V_1(p, y_{N1i}, z_i)d\pi_{1i}/V_{1y}] - (d\tau_1{}^E + dP) - \Sigma_{h \neq 1}d\tau_h{}^E$$
$$= \mathrm{dCV}_{1B} - d\tau^E - dC = \mathrm{dCV}_{1B} - d\tau^E - (dC_m + dC_s + dC_d - dC_s)$$
$$(7.9')$$

where λ is the uniform marginal social utility of income as defined in (7.7), V_{1y} is the state-independent marginal utility of income of the treated individual, dCV_{1B} is his or her non-contingent gross WTP for the treatment's uncertain effects on health and disposable income, keeping out-of-pocket payments and tax payments constant ($dP = d\tau_{1i} = 0$ for $\forall i$), $d\tau_h{}^E$ is the expected change in tax payments for individual h, $d\tau^E$ is the expected change in aggregate tax payments $\Sigma_h d\tau_h{}^E$ *plus* dP *less* the total treatment cost dC, dC_m includes all direct medical and health care costs, dC_s includes all health care costs associated with any adverse side effects of the treatment, dC_d includes the present value costs of treating diseases that would not have occurred if the patient had not lived longer as a result of the original treatment, dC_s refers to present value savings in health care, rehabilitation and custodial costs due to the prevention or alleviation of disease; this classification of costs has been borrowed from Weinstein and Stason (1976).

Thus we explicitly interpret costs in terms of the individual's entire future health profile, both with and without the considered treatment. The benefits, as covered by dCV_{1B} or equivalently by dEV_{1B}, should then be given a corresponding interpretation, i.e. refer to the entire health and disposable income profiles with and without the treatment. Due to the fact that the treatment may affect the individual's working capacity and hence his or her future tax payments, the term $d\tau^E$ in (7.9') is a residual. This implies that the cost dC in (7.9') need not coincide with the expected change in total taxes (*plus* dP). If the individual is able to work more with the treatment than without it, then $-d\tau^E$ is positive; s/he will pay more in taxes even for fixed tax rates τ_{hi}. In this case tax rates do not have to be raised to fully cover dC.

It is important to stress that our money measures CV and EV in a single figure provide the same information as the different components in (7.9) and (7.9'). Thus (7.9) and (7.9') represent just another way of expressing the change in social welfare. The more general project evaluation criteria stated in (7.6) and (7.6'') can of course also be decomposed in the way suggested by (7.9) and (7.9') above.

Altruism

It is often claimed that people are concerned not only about their own health (welfare) but also about the health (welfare) of others. Even if a person is unaffected by a particular project, s/he may be concerned about the project's impact on the health of others, i.e. express altruistic concerns. Such altruistic concerns are usually not valued on the market and are hence difficult to capture using market data, i.e. it is difficult to estimate from market data the *total* monetary value which people place on changes in morbidity and mortality risks. As noted in chapters 5 and 6, the CVM has therefore become an important tool for evaluating changes in health status caused by pollution and measures such as public safety expenditure and medical treatments.

In a recent paper, Milgrom (1993), drawing on results derived by Bergstrom (1982), has argued forcefully that one can completely forget any altruistic components in a social cost-benefit analysis. Milgrom thus implicitly claims that one should ask people about their WTP for changes in their *own* safety. Moreover in two recent papers, Jones-Lee (1991, 1992) has derived a set of results on the valuation of a statistical life in the presence of different kinds of altruism. In particular, Jones-Lee shows that one should take full account of people's WTP for the safety of others if and only if altruism is exclusively safety-focused; definitions of different forms of altruism are given below. If altruism is pure, one can simply forget about a WTP for improvements in the safety of others, i.e. concentrate on the value of a statistical life. The intuition behind this result is that the pure altruist values both benefits and costs that accrue to others (the overall change in utility). These benefits and costs net out if we are close to a social welfare optimum.

These results may give the impression that in a WTP study using the CVM one must ask a question which covers only part of the respondent's total WTP for such things as changes in safety, unless one is prepared to assume that altruism is exclusively safety-focused. The aforementioned results relate however to infinitesimally small projects/changes evaluated at a (constrained) social welfare optimum. In this and the next section, which draw on Johansson (1994), the treatment of altruism in empirical evaluations of projects of an arbitrary size and 'distance' from the social welfare optimum will be discussed.

The Hicks–Allais type of model used in this section is due to Jones-Lee (1991, 1992), and is similar to the endogenous risk model used in previous chapters. That is, it is a simple single-period model in which individuals, as viewed from the beginning of the period, face two possible future states of the world: being alive or being dead. Given the purpose of this section, using such a simplified model saves us from an unnecessarily complex mathematical presentation without loss of generality. It is assumed that individuals have preferences over their own survival probabilities and levels of wealth, and those of others. The well-behaved cardinal utility function of individual h is written as follows:

$$V_h = V_h(\pi_1, y_1, \ldots, \pi_H, y_H) \qquad \forall h \tag{7.10}$$

where π_h is the survival probability of individual h, and y_h is his or her wealth. The function $V_h(.)$ is assumed to be strictly increasing in π_h and y_h and non-decreasing in its other arguments. As noted by Jones-Lee (1992, p. 82), this formulation of the utility function is sufficiently general to include as special cases virtually all of the main approaches to the treatment of choice under uncertainty, for example the expected utility approach. Note also that for a purely selfish person $\partial V_h / \partial \pi_j$ and $\partial V_h / \partial y_j$ are equal to zero for all $j \neq h$, while they are strictly positive for a pure altruist.[3] In the present context, a person for whom $\partial V_h / \partial \pi_j > 0$ while $\partial V_h / \partial y_j = 0$ is said to be a paternalistic or safety-focused altruist since s/he cares about only one aspect of person j's well-being, namely his or her safety. It should be pointed out, however, that safety-focused altruism is just one (rather extreme) form of paternalistic altruism. For example, another (equally extreme) form of paternalistic altruism is wealth-focused altruism, in which one cares only about the other person's income or wealth and is indifferent to variations in his or her safety.

There are also other forms of altruism, such as impure altruism where a person derives satisfaction from the pure act of giving, and intergenerational altruism. The latter can however be viewed as covered by our analysis since individual h's utility function can be thought of as covering all generations s/he cares about. For more on the concept of impure altruism, the reader is referred to Andreoni (1989, 1990).

Let us now consider a project/treatment that changes survival probabilities (π) and net or after-tax wealth ($y - \tau$) from $\pi_{h0}, y_{h0} - \tau_{h0}$ to $\pi_{h1}, y_{h1} - \tau_{h1}$ for $h = 1, \ldots, H$, where a subscript 0 (1) refers to before-project (with-project) values, y is before-tax wealth and τ is a tax. Note that we here treat the survival probabilities as fixed to the individuals since we want to evaluate, for example, a new medical treatment or some public safety measure. Our H individuals are asked three different questions regarding their WTP for this project. First, we inquire about each individual's *total* WTP for the above specified project, regardless of his or her motives for paying. Secondly, s/he is asked about his or her WTP for the project, provided that everybody else pays so as to remain at their initial levels of utility. Thirdly, each person is asked about his or her WTP for the change in his or her *own* survival probability and *own* wealth. Using (7.10), we arrive at the following three money measures of the project:

$$V_h(\pi_{11}, y_{11} - \tau_{11}, \ldots, \pi_{h1}, y_{h1} - \tau_{h1} - CV_h, \ldots, \pi_{H1}, y_{H1} - \tau_{H1}) = V_{h0}$$

$$V_h(\pi_{11}, y_{11} - \tau_{11} - CV_{1c}, \ldots, \pi_{h1}, y_{h1} - \tau_{h1} - CV_{hc}, \ldots, \pi_{H1}, y_{H1} - \tau_{H1} - CV_{Hc}) = V_{h0}$$

$$V_h(\pi_{10}, y_{10} - \tau_{10}, \ldots, \pi_{h1}, y_{h1} - \tau_{h1} - PCV_h, \ldots, \pi_{H0}, y_{H0} - \tau_{H0}) = V_{h0}$$

$$(7.11)$$

where V_{h0} is the initial (i.e. pre-project) level of utility of individual h, CV_h is his or her *total* non-contingent CV, CV_{hc} is the non-contingent CV *provided* everybody else pays so as to remain at their initial levels of utility, PCV_h is his or her non-contingent CV when s/he is induced to act as if s/he is purely selfish, and τ_h is a tax paid by individual h. In other words, CV_h yields the total WTP for a project/treatment that changes survival probabilities, taxes and initial wealth for possibly all individuals in society, while CV_{hc} yields the WTP provided everybody pays (is compensated) so as to remain at their initial levels of utility. Alternatively, the analysis can be based on the EV measure, but this exercise is not undertaken here.

One expects that a pure altruist would report $CV_h > CV_{hc}$, though the exact outcome hinges upon the project's impact on the welfare of the individuals s/he cares about. Moreover, such a person would report $CV_{hc} = PCV_h$, since both questions assume that others remain at their initial levels of utility.

For a paternalistic altruist $CV_h = CV_{hc} > PCV_h$, with the inequality holding at least if $\pi_{j1} \geq \pi_{j0}$ for $\forall j \neq h$, with the strict inequality holding for at least one person for whom h cares, since such a person cares only about the project's impact on the survival probabilities of others, i.e. does not care about the utility/wealth of others *per se*. If individual h is strictly selfish, then $CV_h = CV_{hc} = PCV_h$.

Also note that by keeping the respondent's own tax payments constant in, for instance, the second line of (7.11), we would arrive at a gross WTP measure, denoted GCV_{hc}, which is equal to $CV_{hc} + \Delta\tau_h$, where $\Delta\tau_h = \tau_{h1} - \tau_{h0}$. This gross WTP measure corresponds to those used in previous sections and chapters, where taxes have usually been kept constant. It illustrates the fact that we may ask a person for his or her WTP either inclusive or exclusive of his or her direct contribution to a project. This is noted here because we will make use of gross WTP measures below.

Altruism in cost-benefit analysis

Ultimately, the purpose of a valuation study is to provide information that can be used to assess a project. As illustrated in the previous section, there are many ways in which the valuation question can be formulated in the presence of altruism. This raises the question of how to design the WTP question so that it will be useful for a cost-benefit analysis. This issue is addressed in this section.

As on p. 120, it is assumed that the social welfare function is generalized utilitarian and can be written as follows:

$$W = \Sigma_h W_h V_h(\cdot) \tag{7.12}$$

where W_h is the distributional weight attributed to individual h. Using this function we can define the change in social welfare ΔW caused by the considered project. Using (7.11), we have three different ways of characterizing ΔW.

Substitution of the *first* line of (7.11) into the expression for ΔW yields the following social welfare change measure:

$$\Delta W = \Sigma_h W_h \big[V_h(\pi_{11}, y_{11} - \tau_{11}, \ldots, \pi_{h1}, y_{h1} - \tau_{h1}, \ldots, \pi_{H1}, y_{H1} - \tau_{H1})$$
$$- V_h(\pi_{11}, y_{11} - \tau_{11}, \ldots, \pi_{h1}, y_{h1} - \tau_{h1} - CV_h, \ldots, \pi_{H1}, y_{H1} - \tau_{H1}) \big]$$
$$= \Sigma_h \int_0^{CV_h} (W_h V_{hyh}) dCV_h = \Sigma_h (W_h v_{hyh}) CV_h \tag{7.13}$$

where V_{hyh} is the marginal utility of *own* income, the integral is a line integral, expressed as the sum of H integrals, changing CV in order from 1 to H, as is explained in Johansson (1993), for example, and the intermediate value theorem has been used in order to arrive at the final expression in (7.13), i.e v_{hyh} is the marginal utility of own income evaluated somewhere between initial and final level values of V_{hyh}.

(7.13) shows that a WTP question allowing individuals to pay for a project's *total* effects yields a project evaluation rule which is parallel to the one stated in (7.6). However, as will be shown below, the presence of altruism causes a problem if one uses the valuation question in the first line of (7.11).

In order to see the problem clearly, let us repeat the experiment but now use the *second* line in (7.11). One finds that the change in social welfare can be expressed as follows:

$$\Delta W = \Sigma_h [(\Sigma_j W_j v_{jyh}) CV_{hc}] \tag{7.14}$$

where $v_{jyh} = \partial V_j / \partial y_h$ is the marginal utility, if any, that individual j derives from individual h's wealth evaluated at some intermediate level as explained above, and the *sum* within parentheses yields the marginal social utility of income assigned to individual h. Individual h's CV is now valued by all individuals who care about h's wealth, i.e. for whom $v_{jyh} \neq 0$. This explains the sum within brackets in (7.14). Summing across all h yields the change in social welfare.

At a social welfare optimum, the term within parentheses in (7.14), i.e. the marginal social utility of income, is equal across individuals, as is shown in the appendix to this chapter. Thus for a small project evaluated at the social welfare optimum, $dW = \Sigma_h \lambda dCV_{hc}$, where λ is the uniform marginal social utility of income and dCV_{hc} is the marginal non-contingent CV of individual h (when everybody pays so as to remain at initial utility levels).

On the other hand, this is not true for the small project version of (7.13), i.e. $\Sigma_h dCV_h$ need not reflect the sign of dW even at a social welfare optimum since the weights $W_h V_{hyh}$ differ from the marginal social utility of income (λ), in general; see the appendix. As a consequence, the fact that $\Sigma_h dCV_h > 0$ for a small project (producing both gainers and losers) evaluated close to a social welfare optimum does not guarantee that the project increases social welfare, unless all individuals are paternalistic safety-oriented altruists (or purely selfish). Recall that $\Sigma_h CV_h = \Sigma_h CV_{hc}$ for a society consisting of paternalistic altruists since $v_{jyh} = 0$ for all $h \neq j$ in (7.14) for such a society.

Consider finally the outcome if we ask people about their WTP for the project, disregarding any impact of the project on the safety and wealth of others. Using the *third* line of (7.11) in the social welfare change measure, one arrives at the following awkward expression:

$$\Delta W = \Sigma_h W_h V_h(\pi_{11}, y_{11} - \tau_{11}, \dots, \pi_{h1}, y_{h1} - \tau_{h1}, \dots, \pi_{H1}, y_{H1} - \tau_{H1})$$
$$- \Sigma_h W_h V_h(\pi_{10}, y_{10} - \tau_{10}, \dots, \pi_{h1}, y_{h1} - \tau_{h1} - PCV_h, \dots, \pi_{H0}, y_{H0}$$
$$- \tau_{H0})$$
$$= \Sigma_h W_h \left\{ \int_0^{PCV_h} (V_{hyh}) dPCV_h + \Sigma_{j \neq h} \left[\int_{\pi_{j0}}^{\pi_{j1}} (\partial V_h / \partial \pi_j) d\pi_j \right. \right.$$
$$\left. \left. + \int_{y_{j0}}^{y_{j1}} (\partial V_h / \partial y_j) dy_j - \int_{\tau_{j0}}^{\tau_{j1}} (\partial V_h / \partial y_j) d\tau_j \right] \right\} \qquad (7.15)$$

where the line integral has been expressed as the sum of integrals, and the sum of the terms within brackets in the final line of (7.15) yields the welfare change of a person due to his altruistic concerns. This sum differs from zero unless the person is strictly selfish. Note that all the partial derivatives within brackets in the final line of (7.15) are strictly positive for a pure altruist, while only the first one is strictly positive for what is here called a paternalistic altruist.

(7.15) reveals that a WTP question forcing people to pay for only some motives while ignoring other motives does not provide us with the information needed in a social cost-benefit analysis. Instead we face the difficult problem of somehow estimating the terms within brackets. (7.15) also highlights the fact that ignoring altruistic motives in a CVM question provides no solution to the aggregation problem. In particular, and as explained above, since the weights V_{hyh} differ from the marginal social utility of income, $\Sigma_h dPCV_h > 0$ for a small project evaluated close to a social welfare optimum does not imply that $dW > 0$, unless all individuals are pure altruists (or purely selfish); then $dPCV_h = dCV_{hc} \; \forall h$ as was shown below (7.11) (p. 130).

Using the second line in (7.11) but keeping the respondent's own tax payments constant, one arrives at the gross WTP measure denoted GCV_{hc} on p. 130. This measure is equal to CV_{hc} *plus* the increase in own tax payments. If we are at a (constrained) social welfare optimum, the sum of marginal *gross* compensating variations $\Sigma_h dGCV_{hc}$ reduces to the change in public safety expenditure, denoted ds in Jones-Lee (1992), i.e.:

$$\Sigma_h(dGCV_{hc}) = \Sigma_h(dCV_{hc} + d\tau_h) = ds = \Sigma_h d\tau_h \qquad (7.14')$$

where we follow Jones-Lee and keep y_h constant. This means that in the aggregate a total WTP question, specified as in the *second* line in (7.11), produces as a *special case* the theoretical cost-benefit rules for small projects evaluated at a constrained social welfare optimum provided in Jones-Lee (1992).

According to the above analysis, the WTP question can be formulated so as to generate the small project evaluation rules stated on p. 124, and also those rules found in Jones-Lee (1992), for example. The analysis also reveals the formidable problems one faces in going from individual WTPs to (signing) aggregate social welfare changes; determining the magnitude of the terms within brackets in (7.14), for example, for each individual is no easy task. Often, the only possibility seems to be to *assume* that the project is small and that we are reasonably close to a social welfare optimum so that the sign of $\Sigma_h dCV_{hc}$ indicates the sign of the change in social welfare. In addition, the comparison of different money measures undertaken below (7.11) can possibly be used to establish a *lower bound* for a project's social profitability.

In any case, I would recommend the cost-benefit practitioner to collect information on both people's total WTP and their WTP for their own safety. The reason is as follows. The CVM, which may be the only available method for estimating an individual's total WTP, is based on *hypothetical* choices and payments and is therefore questioned by many economists; see chapter 5, pp. 71–9. One also faces the risk that altruistic individuals will devote their entire 'altruism' budget to the project under investigation, i.e. that they may overlook the fact that there are many other projects which they may want to 'sponsor'. Moreover, as this section illustrates, there are many different ways in which the total WTP question can be formulated, each variation having its own drawbacks (unless the respondents and the investigator have perfect information, i.e. know (7.11) and (7.12)). On the other hand, in estimating a WTP for people's own safety one can (hopefully) rely on a method revealing *actual* behaviour. In addition, the latter approach provides us with a reasonable lower bound for the project's social profitability, at least for a small project evaluated close to a social welfare optimum; see the discussion in Jones-Lee (1992). More generally, the kinds of rules derived above and in Jones-Lee (1992) provide extremely useful information for the practitioner on how to evaluate a small project in the presence of altruism, for example how to incorporate different kinds of altruistic behaviour in the set of evaluation rules.

Appendix

Maximization of the social welfare function (7.12) subject to $s = \Sigma_h \tau_h$ with respect to s and taxes yields the following first-order conditions for an interior solution when π_{h1} for all h is a well-behaved function of public expenditure s on safety:

$$\Sigma_j \Sigma_h W_h V_{h\pi j} \partial \pi_j / \partial s = \lambda$$
$$\Sigma_h W_h V_{hyj} = \lambda \qquad \forall j \tag{A7.1}$$

where $V_{h\pi j}$ is the marginal utility that h derives from increased safety for person j, V_{hyj} is the marginal utility that h derives from an increase in person j's wealth, and λ is the Lagrange multiplier associated with the government's budget constraint $s = \Sigma_h \tau_h$. Note that the second line yields the marginal social utility of income attributed to person j. If nobody else cares about his or her wealth, the expression reduces to V_{jyj}, i.e. to the marginal utility of own income. The first line expression is an altruism version of the condition (A4.4) in the appendix to chapter 4, i.e. it can be used to calculate an altruism-augmented value of statistical life.

The aggregation problem faced in using the CV_h measure in the presence of pure (and wealth-oriented) altruism is that V_{hyh} differ from the marginal social utility of income as defined by the second line in (A7.1), since other individuals than h also care about his wealth.

8 Further evaluation issues in a risky world

In this chapter we will consider some further evaluation issues in a risky world. An important issue seldom touched upon in health economics is the value of information in a situation where a measure may have some irreversible effects. This kind of problem gives an extra dimension to the valuation issue. That is, how do we define and measure the value of the option to delay a decision when there is independent R&D going on which may reveal whether the consequences are in fact irreversible?

A second issue to consider is the health production function approach and further illustration of how the intertemporal version can be used to evaluate health changes. In particular, time used up in the production of health is now introduced, and the individual has a job so that his health status may affect the number of hours s/he works or the hourly wage s/he receives.

The final issue to be considered is an intertemporal model in which the survival probability is age-dependent but may also be affected through investment in health capital. In turn, the health production function is age-dependent. The model is used to define money measures of a parametric change (say, a medical treatment) in the health production function or in the survival probability. As an important by-product it is shown how to handle a death risk which depends on a state variable (health); it is easy to overlook the fact that such a problem is not a standard optimal control problem.

The value of information

Information plays a key role in all decision-making. This is of course also true for decisions involving medical treatments. There is sometimes a trade-off between the extra benefits which can be obtained by postponing a project/treatment in order to learn more about its consequences, and the extra costs incurred, in terms of extra pain or income foregone, for example. There are other informational problems, such as the principal–agent problem, but these are ignored here; see, for example, Kreps (1990) for details.

A simple way to illustrate the value of perfect information is to consider a risk neutral hospital under two different scenarios. The hospital is one among many hospitals providing a particular medical treatment. In advance, the hospital is uncertain about the value of the treatment, say patients' WTP for the treatment or the principal's economic valuation of the treatment. The hospital's costs of providing the treatment are known with certainty.

If the hospital treats z patients, its expected profitability is defined as follows:

$$PS^E = \Sigma_i \pi_i p_i z - c(z) \tag{8.1}$$

where π_i is the probability that the WTP for the treatment is $\$p_i$ for $i = 1, \ldots, k$, and $c(.)$ is the hospital's strictly convex cost function.

In the first scenario to be considered, the hospital must decide on its scale of production before uncertainty is revealed. The best the hospital can do is to equate the expected WTP with the marginal cost of providing the treatment. In terms of figure 8.1, it will supply $z_i = z^*$ treatments for all i. The cost of treating an additional patient is then equal to the amount p^* which the principal (or the patient) is expected to be willing to pay. The actual amount, however, will be p_1 (with a probability of one-half) or p_2 (with a probability of one-half). That is, *ex post* the profitability of the treatment is either $p_1 z^* - c(z^*)$ or $p_2 z^* - c(z^*)$, depending on whether the WTP for the treatment turns out to be low or high.

If the hospital could postpone its output decision until uncertainty is revealed, it would either treat z_1 *or* z_2 patients, depending on whether the price/WTP of a treatment turns out to be low or high. As a result, the hospital's *social* profitability increases by an amount corresponding to either area A or area B in figure 8.1, as compared with the case where $z = z^*$ units. In other words, in the simple case under discussion, the value of perfect information is equal to the extra social surplus which the hospital can earn by postponing a decision on its production level until the WTP is known. The expected value of perfect information is simply $\pi_1 A + \pi_2 B$, where $\pi_i = 0.5$ for $i = 1,2$ in figure 8.1.

The extra benefits must, however, be compared to the extra costs of delaying a decision. For example, the adjustment costs may be so high that the hospital prefers to take its decisions before the WTP is revealed. In any case, the simple example provided here illustrates the fact that the combination of uncertainty and irreversible consequences means that the conventional investment rule need not hold. This rule says that you should invest if the expected revenues exceed the expected costs. Apparently, this simple rule is no longer valid if you can acquire more information about a project's

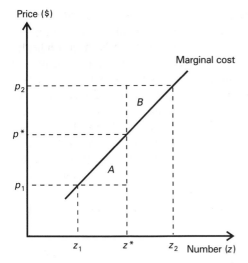

Figure 8.1 An illustration of the value of perfect information

possibly irreversible consequences by postponing the decision to undertake the project.

In order to give the concept of the value of information a more precise meaning within a health economic context, a two-period model will be used. The model is the one given in (2.24) and (4.19). Suppose we consider a new treatment or a new drug whose future, that is period 2, consequences are uncertain as viewed from today. The consequences are also irreversible, i.e. undergoing the treatment or taking the drug cannot be undone if the side effects turn out to be severe. As above, we will compare two scenarios with respect to information or learning. In the first scenario, no further information is acquired as time goes by. In the second scenario, uncertainty is revealed at the beginning of period 2, perhaps due to independent research.

Using a slightly modified version of the model in (2.24), the decision problem in the no-learning scenario can be viewed as:

$$\max_{x_1, s} [u(x_1, z_1) + \max_{D} \int_{z_2} v_2(p_2, y_2 + s, z_{2_\epsilon}(D)) dF(z_{2_\epsilon})] \qquad (8.2)$$

subject to the first-period budget constraint $y_1 - s - p_1 x_1 = 0$, where D is a binary variable equal to unity if the treatment is undertaken and zero otherwise. For simplicity, we assume that $z_2(D) = z^E + D(a + \epsilon)$, where a is a constant and ϵ is a random variable whose expected value is equal to zero.

According to this decision problem, a decision on D *must* be taken before uncertainty is revealed: the decision-maker (or the individual) compares utility attained for $D = 1$ and $D = 0$ *before* the treatment's effects on health have become known, and chooses the alternative that provides the highest level of expected utility. It is assumed that $D = 0$ in period 1 since setting $D = 1$ in period 1 means that no choice is available in period 2. A policy rule such as the one captured by (8.2) is called an *open-loop policy* since a decision is taken conditional on the information initially available.

In the second scenario, a decision on D can be taken after uncertainty is revealed (due to, say, successful research on the consequences of the treatment or the drug). The decision problem is therefore as follows:

$$\max_{x_1, s} \left[u(x_1, z_1) + \int_{z_2} [\max_D v_2(p_2, y_2 + s, z_{2_\epsilon}(D)) dF(z_{2_\epsilon})] \right] \tag{8.3}$$

where, as before, it is assumed that $D = 0$ in period 1 so as to maintain a choice set. According to (8.3), the decision-maker (or the individual) compares utility attained for $D = 1$ and $D = 0$ *after* the treatment's effects on health have become known, i.e. the actual value of z_2 with $D = 1$ and $D = 0$, respectively, is known. The decision-maker (the individual) then chooses the treatment if it yields higher utility than no treatment. Moving back to period 1, the decision-maker (the individual) maximizes two-period expected utility in the way specified by (8.3). This is a *closed-loop policy*, since at each decision point current as well as anticipated future information is exploited.

The difference between (8.2) and (8.3) represents the *expected value of perfect information* conditional on $D = 0$ in period 1; see Arrow and Fisher (1974) and Henry (1974). This value is sometimes called an option value or a quasi-option value in environmental economics. It shows the increase in expected utility of not undertaking a treatment/project in period 1, when it is possible to take a decision after uncertainty is resolved instead of before. Note the importance of irreversibility here. If the decision so to speak can be reversed or neutralized if its consequences are unwanted, then we have the conventional flexibility which eliminates the possible advantages of postponing the decision.

Returning to the simple example illustrated in figure 8.1, suppose $p_1 < 0$, possibly due to severe side effects of the treatment while p_2 is still positive. In the first scenario, expected benefits are defined as before. On the other hand, if a decision can be taken after the treatment's effects are known, it will obviously not be undertaken if its benefits are negative. Its expected benefits are therefore $\pi_2 p_2 z_2 + 0$.

In discussing new treatments or new drugs, the apparatus developed here could possibly be fruitful. Often there is something to be gained by awaiting further research, but also a cost of postponing the introduction of the new medical method or drug. There may also be intermediate cases in the sense that the problem may allow for active learning so that we learn more by a small-scale introduction of the method or drug. Moreover, two-period models tend to produce strong results. Once the possibility of a third or fourth period is opened up, results usually become much more ambiguous. This is also true for models involving a quasi-option value, as has been shown by Fisher and Hanemann (1990). The reader is also referred to the review articles on investment decisions in the presence of irreversibilities and risk by Dixit (1992), Dixit and Pindyck (1994) and Pindyck (1991).

To the best of my knowledge there are no empirical studies of the expected value of information. In principle, one can use (8.2) and (8.3) to design valuation questions which capture the conditional expected value of perfect information. It seems to be an important task for health economists and environmental economists interested in the valuation issue to undertake empirical studies capturing the value of improved information.

A further development would be to assume that the decision-maker faces uncertainty rather than risk. For example, s/he may have a probability distribution function for each possible p value in figure 8.1, which is updated as more information arrives. The reader is referred to Dobbs (1991) for such a model, and also to Taylor et al. (1993) for an empirical illustration of how value of information analytic techniques can be used to evaluate the benefits of acquiring more information about the cancer potency of specific chemical compounds.

A health production function model

In this section, the health production function approach, already touched upon on several occasions, will be further explained and explored. The main difference between the model used in this section and those employed earlier is the treatment of time. The individual is now allowed to allocate his or her time between working time, leisure time, and time used for health production.

Let us consider an individual who consumes private goods, supplies labour, and produces health in each of T periods. For the sake of simplicity the utility function of the individual is assumed to be separable in time and is written as follows:

$$U = \Sigma_t \rho^{t-1} u(x_t, L_t, z_t) \tag{8.4}$$

where $\rho = (1+\theta)^{-1} < 1$ is a discount factor, θ is the discount rate, x_t is a vector of private goods consumed in period t with $t = 1, \ldots, T$, L_t is leisure time in period t, and z_t is a health index for period t. The cardinal sub-utility functions are assumed to be strictly increasing in each of their arguments, and to possess all other properties indicated in chapter 2 so as to generate well-behaved solutions to the utility maximization problems to be considered.

Health is viewed as being produced using private goods and time as variable inputs. The period t health production function is written as:

$$z_t = f_t(X_t, L_{zt}, h_t) \tag{8.5}$$

where X_t is a vector of health goods used in the production of period t health, L_{zt} is time devoted to health production, and h_t is initial health status in period t, viewed as being carried over from period $t-1$, i.e. as a special case, $h_t = z_{t-1}$. The production function is assumed to be strongly concave and increasing in each of its arguments. According to (8.5), the individual carries over his or her period $t-1$ health status or health capital to period t. Conditional on the realized value of h_t, the individual can affect his or her perceived period t health by 'investing' in health services and time.

The only source of uncertainty considered initially is the initial level of health in each future period. As in chapter 4, p. 67, it is assumed that h_t can be written as follows:

$$h_t = h_t^E + \beta_t \epsilon; \int_{h_t} h_{t\epsilon} dF(h_{t\epsilon}) = \int_a^b h_{t\epsilon} dF(h_{t\epsilon}) = h_t^E. \tag{8.6}$$

Hence h_t is a random variable with distribution function $F(.)$ defined over the support $[a,b]$, i.e. $F(h_{t\epsilon}) = \text{prob}\{h_t \leq h_{t\epsilon}\}$ for $h_{t\epsilon} \in [a,b]$, and h_t^E is its expected value. The parameter β_t is interpreted as the standard deviation of h_t since ϵ, whose mean is equal to zero, is assumed to have variance $\sigma^2 = 1$. Moreover, it is assumed that $Pr[\epsilon \geq -h_t^E/\beta_t] = 1$ so as to ensure that h_t does not take on negative values. As explained on p. 67, the formulation in (8.6) allows us to cover spread-preserving changes in the mean as well as mean-preserving changes in the variability of h_t. If there is no uncertainty and no depreciation of health capital, h_t would reduce to z_{t-1}.

In what follows, we will consider a two-period variation of the model outlined above. Period 1 is interpreted as representing the present while period 2 represents the future. Assume that the individual has arrived at period 2 (and hence that s/he has survived period 1). Solving the period 2 utility maximization problem, as stated in the appendix to this chapter, yields a health 'demand' function which can be written as follows:

$$z_2 = z_2(p_2, P_2, w_2, y_2 + s, h_2^r) \tag{8.7}$$

where a subscript 2 refers to period 2, p_2 is a vector of present value prices of consumption goods, P_2 is the price of the, for simplicity, single health good,

w_2 is the present value wage, y_2 is the present value of a lump-sum income, s is savings carried over from period 1, and h_2^r is the realized beginning of the period 2 value of the stochastic h_2 variable. The individual is assumed to treat all prices as fixed and to have access to a perfect capital market, allowing him or her to freely transfer income between the two periods at a fixed market rate of interest.

The formulation of the health demand function in (8.7) implies that uncertainty is revealed at the beginning of period 2, i.e. before decisions are taken. This seems to be a reasonable assumption within the context considered here, since you don't take a headache tablet until you know that you are getting a headache. Note also that the demand functions for consumption goods and health goods as well as the time used in health production are functions of the same arguments as the function in (8.7); see the appendix. Since labour supply here is viewed as endogenous, the market wage has an impact on the individual's allocation of time between work, health production and pure leisure.

The problem for the individual in period 1 is to choose consumption goods, savings, leisure and health production so as to maximize expected utility over both periods:

$$\max_{x_1, X_1, L_1, L_{z1}, s} [u(x_1, L_1, z_1) + \int_{h_2} \rho[v(p_2, P_2, w_2, y_2 + s, h_{2\epsilon})dF(h_{2\epsilon}; \phi)]] \quad (8.8)$$

subject to the period 1 budget constraint and the period 1 health production function:

$$y_1 + w_1(L^{to} - L_1 - L_{z_1}) = p_1 x_1 + P_1 X_1 + I + s \quad (8.8')$$

$$z_1 = f_1(X_1, L_{z_1}, h_1^r) \quad (8.8'')$$

where L^{to} is total time, I is an insurance premium permitting the individual to buy health services at prices P_1 and P_2, and ϕ is interpreted as a vector containing the parameters or moments, such as the mean and the variance, characterizing the stochastic properties of the distribution function.

Solving the above maximization problem yields period 1 and period 2 health demand functions, see the appendix, which can be written as follows:

$$\begin{aligned} z_1 &= z_1(p, P, w, y, h_1^r, \phi) \\ z_2 &= z_2(p, P, w, y, h_1^r, h_2, \phi) \end{aligned} \quad (8.9)$$

where $y = y_1 + y_2 - I$, $p = [p_1, p_2]$ and so on to avoid clutter. The first line of (8.9) shows that today's health demand function is non-stochastic, although it depends on the mean and moments about the mean, as captured by ϕ, of the beginning of period 2 health status h_2 which is stochastic as viewed from today. The second line of (8.9) shows that future health demand is stochastic as viewed from today since the random variable h_2 appears as an argument. This is in sharp contrast to the period 2 demand function in (8.7), which refers to the beginning of period 2 when uncertainty has been revealed. The remaining behaviour functions, such as those capturing demand for consumption goods and leisure time, will contain the same arguments as the functions in (8.9).

Substitution of the period 1 and period 2 demand and supply functions into the utility function (8.8) yields an expected indirect utility function which can be written as follows:

$$V^E = V^E(c,P,h_1^r,\phi) = v_1(c,P,h_1^r,\phi) + \int_{h_2} [v_2(c,P,h_1^r,h_{2e},\phi)dF(h_{2e};\phi)]$$

(8.10)

where $v_2(.) = \rho v(.)$, and $c = [p,w,y_1+y_2-I]$; see the appendix for details. (8.10) expresses the level of utility that the individual is expected to attain as a function of prevailing prices, wages, lump-sum incomes, current health and future health. This concludes the presentation of the model.

Using the model to assess health changes

Let us assume that the individual whose expected utility is captured by (8.10) is asked about his WTP for a medical treatment which changes initial health in period 2. In advance it is not possible to say how h_2 is changed. Rather, the treatment changes the probability that h_2 will take on different values. The individual's non-contingent WTP is implicitly defined by:

$$V^E(p,P,w,y-\text{CV},h_1^r,\phi^1) = V^E(p,P,w,y,h_1^r,\phi^0)$$

(8.11)

where the insurance premium I is suppressed, and CV denotes the maximum non-contingent payment (CV) that the individual is willing to make in exchange for a medical treatment. This treatment changes the probability distribution for the health status at the beginning of period 2. For example, its mean or variance or skewness (or any or all of them) may be believed to change. This is captured by the shift from ϕ^0 to ϕ^1 in (8.11). Through the health production function the shift in the probability distribution is translated into health changes. The associated change in expected utility determines the magnitude of CV in (8.11). Alternatively, we may define a uniform WTP measure based on the concept of EV. The individual is then held at his or her final level of expected utility, implying that s/he is compensated so as to achieve the same level of expected utility as with a utility-improving shift in ϕ, and pays to avoid a utility-reducing shift in ϕ.

In order to further illustrate the meaning of the CV measure, let us consider a *ceteris paribus* small change in the mean and variance (standard deviation) of h_2. Using (A8.5) in the appendix, the marginal non-contingent compensating variation can be shown to be equal to:

$$dCV = \rho(v_z^E/\lambda)dh_2^E + \int_\epsilon \rho((v_z\epsilon_\epsilon)/\lambda)d\beta_2 dF_\epsilon(\epsilon_\epsilon) \qquad (8.11')$$

where $F_\epsilon(.)$ is the distribution function for ϵ, $F_\epsilon(\epsilon_\epsilon) = \text{prob}\{(\epsilon \leq \epsilon_\epsilon)\} = F(h_2^E + \beta_2\epsilon_\epsilon) = \text{prob}\{(h_2 \leq h_2^E + \beta_2\epsilon_\epsilon)\}$, i.e. in terms of (8.6) we have made a transformation from the random variable h_2 with mean h_2^E and variance $(\beta^2)^2$ to the random variable ϵ with zero mean and unit variance (see any textbook on probability theory) and λ is the expected marginal utility of income as can be seen from (A8.4) in the appendix. The first term in the right-hand side expression is the positive marginal WTP for a marginal increase in initial mean health h_2^E for period 2. The second term covers the value of a mean-preserving marginal increase in the variability of initial period 2 health (through a marginal increase in β_2). Note that both v_z and ϵ are stochastic variables; see (A8.5) in the appendix, where it can be seen that v_z is a function of the stochastic variable h_2. Thus $E[v_z\epsilon]$ does not reduce to the product of their means, i.e. to zero since $E[\epsilon] = 0$, but to the covariance between v_z and ϵ. A useful result derived in Chavas and Bishop (1984) states that the sign of the covariance between two functions $f(\epsilon)$ and $g(\epsilon)$ is equal to the sign of the product of their derivatives with respect to ϵ. Thus if v_{zz} is negative, i.e. the individual is risk averse with respect to health risk, see chapter 2, p. 21, the non-contingent CV is negative in (8.11') for a marginal *ceteris paribus* increase in β_2. That is, the individual needs a compensation in order to voluntarily accept a mean-preserving increase in the variability of initial period 2 health. A medical treatment, say, causing increases in both the mean and variability of health may thus increase or decrease expected utility, depending on the magnitudes of the two opposing forces dh^E and $d\beta$.

It is important to stress that our money measure covers all aspects of a health change. That is, any change in expected utility due to adjustments in labour supply (labour income) and purchases of the health good are captured by CV in (8.11). In fact, so long as prices (wages) remain constant, the marginal WTP for a good (including time) is equal to its price throughout the considered shift in ϕ. This means that there is no utility gain or loss due to adjustments in, for example, x_2 and L_{z_2} for fixed prices and wages. It would thus be erroneous to add separate estimates of changes in labour income and purchases of health goods to CV in a cost-benefit analysis of the considered medical treatment. Even if prices or wages change, the resulting impact on utility will be covered by our money measure. This can be seen by adding an index 1 (0) to the prices in the left-hand side (right-hand side) expression in (8.11), indicating their final (initial) level values. One can also allow future income y or the future wage

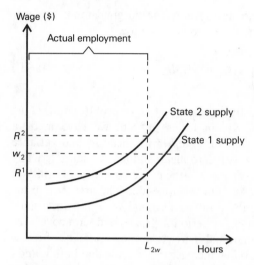

Figure 8.2 A fixed number of working hours when labour supply is state-dependent

rate to depend on health status, i.e. to be functions of h_2, but CV will still cover the overall change in expected utility.

Sometimes, however, individuals are constrained to work a pre-specified number of hours per day. Due to variations in health, the actual number of hours worked can differ from the pre-specified number, say 8 hours per day. In what follows, period 2 working time is written as $L_{2w}(h_2)$. Actual working time is thus a function of the health status at the beginning of the period. The best the individual can do in period 2 is now to allocate the remaining, i.e. non-working, time between leisure and health production so as to even out the marginal utility of leisure time and the marginal utility of time spent in health production. This common marginal utility of leisure time divided by the marginal utility of income is denoted the *reservation wage*. If the individual is compelled to work more hours than s/he would if unconstrained, the market wage falls short of the reservation wage. This inequality is reversed if the individual would like to work more hours than the market can offer given the prevailing wage rate. Note that the period 2 reservation wage is stochastic as viewed from today. This is illustrated in figure 8.2, where the marginal reservation wage is either R^1 or R^2 depending on what (health) state of the world is realized.

In order to further illustrate these ideas it is useful to consider a small change in h_2. Using an appropriately modified version of (8.8), see (A8.6) in the appendix, one obtains the following change in expected utility:

$$dV^E = \int_{h_2} \rho[v_z dh_{2\epsilon} + v_y(w_2 - (v_L/v_y))dL_{2w\epsilon}]dF(h_{2\epsilon}; \phi^0) \qquad (8.12)$$

where $v_z = \partial v/\partial h_2$ is the marginal utility of initial health status, $dh_{2\epsilon} = dh_2^E + \epsilon_\epsilon d\beta_2$, $-v_L = -\partial v/\partial L_2$ is the marginal disutility of work effort as is explained below (A8.6) in the appendix, v_y is the marginal utility of lump-sum income, and $dL_{2w\epsilon} = (\partial L_{2w}/\partial h_2)dh_{2\epsilon}$. The first term within brackets captures the state-dependent marginal utility of health, while the expression within bold parentheses yields the state-dependent difference between the market wage w_2 and the marginal reservation wage v_L/v_y; both v_L and v_y are state-dependent. We can use (8.12) to calculate the expected value of this difference between the market wage and the reservation wage:

$$\Delta PS^E = \int_{h_2} \rho[v_y(w_2 - (v_L/v_y))dL_{2w\epsilon}]dF(h_{2\epsilon}; \phi^0) \qquad (8.13)$$

where ΔPS^E denotes the change in expected producer surplus (expressed here in units of utility since, for reasons to be explained below, we multiply by v_y). If the reservation wage is equal to zero for all states of the world, (8.13) reduces to the change in expected income due to the considered marginal treatment. Note, however, that this change is quite complicated if both the mean h_2^E and the standard deviation β_2 change.

What this analysis shows in addition to the one on pp. 64–5 is that changes in expected income are even less appealing as a welfare change measure once one allows for an opportunity cost of time plus a constraint in the labour market. Note that the sign of ΔPS^E can be opposite to the sign of the change in expected income, depending on whether the marginal reservation wage exceeds or falls short of the market wage. There is also the problem that we cannot easily factor out the marginal utility of income from (8.13) so as to convert the expression from units of utility to monetary units. The reason is that both v_y and dL_{2w} are stochastic in (8.13), implying that their product in (8.13) does not reduce to the product of their expected levels. This is parallel to the case considered in (8.11′). In addition we have the usual problem that neither the change in expected income nor ΔPS^E covers the value of the change in health *per se*, i.e. the first term in (8.12).

One faces similar problems in using period 2 market prices to evaluate the WTP for risk reductions. This can be seen from the second line of (A8.5′) in the appendix. The marginal utility of income as well as the future demand for the health good X_2 are stochastic as viewed from today. This means that the future expected demand for the good does not reflect the marginal WTP for a small decrease in the price of the good (in the simple way that it does in a certain world). For further discussion of this kind of complication in using market data to assess (environmental) health risks, the reader is referred to Shogren and Crocker (1991).

On the value of changes in life expectancy

In this section we will return to the intertemporal models considered in the final section of chapter 2 in order to derive money measures of a change in the survival probability in models where health and the survival probability are age-dependent.

Let us use the same simple utility function $u(t) = u[x(t), h(t)]$ as in the deterministic case considered in chapter 2, p. 27. Instantaneous utility depends on the levels of consumption of goods and the stock of health capital. Integrating this function between zero and T yields the total utility of living for T years. However, the length of life, i.e. T, is stochastic. The distribution of T is given by the hazard function (the probability that the individual dies in the short interval $(T, T + dT)$ conditional on having survived to T):

$$[F_d(T)/(1 - F(T))]dT = \delta[h(T), T]dT \qquad (8.14)$$

where $F(.)$ is the cumulative distribution function for the time of death, i.e. T, and $F_d(.)$ is the density function for T. Thus the hazard is a function of both the stock of health capital at time T, and the age of the individual. We assume that the intensity parameter $\delta(.)$ is non-negative, bounded away from zero, and decreasing in h and increasing in T.

Integration of (8.14) yields:

$$1 - F(T) = e^{-\int_0^T \delta[h(s), s]ds} = e^{-\Delta(T)} \qquad (8.15)$$

where $1 - F(T)$ is the survival probability for the individual at time ('age') T. (8.15) means that we assume that health capital not only increases the quality of life through its presence in the utility function, but also has an impact on the expected life-length of the individual. These assumptions seem realistic. Expected present value utility can thus be written as follows:

$$E[u_0] = \int_0^\infty u[x(t), h(t)]e^{-[\theta t + \Delta(t)]}dt \qquad (8.16)$$

where θ is the marginal rate of time preference; the reader is referred to (A8.7) and (A8.8) in the appendix for further details.

The accumulation of health follows the equation:

$$\dot{h} = f^*(X, t, a) - \gamma h = f(X, h, t, a, \gamma) \qquad (8.17)$$

where a is a shift parameter, γ is a depreciation factor, and $f^*(X, t, a)$ is a strictly concave production function in $X, f^* \in C^2$, which is increasing in X

and decreasing in time. Thus the individual's age has a direct impact on his ability to produce health capital.

The individual's dynamic budget constraint is written as follows:

$$x(t) + X(t) + \dot{k}(t) = w(t) + [r(t) + \delta(t)]k(t). \tag{8.18}$$

The left-hand side of the dynamic budget constraint is the sum of consumption, resources set aside for health investments, and the net accumulation of assets at time t. The right-hand side consists of labour income, $w(t)$, and capital income at time t. The latter consists of two components: interest income, $r(t)k(t)$, and income from the insurance system, $\delta(t)k(t)$. The insurance system is the one described on p. 29.

The dynamic budget constraint (8.18) in combination with a No-Ponzi game condition (see (2.31)), can be used to show, by integrating the budget constraint forwards, that the present value at time 0 of total consumption, $(x + X)$, equals the present value of wage plus capital income, where the discount factor at time t is equal to the sum of the interest rate r and the death intensity parameter δ:

$$\int_0^\infty [x(t) + X(t)]e^{-[\Delta(t) + rt]}dt = k(0) + \int_0^\infty [w(t)]e^{-[(\Delta(t) + rt]}dt \tag{8.18'}$$

where, for the sake of simplicity, the rate of interest $r(t)$ is assumed to be constant over time. In what follows, we will use (8.18) but one can as well employ (8.18') instead of (8.18). This is due to the assumption of a perfect insurance market, which enables the individual to equate the expected present value of expenditures with the expected present value of wealth. In the absence of annuities, this is not possible; this implies that (8.18) with income from the insurance system, i.e. δk, ignored is the relevant dynamic budget constraint until the individual dies.

In terms of the models on pp. 27–30, we should simply maximize expected present value utility subject to the dynamic budget constraint and the health accumulation equation. Unfortunately, the problem under investigation is *not* such a standard optimal control problem with an infinite planning horizon. The reason is the fact that the discount factor contains the state variable h. However, using equation (8.16) and a standard trick, expected present value utility at time 0 can be written as follows:

$$E[u_0] = \int_0^\infty u[x(t), h(t)]e^{-[\theta t + \Delta(t)]}dt \tag{8.16'}$$

with $\Delta(t)$ defined as:

$$\Delta(t) = \int_0^t \delta[h(\tau), \tau]d\tau \tag{8.19}$$

i.e. $\Delta(t)$ is given by the differential equation:

$$\dot{\Delta}(t) = \delta[h(t), t] \qquad ; \Delta(0) = 0. \tag{8.20}$$

By maximizing (8.16') with respect to x and X subject to (8.17), (8.18) and (8.20) the problem is turned into a standard control problem with an infinite planning horizon. This approach should be useful for health economists working with intertemporal problems where the survival probability depends on health capital or other state variables.

The current value Hamiltonian can now be written as follows:

$$H(t) = u[x(t), h(t)] + \mu_k(t)\dot{k}(t) + \mu_h(t)\dot{h}(t) + \mu_\delta\dot{\Delta}(t) \tag{8.21}$$

where the following holds for the current value costate variables:

$$\mu_k(t) = \mu_{rk}(t)e^{\theta t + \Delta(t)}, \mu_h(t) = \mu_{rh}(t)e^{\theta t + \Delta(t)}, \mu_\delta(t) = \mu_{r\delta}(t)e^{\theta t + \Delta(t)},$$

a subscript r refers to present value, it is assumed that $r(t) = \theta$, and the *present value* Hamiltonian is equal to $H^p(t) = H(t)e^{-[\theta t + \Delta(t)]}$. This concludes the presentation of the model. The necessary conditions for an interior solution to the individual's maximization problem are stated in the appendix.

The model is now used to derive a couple of results on the individual's WTP for changes in health. The most obvious approach is provided in the elegant paper by Rosen (1988), where one can find valuation formulae for age-specific mortality risks. However, since the publication of Rosen's paper, new results have appeared on the envelope theorem in dynamic optimization; see Caputo (1990) and LaFrance and Barney (1991), for example. Roughly speaking, the dynamic envelope theorem says that the total effect on the objective function, i.e. optimal expected present value utility, of an infinitesimally small change in a parameter is obtained by taking the partial derivative of the present value Hamiltonian (or more generally the Lagrangian) with respect to the parameter and integrating along the optimal path over the planning horizon. Johansson and Löfgren (1994b) have generalized the theorem to an infinite horizon problem with fundamental time dependency (as in (8.17)). The assumptions needed in using the envelope theorem are assumed to hold, but will not be presented here; see Caputo (1990), LaFrance and Barney (1991) and Johansson and Löfgren (1994b) for details.

Let us assume that the individual has attained age s and consider a marginal change in the parameter α (medical technology, say) in the health production function. We thus want to evaluate $\partial E[u_s]/\partial \alpha$. Using the envelope theorem, one finds that:[1]

$$dE[u_s] = \int_s^\infty [(\partial H^p(t)/\partial \alpha)d\alpha] \, dt = \int_s^\infty \mu_h(t)f_\alpha^*(.)d\alpha \, e^{-[\theta(t-s) + \Delta(t)]}dt \tag{8.22}$$

where $H^p(t)$ is the present value Hamiltonian, $f_a^*(.)$ is the partial derivative of the age-dependent health production function in (8.17) with respect to a, and the expression is evaluated along the optimal path; see the dynamic envelope theorem in Caputo (1990) or Theorem 1 in LaFrance and Barney (1991). (8.22) shows that the increase in a must increase expected present value utility, regardless of the age of the individual. The reader can easily verify that a marginal increase in the health depreciation rate γ means that $f_a^*(.)$ is replaced by $-h(t)$ in (8.22), i.e. expected present value utility is reduced by an increase in γ.

If there is a parametric change in income, denoted dy, the envelope theorem ensures that:

$$dE[u_s] = \int_s^\infty \mu_k(t)\, dy\, e^{-[\theta(t-s)+\Delta(t)]}\, dt. \tag{8.23}$$

This yields the expected present value in utility units of adding $\$dy$ to the right-hand side of the dynamic budget constraint (8.18). One can easily combine (8.22) and (8.23) so as to define the WTP for the parametric change in the health production function; simply change (reduce) y so as to obtain $dE[u_s] = 0$ in (8.22).

Finally, let us consider a parametric shift in the death probability. Using the same envelope technique as above, the effect on expected present value utility of a parametric shift in $\delta[h(t), t, a]$ can be shown to equal:

$$dE[u_s] = \int_s^\infty [-\Delta_a(t)H(t) + \mu_k(t)k(t) + \mu_\delta(t)\delta_a(t)]\, da\, e^{-[\theta(t-s)+\Delta(t)]}dt \tag{8.24}$$

where a subscript a refers to the partial derivative with respect to a, and the right-hand side expression within brackets (times the discount factor $e^{-[\cdot]}$) is the partial derivative of the present value Hamiltonian with respect to a. The envelope property considerably simplifies the calculations in Rosen (1988) and Chang (1991), for example. Note that if the death probability is constant and equal to δa, with $a = 1$, then $\Delta_a(t)da$ reduces to $(t-s)\delta da$; also, the term $\mu_\delta\delta$ vanishes from the Hamiltonian implying that the term $\mu_\delta\delta_a$ in (8.24) also vanishes. It is well known, see Chang (1991), for example, that an increase in a constant death risk reduces expected present value utility, and Rosen (1988) derives the same result for the case in which the death risk is age-dependent. Adding the *negative* term $\mu_\delta\delta_a$, will not alter this qualitative result, i.e. the sign of (8.24) must be negative.[2]

In closing, it should be mentioned that models similar to the one used here have recently been used to show how the conventional national income measure, which is often used as a welfare measure, should be augmented so as to cover changes in health; see Aronsson *et al.* (1994) and Johansson and Löfgren (1994a) for details. This is an important valuation issue, which thus far has been dominated by environmental economists; see, for example, Dasgupta and Mäler (1991), Hartwick (1990, 1991), Mäler (1991) and Weitzman (1976). Changes in the population's health caused by pollution or other factors may reasonably be assumed to be an important welfare indicator, which deserves as much attention as changes in the stocks of natural resources and pollutants.

Appendix

Assume that the individual considered on pp. 139–40 has arrived at the final (second) period. His problem is to maximize:

$$u = u[x_2, L_2, f(X_2, L_{z_2}, h'_2)] \tag{A8.1}$$

subject to the budget constraint:

$$y_2 + s + w_2(L^{to} - L_2 - L_{z_2}) - p_2 x_2 - P_2 X_2 = 0 \tag{A8.2}$$

where $z_2 = f_2(X_2, L_{z_2}, h'_2)$ and the market rate of interest has been used to convert current prices to present values. Throughout it is assumed that there exist well-behaved interior solutions to the maximization problems under consideration. Note that the individual leaves no bequests.

An interior solution to this conventional maximization problem yields the demand and supply functions:

$$
\begin{aligned}
z_2 &= z_2(p_2, P_2, w_2, y_2 + s, h'_2) \\
L_2 &= L_2(p_2, P_2, w_2, y_2 + s, h'_2) \\
X_2 &= X_2(p_2, P_2, w_2, y_2 + s, h'_2) \\
x_2 &= x_2(p_2, P_2, w_2, y_2 + s, h'_2)
\end{aligned}
\tag{A8.3}
$$

where the dependence on L^{to} has been ignored.

First-order conditions for an interior solution to the overall maximization problem stated in (8.8)–(8.8″) in the main text include:

$$
\begin{aligned}
\partial u / \partial x_1 &= \lambda p_1 \\
\partial u / \partial L_1 &= \lambda w_1 \\
(\partial u / \partial z_1)(\partial f_1 / \partial L_{z1}) &= \lambda w_1 \\
(\partial u / \partial z_1)(\partial f_1 / \partial X_1) &= \lambda P_1 \\
\lambda &= \int_{h_2}^{r} \rho v_y dF(.)
\end{aligned}
\tag{A8.4}
$$

where λ is the Lagrange multiplier associated with the budget constraint, equal to the expected present value marginal utility of (period 2) income, and $v_y = v_y(p_2, P_2, w_2, y_2 + s, h_{2\epsilon})$. The final line in (A8.4) shows that the stochastic properties of h_2, captured by the vector ϕ, affect period 1 demands and supplies. Solving (A8.4) yields period 1 behaviour functions of the form stated in (8.9). Substitution of the savings function $s = s(p, P, w, y, h_1^r, \phi)$ into the period 2 behaviour functions in (8.7) yields the behaviour functions in the second line of (8.9). Note that h_2 and not the actual health h_2^r at the beginning of period 2 shows up in the second line of (8.9) since in (8.9) we view the world from the beginning of period 1.

In order to illustrate some of the results stated in the main text, totally differentiate (8.8) with $dp = dP = dw = 0$ using the budget constraint (8.8') and equations (A8.4). Then:

$$dV^E = \lambda(dy_1 + dy_2) + \int_{h_2} \rho v_z dh_{2\epsilon} dF(.) \tag{A8.5}$$

where $v_z = \partial v(.)/\partial h_2 = v_z(p_2, P_2, w_2, y_2 + s, h_{2\epsilon})$. If the period 1 and period 2 health good prices are changed, then the following terms show up in (A8.5):

$$-\lambda X_1 dP_1$$
$$-\int_{h_2} \rho v_y X_2 dP_2 dF(.) \tag{A8.5'}$$

where both v_y and X_2 are stochastic as viewed from today.

If period 2 labour demand is fixed in each state of the world from the point of view of the individual but still varies across health states, the wage w_2 no longer shows up as a separate argument in the behaviour functions. Instead $w_2 L_{w_2}(h_2)$ is like a lump-sum income in each state and hence shows up together with other lump-sum incomes, i.e. y. Therefore the individual maximizes:

$$\max_{x_1, X_1, L_1, L_{z1}, s} [u(x_1, z_1) + \int_{h_2} \rho[v(p_2, P_2, y_2 + w_2 L_{2w}(h_{2\epsilon}) \\ + s, h_{2\epsilon}, L_{2w}(h_{2\epsilon})) dF(h_{2\epsilon}; \phi)]] \tag{A8.6}$$

subject to the period 1 budget constraint and the health production function. Note that $L_2 = L^{to} - L_{2w} - L_{z_2}$, a fact which explains why L_{2w} shows up as a separate argument in $v(.)$ in (A8.6), i.e. we can no longer completely 'maximize out' L_2 from the utility function; L^{to}, which also should appear in (A8.6), is suppressed as before. The partial derivative $-v_L$ in (8.12) and (8.13) refers to the derivative of $v(.)$ with respect to L_{2w} holding labour income constant.

In order to arrive at the objective function (8.16), let us start by introducing the following definition:

$$U(t) = \int_0^t u(s)e^{-\theta s} ds. \tag{A8.7}$$

Next, define expected present value utility as follows:

$$E[u_0] = \int_0^\infty \int_0^t u(s)e^{-\theta s}F_d(t)\,ds\,dt = \int_0^\infty U(t)F_d(t)dt$$

$$= \int_0^\infty U(t)F'(t)dt = \int_0^\infty U'(t)[1-F(t)]dt \qquad \text{(A8.7$'$)}$$

where a prime denotes a partial derivative, $F'(t) = F_d(t)$, the term $[1-F(t)]$ is defined in (8.15), the final equality is obtained by integration by parts and the term $U'(t)$ is equal to:

$$U'(t) = (d/dt)\int_0^t u(s)e^{-\theta s}ds = u(t)e^{-\theta t}. \qquad \text{(A8.8)}$$

This explains the formulation of expected present value utility in (8.16).

The necessary conditions for an (interior) optimal control are that for each t it holds that:

$$\partial H/\partial x = u_x(x,h) - \mu_k = 0 \qquad \text{(A8.9)}$$

$$\partial H/\partial X = \mu_h f_X(X,h,t,\gamma) - \mu_k = 0$$

$$\dot{\mu}_k - (\theta + \dot{\Delta}(t))\mu_k = -\partial H/\partial k$$

$$\dot{\mu}_h - (\theta + \dot{\Delta}(t))\mu_h = -\partial H/\partial h$$

$$\dot{\mu}_\delta - (\theta + \dot{\Delta}(t))\mu_\delta = -\partial H/\partial \Delta$$

$$\dot{k} = w + (r+\delta)k - x - X$$

$$\dot{h} = f(X,h,t,\gamma)$$

$$\dot{\Delta} = \delta(h,t)$$

$$\lim_{t\to\infty} \mu_k k e^{-(\theta t + \Delta(t))} = 0$$

$$\lim_{t\to\infty} \mu_h h e^{-(\theta t + \Delta(t))} = 0$$

$$\lim_{t\to\infty} \mu_\delta \Delta e^{-(\theta t + \Delta(t))} = 0$$

where in addition $\partial H/\partial k = \mu_k(r+\delta)$, $\partial H/\partial h = u_h(.) + \mu_h f_h(.) + \mu_\delta \delta_h(.)$, and $\partial H/\partial \Delta = 0$ since the current value Hamiltonian (in contrast to the present value Hamiltonian) is not a direct function of Δ. The transversality conditions written as in (A8.9) presuppose certain growth conditions on the state variables. For details the reader is referred to Theorem 3.17 in Seierstad and Sydsæter (1987).

9 Concluding remarks on related approaches

This book is devoted to the conventional economic approach to the evaluation of a project/treatment. A main purpose has been to show how one can define and estimate WTP measures for changes in health risks. An important aim has also been to point out advantages as well as disadvantages and limitations of this approach. As pointed out in chapter 1, most health economists have chosen not to strive at cost-benefit analysis. This is probably one important reason for their lack of interest in money measures of utility change. Instead they have concentrated on a kind of cost-effectiveness analysis, and based their analysis on the concepts of quality-adjusted life-years (qalys) and, more recently, healthy-years equivalents (hyes). It is outside the scope of this book to examine in detail these concepts and their properties. In closing this book, we will however briefly review the concepts of qalys and hyes and their usefulness in decision-making. In so doing, the results presented in previous chapters will be used in order to indicate some of the similarities and differences between qalys and hyes on the one hand and WTP measures on the other. The risk–risk trade-off and risk–dollar trade-off approaches are also briefly described. Under certain circumstances, the risk–dollar method provides a link between money measures and qalys. The book closes with a brief discussion of cost-effectiveness analysis and cost-benefit analysis.

Qalys and hyes

The typical decision criterion used within the health care system is based on cost-effectiveness analysis. One may, for example, strive at maximizing the health effects per dollar 'invested' in the system. One then needs a measure of the health effects of different treatments. The two most well known output measures are qalys and hyes.

The basic idea behind qalys is to let the individual indicate the 'relative' utility s/he derives from a particular health profile. Let $v(y, z_t)$ denote the (relative or normalized, as explained below) utility derived from income y, assumed to be constant over time, and health status z_t in period t. The individual is called a discounted qaly maximizer if s/he maximizes:

$$v = \sum_{t=1}^{T} \rho^{t-1} v(y, z_t) \tag{9.1}$$

where $\rho \leq 1$ is a discount factor, and the individual lives for T periods (years) with certainty. Typically, income is kept constant, as in (9.1), and $v(.)$ is normalized so that $v(y, z_{0t}) = 0$ and $v(y, z_{ft}) = 1$, where z_0 is the worst possible health status and z_f is full health; this normalization can be interpreted as if $v(.)$ is defined as $v(y, z_t) = V(y, z_t)/V(y, z_{ft})$, where $V(.)$ yields the absolute level of utility and the absolute level of utility of being dead is equal to zero.

According to (9.1), the individual is maximizing the sum of present value qalys. If ρ is equal to one, the number of qalys from having health z_c for T years is simply $v(y, z_c)$ times T. Thus, if $v(y, z_c) = 0.6$ and $T = 10$, the number of qalys is equal to 6.

In a risky world, the approach is often used as follows. The individual is assumed to be an expected utility maximizer. Suppose that the individual is offered a choice between living T years with health quality z_c, possibly interpreted as his or her current health status, and a gamble according to which the probability is π that s/he will live with full health for T years and the probability is $1 - \pi$ that s/he will die immediately. It obviously holds that:

$$\sum_{t=1}^{T} \rho^{t-1} v(y, z_{ct}) \gtreqless \pi \sum_{t=1}^{T} \rho^{t-1} v(y, z_{ft}) + (1 - \pi) \cdot 0 \tag{9.2}$$

where the final term equals zero since, by assumption, $v(y, z_{0t}) = 0$. The sign of the inequality in (9.2) depends on the magnitude of π. Next, find the probability π' that will make the individual indifferent between the two alternatives. This technique is known as the *standard gamble* technique. It follows that the probability π' must be equal to the utility derived from current health status, i.e. $\pi' = v(y, z_{ct})$. Repeating the experiment but with current health replaced by the health status z_{mt} achieved with a particular medical treatment yields the utility $v(y, z_{mt})$ associated with the treatment. This approach can be used to calculate the present value of the number of qalys gained from the treatment, i.e. $\Sigma_t \rho^{t-1}[v(y, z_{mt}) - v(y, z_{ct})]$.

The following example of a standard gamble question is taken from Dolan *et al.* (1993):

Suppose you were in a road accident and suffered the injuries shown on R (the card is not shown here). However, you are told by the hospital that a special treatment is available which, if it succeeds, will put you in condition J (not shown here). But there is a chance that the treatment could fail and if so you will die/suffer the disabilities shown on card K (not shown here).

You have to decide whether to have the treatment or not.

(i) Highest chance of failure at which definitely have treatment: .... in ....

(ii) Chance of failure at which definitely not have treatment: .... in ....

You've said that you would definitely have the treatment if there were .... chances in .... (i) of the treatment failing, but definitely not have the treatment if there were .... chances in .... (ii) of failure. If you had to give one answer, what chances between these two would make it most difficult for you to decide whether or not to have the treatment?

Alternatively, one may use a *time trade-off* technique to estimate the utility function $v(y, z_{ct})$ in (9.2). That is, change the time horizon T in the left-hand side expression so as to turn the inequality into an equality. This yields the time, say T' years, with current health which the individual finds equivalent to living for T years with full health with probability π and dying immediately with probability $1 - \pi$. Given the time horizon T' (and the discount rate), one can directly figure out $v(y, z_{ct})$.

Typically, the two methods described here require in-person interviews, and the respondent is asked to provide a hypothetical answer (ultimately about his *unobservable* level of utility) to a hypothetical change in health and/or health risks. Thus the problems in using standard gambles and time trade-offs are similar to those one faces in a CVM study where the respondent is asked to make a hypothetical payment in exchange for a hypothetical change in health and health risks. For a discussion of all the problems or biases one may encounter in estimating qalys/hyes the reader is referred to chapter 5, pp. 71–9. There is however a difference between the two approaches since one can undertake experiments with real (and hence *observable*) payments in order to examine the properties of our money measures of utility change; see the outline of such an experiment at the end of chapter 6 (pp. 112–13). There seems to be no similar observable mechanism available in the case of qalys/hyes.

Our qaly maximizer in (9.1) is risk neutral with respect to uncertainty with respect to the time horizon T, at least this is so if s/he does not discount future qalys. This is because v in (9.1) is linear in time if ρ is equal to unity. In the literature, this is sometimes handled by assuming that $v = v(y, z)T^{\alpha}$, where α is a risk aversion parameter, i.e. $\alpha < 1$ for a risk averse individual,[1] or one assumes that $v = u[\Sigma_t v(y, z_t)]$, where $u(.)$ is a strictly concave function for an individual who is risk averse with respect to risk in the total number of qalys. The reader is referred to Pliskin *et al.* (1980) for the former and to Broome (1993) for the latter approach. An attempt to estimate the risk aversion parameter a can be found in Miyamato and Eraker (1985).

The second benefits measure often used by health economists is healthy-years equivalents or hyes; see Mehrez and Gafni (1989, 1991) for a detailed presentation of this approach. In order to illustrate the approach, let us assume that the individual's actual health profile is z_t for $t = 1, \ldots, T$. Then hyes is defined as the number of years T^* in full health such that:

$$\sum_{t=1}^{T^*} \rho^{t-1} v(y, z_{ft}) = \sum_{t=1}^{T} \rho^{t-1} v(y, z_t). \tag{9.3}$$

Thus the individual is indifferent between living a healthy life during T^* years ($z = z_f$ for all t) and living for T years with a health profile z_t. For example, if the individual is indifferent between living 6 years with full health (and then dying) and 10 years with chronic renal failure (and then dying), then $T^* = 6$.

To an economist it seems more natural to explicitly introduce uncertainty about the future health profile. For example, if there are just two intermediate health states z_i and z_j, the number of hyes, denoted T^{**}, is obtained from the following equality:

$$\sum_{t=1}^{T^{**}} \rho^{t-1} v(y, z_{ft}) = \sum_{t=1}^{T} \rho^{t-1} [\pi_i v(y, z_{it}) + (1 - \pi_i) v(y, z_{jt})] \tag{9.4}$$

where π_i is the probability of experiencing health state i. In this case, the individual is faced with probabilities that he will experience different health states in the future. Thus T^{**} is such that the individual is indifferent between living T^{**} years with full health and living a longer life with some chronic disease if s/he survives (i.e. z_j is here interpreted as being dead). Thus the individual may be indifferent between living 6 years (T^{**}) with full health and living 10 years (T) with a particular chronic disease with a probability of 0.6 and dying immediately with a probability of 0.4.

There is a huge literature on the properties of qalys and hyes, and we will make no attempt whatsoever to summarize the still ongoing debate between proponents of qalys and proponents of hyes; the reader is referred to Broome (1993), Mehrez and Gafni (1989, 1991), Johannesson, Pliskin and Weinstein (1993), Pliskin *et al.* (1980) and Wakker (1994) for discussion as well as references. A few comments are however in order. First, the assumptions used in arriving at expressions such as (9.1) or (9.3) are extremely strong and restrictive, and we don't know if people really behave in the way these models assume. Obviously, however, they are not compatible with more general utility maximization problems of the kind specified in previous chapters; such problems result in more complicated indirect utility functions than those in (9.1) and (9.3). There is therefore no reason to believe that measures based on qalys or hyes generally rank treatments in the same order as the individual's indirect utility function.

Even if some would argue that output measures are not aimed at covering non-health considerations, it is not self-evident that the individual is able to ignore such considerations. To illustrate, income variations are ignored in (9.1)–(9.4); in the literature, it is typical that income does not show up at all in the value functions. It is not obvious that an individual asked while participating in a qaly study is able or prepared to ignore the income consequences of a medical treatment, i.e. one faces an embedding problem similar to the one discussed on p. 77.

The comparison between two treatments in chapter 3, pp. 40–1 illustrates this problem. Let the value function used in defining qalys be $v(z) = (1 - a)\ln z/[(1 - a)\ln z_f]$, where z_f is full health; the normalization means that $v(z)$ is restricted to taking on values in the interval $[0,1]$. The first treatment increases z (from $z = 1$) to $z = 2$ while the second treatment increases z to $z = 3$. Thus the second treatment produces more qalys than the first treatment.[2] As was shown on p. 41, the individual is indifferent between the two treatments if their consequences for his or her income are accounted for. Thus our qaly measure provides us with incorrect information about the individual's overall valuation of the two treatments; note, however, that this is also true for the CV measure, while the EV measure correctly tells us that the individual is indifferent between the two treatments. In addition, even if the qaly measure may tell us that a particular treatment increases the number of qalys, the CV and EV measures, just like the individual's utility function, may tell us that the individual's total utility decreases if s/he participates in the treatment (due to, say, a large loss of income during the treatment). A proponent of qalys would probably argue that qalys is a reasonable output measure for a decision-maker within the health sector; his or her target is to provide health/treatments at the lowest possible cost (though it is a bit disturbing if this means that a patient does not get the most preferred treatment).

Secondly, there is no age-dependency in our measures of qalys and hyes. That is, the number of qalys/hyes gained from a treatment does not depend on one's age, as can be seen from (9.1)–(9.4). Still, risks as well as health changes as such may be valued differently depending on whether one is young or old; see Jones-Lee (1976) or Rosen (1988) and chapters 2, 4 and 8, pp. 30, 68 and 148–9, for example. This age-dependency is covered by properly defined money measures, though this dependency has often been ignored in this book. Similarly, in contrast to qalys/hyes, the money measures can be designed so as to reflect altruistic concerns; see chapter 7 for details. Altruism is probably an important factor in discussions of how to allocate resources between different programmes within the health care sector; for example, if one programme is oriented towards diseases often faced by elderly people while another is more oriented towards diseases typically faced by children, altruistic considerations may play an important role in people's views on the relative merits of the programmes.

Thirdly, it is not obvious to the present author how a social welfare function should be specified in order to generate the sum across individuals of qalys or hyes as the number to be maximized. It seems to be a kind of utilitarian social welfare function which devotes the same welfare weights to high income earners and low income earners (and ignores all goods except health). Proponents of the approach seem to view it as egalitarian *within* the health sector. As Broome (1993) points out, this is not generally true since treating an old person produces fewer qalys than treating a young person. Thus in a sense the approach disfavours old people. More generally, the social welfare function in question attributes a higher weight to a rich young person than to a poor old person (in the sense that a particular treatment produces more qalys/hyes if given to the younger person). The approach also ignores altruistic motives, in sharp contrast to the social welfare function specified on pp. 130–4. (7.15) highlights the fact that ignoring altruistic concerns, i.e. treating people as being purely selfish, can lead to seriously flawed benefits estimates and hence to serious misallocations of resources within the health care system.

In closing this section, it is important to stress that even if one happens to know that society's social welfare function is utilitarian, this fact does *not* allow a cost-benefit analyst to sum WTPs across individuals (unless the welfare distribution in society is optimal); see chapter 7 for details. An important part of a properly conducted cost-benefit analysis is to show the distributional consequences of the project, i.e. to point out who gains and who loses from the project. The ethical question of how to weight different (groups of) individuals is ultimately left to the decision-maker, since this question is considered to be outside the domain of the investigator. This does not rule out the possibility that, as a special case, one may choose to illustrate the social profitability of the project by summing monetary benefits and costs across individuals. The underlying assumption, i.e. that social welfare is optimally distributed, must however be stressed by authors using this approach.

Risk–risk and risk–dollar trade-offs

Recently, there has been a growing interest in two methods known as risk–risk trade-offs and risk–dollar trade-offs, respectively. Some empirical results were reported in chapter 5, p. 87. A brief description of the principles of these methods is given below, and a possibility of switching from qalys to money measures, or vice versa, is indicated.

In order to illustrate the methods of risk–risk trade-offs and risk–dollar trade-offs let us follow Viscusi *et al.* (1991) and assume that the one-period utility function is separable in health and income and that the marginal utility of income is constant and equal to one: $V(z, y) = u(z) + y$. The risk–risk trade-off approach can then be illustrated as follows. Let us consider three health states: full health (z_f), imperfect health, say angina pectoris, (z_c) and death (z_0). The individual, who at the beginning of the period suffers from the disease, can choose between two different treatments. The first treatment yields probabilities π_{f_1}, π_{c_1} and π_{0_1} of experiencing the different health states, i.e. there is no guarantee that the treatment improves the health of the patient. The second treatment yields a lower probability of staying in the bad-health state but increases the probability of dying, i.e. $\pi_{c_2} < \pi_{c_1}$ while $\pi_{0_2} > \pi_{0_1}$. If the patient faced with these probabilities selects the first treatment, the probability of dying from the second treatment is reduced until the patient becomes indifferent between the two treatments. If s/he initially prefers the second treatment, the risk that this treatment leaves the patient in the imperfect health state is increased until indifference is achieved.

It can easily be verified that the following holds:

$$u(z_c) = (1 - a)u(z_f) + au(z_0) \tag{9.5}$$

where $a = (\pi_{0_2} - \pi_{0_1})/(\pi_{c_1} - \pi_{c_2})$ and the probabilities are those which make the individual indifferent between the two treatments; see Viscusi *et al.* (1991). Thus the problem has been transformed into an equivalent lottery on life with good health and death. At least in theory, i.e. if all the underlying assumptions hold, the risk–risk approach and the standard gamble approach should yield the same result. However, some preliminary evidence reported by Dolan *et al.* (1993) indicates that the two methods produce different results.

In what follows a risk–risk question in Dolan *et al.* (1993) is reported:

Here are two types of injuries that you saw earlier. Could you please glance at these two descriptions, to refresh your memory. The present risk of each of them is shown underneath:
80 in a million each year for K and 120 in a million each year for R.

Suppose a particular road safety feature would reduce your risk of K but only by increasing your risk of R by 60 in a million.

I'd like to know how much you would want your risk of K to be reduced to make up for increasing your risk of R by 60 in a million.

(i) Increase in risk R definitely made up by reduction in risk K by .... in a million
(ii) Increase in risk R definitely not made up by reduction in risk K by .... in a million

You've said that reducing your risk of K by .... (i) in a million would definitely make up for increasing your risk of R by 60 in a million, but that reducing your risk of K by .... (ii) in a million would definitely not make up for it. If you had to give one figure between these two, what would your best estimate be of the reduction in your risk of K which would exactly make up for increasing your risk of R by 60 in a million?

The reader interested in using risk–risk trade-offs to estimate the WTP per statistical case of a disease prevented is referred to p. 87 for a simple numerical illustration of the principal procedure.

The risk–dollar approach is similar to the risk–risk approach, but in terms of (9.5) the second treatment demands an out-of-pocket payment equal to $c (while the first treatment is free of charge). The initial probabilities of different outcomes are (for simplicity) the same as above. If the patient prefers the first treatment, the probability of dying from the second treatment is reduced while if s/he prefers the second treatment the probability π_{c_2} that this treatment leaves the patient in the bad-health state is increased, as described above. Once indifference has been established, the following holds:

$$u(z_c) = u(z_f) - c/(\pi_{c_1} - \pi_{c_2}) \tag{9.6}$$

where the utility of being dead has been set equal to zero. Thus $c/(\pi_{c_1} - \pi_{c_2})$ yields the WTP for achieving full health (or the compensation that the sick person needs in order to achieve the same utility as if s/he were fully healthy), i.e. a kind of value of a statistical life; compare p. 61. In order to illustrate the meaning of (9.6), let us assume that a person is indifferent between having treatment 1 with a risk of staying in the bad-health state of 55/100,000 and paying $100 for the treatment and having treatment 2, which is free of charge, with a risk of staying in the bad-health state of 75/100,000. Then the implied value of the bad-health state is equal to $500,000, and $u(z_c) = -\$500,000 + u(z_f)$; see Viscusi et al. (1991) for details.

This approach indicates one possible way of going from qalys to monetary measures and vice versa. The awkward assumption that the marginal utility of income is constant can be defended if one considers (infinitesimally) small changes in risks (since the marginal utility of income is then evaluated at a 'point' and hence constant), though one still has to determine its magnitude (above set equal to one), a task which seems to require extremely strong assumptions.

Cost-effectiveness analysis

Qalys and hyes are used as output measures in cost-effectiveness analysis of treatments and other measures within the health care field; note that some authors would speak of a cost-utility analysis when utility change indices such as qalys or hyes are used as the output measure, and a cost-effectiveness analysis when the output measure is in natural units such as life-years saved or improvement in functional status. In order to illustrate the approach, suppose that a treatment raises the quality of life from $v = 5$ to $v = 7$. The cost of the treatment is \$1000. Then one calculates the cost per qaly gained, i.e. $1000/2 = 500$. The lower this ratio, the more 'profitable' a treatment is; alternatively one may use hyes instead of qalys. Thus in contrast to a cost-benefit analysis, where all benefits and costs are converted to the same 'dimension', i.e. to monetary units, a cost-effectiveness analysis based on qalys or hyes defines benefits in one dimension and costs in another. Moreover, instead of looking at the difference between benefits and costs, one looks at a ratio.

In the appendix, programming techniques are used to illustrate the properties of cost-effectiveness analysis and its relationship to cost-benefit analysis. Following Weinstein and Stason (1976) one can formulate a cost-effectiveness analysis of a treatment in the following way:

$$C/B_Q = (C_m + C_s + C_d - C_s)/v(y, z_c) \cdot T \tag{9.7}$$

where C denotes the total cost, $B_Q = v(y, z_c) \cdot T$ yields the number of, for simplicity risk neutral, qalys produced by the treatment, C_m includes all direct medical and health care costs, C_s includes all health care costs associated with the adverse side effects of the treatment, C_d includes the costs of treating diseases that would not have occurred if the patient had not lived longer as a result of the original treatment, and C_s refers to savings in health care, rehabilitation and custodial costs due to the prevention or alleviation of disease. Usually, one would also discount future qalys and costs, though this has been ignored in (9.7). The reader is referred to Weinstein and Stason (1976) for further details. See also (7.9') for a cost-benefit analysis involving the same cost components as equation (9.7). Note, however, that the social cost-benefit analysis in addition covers costs and benefits outside the health care system.

A social cost-benefit analysis is more general than a cost-effectiveness analysis in the sense that it represents an attempt to rank treatments in the same order as society would. The *difference* between a project's benefits and costs is ideally a good or sign-preserving measure of the change in social welfare. It is well known and easy to show that *ratios* between benefits and costs may fail to provide a correct ranking of treatments/projects. This is most easily seen by letting benefits and costs be increasing functions of the magnitude of a project: $B = B(z)$ and $C = C(z)$ with $\partial B/\partial z$, $\partial C/\partial z > 0$. A marginal increase in z is profitable if $B' > C'$, i.e. if the marginal benefits, denoted B', exceed the marginal cost, denoted C'. Still, the ratio $R = C(z)/B(z)$ may increase or decrease since:

$$R' = (C' \cdot B - C \cdot B')/B^2 \tag{9.8}$$

where a prime refers to a derivative with respect to z. Thus the marginal cost is multiplied by total benefits while marginal benefits are multiplied by total costs, implying that the ratio between costs and benefits may increase or decrease when a small profitable project is added. This is the reason why economists are reluctant to use ratios to rank the profitability of different projects. There is the further problem that the magnitude of a ratio is sensitive to the precise definition of benefits and costs, respectively. To illustrate, side effects of a treatment may be considered as reducing the benefits or treated as a part of the treatment's costs; the choice will affect the ratio between costs and benefits.

The above discussion refers to the unconstrained case in which one is free to implement any new socially profitable project. In more complicated decision situations one must select projects given a budget or capital constraint and other constraints such as indivisibilities and mutually exclusive projects. One then maximizes the sum of present value benefits *less* the sum of present value costs across the projects, subject to the various constraints faced. This is the approach described by Baumol (1972) and Weinstein and Zeckhauser (1973), for example. As demonstrated by Weinstein and Zeckhauser, the solution to problems involving a fixed budget may be such that one must look at the *ratio* of benefits to resource used for each project, and all projects with a ratio greater than a critical ratio, determined endogenously, are undertaken; see also the appendix to this chapter, which outlines some non-linear and linear programming problems.

It seems to be this last feature which has induced health economists to look at the ratio between net benefits and the resource cost as in (9.7); net benefits are typically defined as the (present value of the) number of qalys or hyes, not as the difference between monetary present value benefits and costs (sometimes motivated by a wish to keep money or ability to pay outside the health domain). Given that the objective is to maximize the number of qalys or hyes subject to a budget constraint the approach is legitimate *per se*. The fundamental problem with the approach is that qalys or hyes do not necessarily reflect individual preferences, as was discussed on pp. 156–8. Thus a social welfare function reflecting individual preferences may rank treatments in another order than a cost-effectiveness analysis using qalys or hyes as the output measure. In addition, one needs a cost-benefit analysis in order to determine whether to devote more or less resources to a particular sector. A cost-effectiveness analysis is not designed to handle such questions since in a health care context it represents an attempt to allocate a fixed overall budget as efficiently as possible given a specified net benefit measure; see the appendix for further details.

In sum, there seems to be no strong reason for arguing emphatically in favour of one or the other approach to benefits measures or in favour of cost-benefit analysis over cost-effectiveness analysis; there is no measure which works in all possible circumstances, and cost-effectiveness analysis and cost-benefit analysis are complementary rather than mutually exclusive approaches. There are even those, such as advocates of the public choice school, who dislike the kind of welfare economics which is behind the decision criteria discussed in this book; see Mueller (1989) for a survey of the public choice school. Nevertheless, all the benefits or output measures taken up in this book will certainly continue to play a role in decision-making. It is reasonable to suppose that cost-effectiveness analysis will continue to be an important tool in decision-making in the future, and for such an analysis one needs some kind of effect measure. At present, qalys and hyes are the favoured effect measures, but new measures may well be developed. Cost-benefit analysis will probably also play an important role in future health care decision-making. In particular, this seems probable with respect to more general allocational issues, where one needs to compare costs and benefits of different programmes. Also, the studies summarized in chapter 6 illustrate the fact that in choosing between different treatments of a particular disease, one may need a money measure in order to cover all kinds of effects of the treatment (including its impact on leisure time, working time and income, health at different points of time, and so on). Still, much research is needed in examining the empirical properties and usefulness of different methods for the measurement of the monetary value of changes in health risks. Though there is a lot of experience in the environmental arena from using methods such as the CVM and various indirect methods, the problems are often slightly different when assessing health care than when assessing environmental (health) risks. In particular, individual risk plays a much more prominent role in the former case than in the case of public goods or bads such as public safety measures and pollution of the air and the water. It is therefore important to examine further the reliability and validity of different methods for the measurement of WTP measures of changes in health risks. It is also an important task to compare the empirical properties of money measures, qalys and hyes in order to check the conditions under which they produce the same ranking of different medical treatments/projects.

Appendix

In this appendix a simple non-linear programming problem is outlined and used to derive some simple cost-efficiency results; the reader is referred to any textbook on mathematical economics, e.g. Léonard and Van Long (1992), for details on linear and non-linear programming techniques. The natural approach, setting aside the distributional issue here, would be to specify the objective function as expressing the difference between aggregate benefits and aggregate costs across a number of projects or medical treatments. However, this approach assumes that benefits and costs are comparable (e.g. expressed in dollars). In order to be able to relate our results to cost-effectiveness analysis, we will choose another approach. The decision-maker is assumed to consider different medical treatments for a particular disease. If z_i patients take treatment i, the benefits are B_i for $i = 1, \ldots, I$, where B_i is an increasing function of the number of patients treated. The decision-maker's objective is to maximize aggregate benefits $(B = \Sigma_i B_i(z_i))$ subject to a resource constraint (and possibly other constraints).

Let us consider the following (function similar to and here denoted the) Lagrangean:

$$L = \Sigma_i B_i(z_i) + \lambda[C - \Sigma_i C_i(z_i)] \qquad (A9.1)$$

where $B_i(z_i)$ denotes the total benefits, however measured, if z_i patients are treated by the ith method, $C_i(z_i)$ denotes the corresponding cost, C is the budget constraint, and λ is a Lagrange multiplier (or a dual variable). It is assumed that all benefits functions are concave, and that all cost functions are convex. If the benefits and cost functions are linear in z, (A9.1) reduces to a conventional linear programming problem. There is a reasonable restraint on the maximization problem not explicitly accounted for in (A9.1): $\Sigma_i z_i \leq Z$, where Z is interpreted as the total number of patients or an upper bound for the number of treatments set by the decision-maker. In what follows, we ignore this restraint, unless otherwise explicitly stated.

First-order conditions (the Kuhn–Tucker conditions) for a maximum read:

$$\partial L / \partial z_i = B_i'(\cdot) - \lambda C_i' \leq 0, \quad z_i \geq 0, \quad z_i(\partial L / \partial z_i) = 0 \quad \forall i$$
$$\partial L / \partial \lambda = C - \Sigma_i C_i(z_i) \geq 0, \quad \lambda \geq 0, \quad \lambda(\partial L / \partial \lambda) = 0 \qquad (A9.2)$$

where a prime refers to a partial derivative with respect to z_i. The first condition states that, at optimum, the marginal benefit of a treatment *less* its marginal cost, weighted by a shadow price λ, must be non-positive. If the difference is strictly negative, the treatment is not undertaken at all; setting $z_i = 0$ in the first line of (A9.2) ensures that $z_i(\partial L / \partial z_i) = 0$ if $\partial L / \partial z_i < 0$. The second condition states that, at an optimum it is the case that $\lambda = dL/dC = dB/dC$. In other words, λ (or rather λdC) yields the extra or marginal benefits obtained by increasing the budget by a dollar; see, for example, Léonard and Van Long (1992) for a derivation of this result. If the budget constraint is binding, it holds that λ is strictly positive in optimum.

Rearranging (A9.2), one finds that $1/\lambda \leq C_i'/B_i'$, where the right-hand side ratio yields the cost-effect or cost-benefit ratio. The ith type of treatment is undertaken only if $1/\lambda = C'_i/B'_i$. (Note the similarity between this ratio and the formula in (9.7) in the main text; the difference is that we have not defined the units (say, qalys or dollars), in which the benefits B_i are measured.) If it is the case that $1/\lambda < C'_i/B'_i$ at the optimum, then z_i is set equal to zero, i.e. the ith treatment is not used at all.

Let us now consider the case in which $B'_i = \lambda C'_i$ for all i, and assume that benefits are measured in monetary units. If the budget is chosen optimally, it must hold that $\lambda = 1$; adding one dollar to the budget produces a one dollar increase in aggregate benefits. This is the conventional cost-benefit case, in which the optimal size of a 'project' is such that the project's marginal benefit is equal to its marginal cost, i.e. $B'_i = C'_i$ for all i.

Consider next what seems to be the typical cost-effectiveness analysis case considered in health economics: the linear programming case in which the objective is to maximize aggregate benefits subject to a fixed budget. All benefits and cost functions are assumed to be linear: $B_i(.) = b_i z_i$ and $C_i(.) = c_i z_i$, where b_i and c_i are strictly positive constants; b_i typically reflects the number of qalys associated with the ith treatment. It should be obvious what modifications the linearity assumption cause in (A9.2); we simply replace B'_i by b_i and C'_i by c_i. In this linear case we simply select the treatment which has the lowest marginal cost-effect ratio c_i/b_i (ignoring here the case in which several treatments have the same cost-effect ratio).

In order to make the linear problem more interesting, let us reintroduce the constraint for the number of patients who can be treated, i.e. $\Sigma_i z_i \leq Z$. In fact, we assume that this constraint is binding, in order to avoid a patient being treated more than once; see Karlsson (1991) for details. It is easily verified that we will now have the following weak 'cost-effect' inequality: $1/\lambda \leq c_i/(b_i - \mu)$, where μ is the dual variable associated with the constraint on the number of patients treated. A particular method of treatment, say the ith one, will be implemented, i.e. $z_i > 0$, if $1/\lambda = c_i/(b_i - \mu)$. The two-treatment case is illustrated in figure 9.1, where the thick kinked line yields the outer boundary of the feasible region. The contours of the objective function, given by $b_1 z_1 + b_2 z_2 = \text{constant}$, have slope $-b_1/b_2$. Hence the maximum of the objective function occurs at A. If the slope of the contours of the objective function are less steep (steeper) than the boundary constraints, the optimum would have been at A^2 (A^1), i.e. only one programme is implemented. Assuming that A in figure 9.1 represents the optimal solution, at A it must hold that $1/\lambda = c_1/(b_1 - \mu) = c_2/(b_2 - \mu)$, where $1/\lambda = dC/dB$. It is easily verified that $1/\lambda = (c_1 - c_2)/(b_1 - b_2)$ at the optimum, i.e. point A in figure 9.1. This is one way of arriving at the interpretation of $1/\lambda$ as the marginal cost-effect ratio between two treatments.

If a number of independent programmes (e.g. blood pressure control,

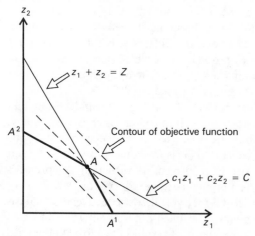

Figure 9.1 A cost-effectiveness analysis problem

ulcer treatment, and so on) compete for the limited budget C, we replace the constraint on the total number of patients (Z) by constraints $0 \leq z_i \leq 1$ for all i; one can view z_i as the proportion treated of those suffering from the ith disease. As a rule, we either undertake a programme or don't, i.e. in general $z_i = 0$ or $z_i = 1$. Accordingly, the decision rule is now to rank the programmes from the lowest to the highest cost-effect ratio, and to select programmes until the budget is exhausted; see Johannesson and Weinstein (1993) for details.

A more general decision problem is obtained by considering different programmes, different diseases, and different sub-budgets. The reason for introducing several sub-budgets is as follows. Often, there are different 'agencies' involved in medical decision-making. These agencies may allocate fixed amounts of money to different medical treatments. The Lagrangean associated with this decision problem can be stated as follows:

$$L = \Sigma_j[\Sigma_i B_{ij}(z_{ij})] + \Sigma_v \lambda_v[C_v - \Sigma_i \Sigma_j C_{ijv}(z_{ij})] + \Sigma_i \mu_i[Z_i - \Sigma_j z_{ij}] \quad \text{(A9.3)}$$

where $B_{ij}(z_{ij})$ denotes the benefits obtained by treating z_i patients suffering from disease i by method j for $j = 1, \ldots, J$, $C_{ijv}(z_{ij})$ is the associated cost borne by the vth 'agency', C_v for $v = 1, \ldots, V$ is the amount of money the vth 'agency' allocates to medical treatments, and λ_v is a Lagrange multiplier associated with the vth sub-budget. For many combinations of diseases and treatments, it is optimal to set z_{ij} equal to zero; it is no cure to undertake a heart operation to heal a broken leg, for example.

We will not work through the necessary conditions for an optimal solution to the above maximization problem, because they represent straightforward generalizations of those stated in (A9.2). In terms of a linear programming problem, the marginal cost-effect ratios are variations of those stated above.

Fixed and binding sub-budgets result in a sub-optimal allocation of resources between patient groups and treatments, i.e. λ_v will not be equal for all v. Thus, in this case, the weight a dollar is attributed in the cost-effectiveness analysis depends on what agency provides it. This is in sharp contrast to (9.7), where unweighted costs are aggregated. For further analysis of health economic decision problems based on cost-effectiveness analysis the reader is referred to Johannesson and Weinstein (1993), Karlsson (1991) and Weinstein and Zeckhauser (1973). In closing, the following should be noted. The kind of budget constraints included in (A9.3) tend to increase the discrepancy between the outcome of a cost-effectiveness analysis and the outcome of a social cost-benefit analysis. This result illustrates the fact that restricting a cost-effectiveness analysis to the agency level (say, a hospital) may result in an allocation of resources which is very different from the allocation which is optimal from a societal point of view.

Notes

2 Some basic tools and concepts

1. For a risk loving individual, (2.19) yields a minimum due to the second-order properties ($V_{yy} > 0$) of his indirect utility function.
2. See (2.33), where it is shown how to arrive at the formulation of expected utility in (2.30).

3 Evaluating health changes in a certain world

1. The sign convention used to define CV (and later EV) is arbitrary but it means that the sign of CV (EV) is equal to the sign of the change in utility ΔV. See (3.5).
2. For a decrease in health status (z) both CV and EV take on negative values but EV is closer to zero than CV and hence larger.
3. Below (p. 47) it is shown that one cannot completely evaluate an essential commodity used to produce health, since the individual dies without the commodity. However, we can evaluate a change in its price so long as the price is not too high, i.e. so high that X_i approaches zero and the individual dies.

4 Money measures in a risky world

1. Since both V_y and CV_i vary across states it holds that: $\Delta V^E \approx E[V_y CV_i]$ $= V_y^E CV_E + \text{cov}(V_y, CV_i)$, where cov(.) is the covariance. Thus, the covariance term may be of such a sign and magnitude that the sign of the change in expected utility $E[V_y CV_i]$ is opposite to the sign of CV^E.
2. If π_0 approaches 1, we may fail to define money measures. This will be discussed further below.
3. If the individual is able to insure, we have to add the term $\pi_1 dy_1 + \pi_2 dy_2$ in order to arrive at the total change in expected income.
4. See p. 30 for how to calculate present value income when the probability of dying in a particular period is strictly positive.
5. It is assumed that such a well-behaved function exists. See the further presentation of the model in chapter 8.

5 Evaluating health risks: practical methodologies

1. In some recent applications, the respondent is asked a second valuation question; if s/he accepts the first bid, the second bid is higher, while if s/he rejects the first bid it is lower. See for example Morey *et al.* (1991) for this double-bounded technique.
2. See chapter 6, p. 114 for the formulae to be used to compute the average WTP in the log-linear case.
3. Note, however, that we have normalized the number of respondents to one, i.e. we actually calculate an average consumer surplus (and later an average WTP). Thus in an actual study, the total consumer surplus (total WTP) is obtained by multiplying the average consumer surplus (average WTP) by the number of persons in the population.

6 Contingent valuation studies of health care

1. The econometric techniques mentioned in this section and how to use them in order to calculate the median and the mean WTP are explained on pp. 106–14.
2. A non-parametric method described on pp. 109–10 was used to calculate the mean and median on each question. Alternatively, since the questions can be viewed as being open-ended one could as well calculate the mean in the usual way, i.e. by dividing the sum across respondents (of the highest bid accepted by each respondent) by the number of respondents.
3. In an open-ended valuation question the respondent is asked about his maximum WTP for the treatment or the minimum compensation s/he needs in order to accept the treatment. If participation in the treatment is voluntary, one can forget about the compensation question.

7 Aggregation

1. The model used here is static. In order to cover ageing, one would need a dynamic model with population growth, i.e. a model where people are born and die.
2. It must be admitted that the author has not checked the properties of this social welfare function under the expected utility hypothesis.
3. A pure altruist respects the preferences of others. This means that $(\partial V_h/\partial \pi_j)/(\partial V_h/\partial y_j) = (\partial V_j/\partial \pi_j)/(\partial V_j/\partial y_j)$, for example.

8 Further evaluation issues in a risky world

1. The reader should note that $e^{-A(t)} = [1 - F(t)]/[1 - F(s)]$ in (8.22)–(8.24) since the individual, by assumption, has survived until age s. Throughout, it is assumed that the assumptions underlying the dynamic envelope theorem in Caputo (1990) are satisfied. Johansson and Löfgren (1994b) show that a fundamental time-dependency, as in (8.17), may, but need not, cause a minor change in the results reported here.

2. μ_δ must be negative since an increase in the death probability δ reduces expected utility.

9 Concluding remarks on related approaches

1. If the time trade-off method is used, the specification is $v = [v(y, z)T]^\alpha$ since one is seeking a ratio between years.
2. The seemingly bizarre baseline for the comparison on p. 41, i.e. $z^0 = 1$ without treatment, so that $v(z^0) = 0$, was chosen only in order to simplify the calculations.

Bibliography

Acton, J.P., 1973. 'Evaluating public programs to save lives: the case of heart attacks', *RAND Report R-950-RC*, Santa Monica, CA

Åkerman, J., Johnson, F.R. and Bergman, L., 1991. 'Paying for safety: Voluntary reduction of residential radon risks', *Land Economics*, 67, 435–46

Amemiya, T., 1981. 'Qualitative response models: a survey', *Journal of Economic Literature*, 19, 1483–1536

Andreoni, J., 1990. 'Impure altruism and donation to public goods: a theory of warm glow giving', *Economic Journal*, 100, 464–77

1989. 'Giving with impure altruism: applications to charity and Ricardian equivalence', *Journal of Political Economy*, 97, 1447–58

Appel, L.J., Steinberg, E.P., Powe, N.R., Anderson, G.F., Dwyer, S.A. and Faden, R.R, 1990. 'Risk reduction from low osmolality contrast media: what do patients think it is worth?', *Medical Care*, 28, 324–337

Aronsson, T., Johansson, P.-O. and Löfgren, K.-G., 1994. 'Welfare measurement and the health environment', mimeo

Arrow, K.J., 1971. *Essays in the Theory of Risk-bearing*, London: North-Holland

1964. 'The role of securities in the optimal allocation of risk-bearing', *Review of Economic Studies*, 31, 91–96

1963. 'Uncertainty and the economics of medical care', *American Economic Review*, 53, 941–73

1951. *Social Choice and Individual Values*, New York: John Wiley & Sons

Arrow, K.J. and Fisher, A.C., 1974. 'Environmental preservation, uncertainty, and irreversibility', *Quarterly Journal of Economics*, 88, 312–19

Arrow, K.J. and Kurz, M., 1970. *Public Investment, the Rate of Return, and Optimal Fiscal Policy*, Baltimore: Johns Hopkins University Press

Arrow, K.J., Solow, R. (co-chairs), Leamer, E., Portney, P., Randner, R. and Schuman, H., 1993. 'Report of the NOAA Panel on contingent valuation', *Federal Register*, Vol. 58, No. 10, Friday January 15 1993

Baumol, W.J., 1972. *Economic Theory and Operations Analysis*, 3rd ed., London: Prentice-Hall

Becker, G.S., 1975. *Human Capital*, 2nd ed., Chicago: University of Chicago Press

1965. 'A theory of the allocation of time', *Economic Journal*, 75, 493–517

Berger, M.C., Blomquist, G.C., Kenkel, D. and Tolley, G.S., 1987. 'Valuing changes in health risks: a comparison of alternative measures', *Southern Economic Journal*, 53, 967–84

Bergson, A., 1938. 'A reformulation of certain aspects of welfare economics', *Quarterly Journal of Economics*, 52, 310–34

Bergstrom, T.C., 1982. 'When is a man's life worth more than his human capital?', in Jones-Lee, M.W. (ed.), *The Value of Life and Safety*, Amsterdam: North-Holland

Bernoulli, D., 1954. 'Exposition of a new theory of the measurement of risk', *Econometrica*, 22, 23–36. English trans. by L. Sommer of Bernoulli (1738): *Specimen theoriae novae de mensura sortis*

Berwick, D.M. and Weinstein, M.C., 1985. 'What do patients value? Willingness to pay for ultrasound in normal pregnancy', *Medical Care*, 23, 881–93

Besley, T., 1989. 'Publicly provided disaster insurance for health and the control of moral hazard', *Journal of Public Economics*, 39, 141–56

Biddle, J.E. and Zarkin, G., 1988. 'Worker preferences and market compensation for job risk', *Review of Economics and Statistics*, 70, 660–7

Bishop, R.C. and Heberlein, J.A., 1979. 'Measuring values of extra market goods: are indirect measures biased?', *American Journal of Agricultural Economics*, 61, 926–930

Blackorby, C. and Donaldson, D., 1986. 'Can risk-benefit analysis provide consistent policy evaluations of projects involving loss of life?', *Economic Journal*, 96, 758–73

Blackorby, C., Donaldson, D. and Moloney, D., 1984. 'Consumer's surplus and welfare change in a simple dynamic model', *Review of Economic Studies*, 51, 171–76

Blanchard, O.J., 1985. 'Debt, deficits, and finite horizons', *Journal of Political Economy*, 93, 223–47

Blanchard, O.J. and Fischer, S., 1989. *Lectures on Macroeconomics*, Cambridge, MA: MIT Press

Blomquist, G., 1979. 'Value of life savings: implications of consumption activity', *Journal of Political Economy*, 87, 540–58

Blomquist, G.C., Berger, M.C. and Hoehn, J.P., 1988. 'New estimates of quality of life in urban areas', *American Economic Review*, 78, 89–107

Boadway, R.W., 1974. 'The welfare foundations of cost-benefit analysis', *Economic Journal*, 84, 926–39

Boadway, R.W. and Bruce, N., 1984. *Welfare Economics*, Oxford: Basil Blackwell

Borch, K., 1990. *Economics of Insurance*, Amsterdam: North-Holland

Bowker, J.M. and Stoll, J.R., 1988. 'Use of dichotomous choice nonmarket methods to value the whooping crane resource', *American Journal of Agricultural Economics*, 70, 372–81

Boyle, K.J. and Bishop, R.C., 1988. 'Welfare measurements using contingent valuation: a comparison of techniques', *American Journal of Agricultural Economics*, 70, 21–8

Boyle, M.H., Torrance, G.W., Sinclair, J.C. and Horwood, S.P., 1983. 'Economic evaluation of neonatal intensive care of very-low-birth-weight infants', *New England Journal of Medicine*, 308, 1330–37

Braden, J.B. and Kolstad, C.D. (eds.), 1991. *Measuring the Demand for Environmental Quality*, Amsterdam: North-Holland

Brent, R.J., 1991. 'A new approach to valuing a life', *Journal of Public Economics*, 44, 165–71

Brookshire, D.S., Randall, A. and Stoll, J.R., 1980. 'Valuing increments and decrements of natural resource service flows', *American Journal of Agricultural Economics*, 62, 478–88

Brookshire, D.S., Thayer, M.A., Schulze, W.D. and d'Arge, R.C., 1982. 'Valuing public goods: a comparison of survey and hedonic approaches', *American Economic Review*, 72, 165–77

Broome, J., 1993. 'Qalys', *Journal of Public Economics*, 50, 149–67

1985. 'The economic value of life', *Economica*, 52, 281–94

1979. 'Trying to value a life: a reply', *Journal of Public Economics*, 12, 259–62

1978. 'Trying to value a life', *Journal of Public Economics*, 9, 91–100

Buchanan, J.M. and Fair, R.L., 1979. 'Trying again to value a life', *Journal of Public Economics*, 12, 245–48

Cameron, A.C. and Trivedi, P.K., 1991. 'The role of income and health risk in the choice of insurance', *Journal of Public Economics*, 45, 1–28

Cameron, T.A., 1988. 'A new paradigm for valuing non-market goods using referendum data: maximum likelihood estimation by censored logistic regression', *Journal of Environmental Economics and Management*, 15, 355–79

Caputo, M.R., 1990. 'How to do comparative dynamics on the back of an envelope in optimal control theory', *Journal of Economic Dynamics and Control*, 14, 655–83

Carson, R.T. and Mitchell, R.C., 1994a. 'Sequencing and nesting in contingent valuation surveys', *Journal of Environmental Economics and Management*, forthcoming

1994b. 'The issue of scope in contingent valuation studies', *American Journal of Agricultural Economics*, forthcoming

Carson, R.T., Wright, J., Alberini, A. and Flores, N., 1993. 'A bibliography of contingent valuation studies and papers', La Jolla, CA: Natural Resource Damage Assessment

Chang, F.-R., 1991. 'Uncertain lifetimes, retirement and economic welfare', *Economica*, 58, 215–32

Chavas, J.-P. and Bishop, R.C., 1984. 'Ex-ante consumer evaluation in cost-benefit analysis', Department of Agricultural Economics, Wisconsin, MD: University of Wisconsin

Chipman, J.S. and Moore, J.C., 1980. 'Compensating variation, consumer's surplus, and welfare', *American Economic Review*, 70, 933–49

Cook, P.J. and Graham, D.A., 1977. 'The demand for insurance and protection: the case of irreplaceable commodities', *Quarterly Journal of Economics*, 91, 143–56

Courant, P.N. and Porter, R.C., 1981. 'Averting expenditure and the cost of pollution', *Journal of Environmental Economics and Management*, 8, 321–9

Coursey, D.L., Hovis, J.L. and Schulze, D.W., 1987. 'The disparity between willingness to accept and willingness to pay measures of value', *Quarterly Journal of Economics*, 102, 679–90

Cowell, F.A., 1986. *Microeconomic Principles*, Oxford: Philip Allan

Crocker, T.D., Forster, B.A. and Shogren, J.F., 1991. 'Valuing potential groundwater protection benefits', *Water Resources Research*, 27, 1–6

Cropper, M.L. and Freeman, A.M., 1991. 'Environmental health effects', in Braden, J.B. and Kolstad, C.D. (eds.), *Measuring the Demand for Environmental Quality*, Amsterdam: North-Holland

Cropper, M.L., Aydede, S.K. and Portney, P.R., 1992. 'Rates of time preference for saving lives', *American Economic Review*, 82, 469–72

Culbertson, V.L., Arthur, T.G., Rhodes, P.J. and Rhodes, R.S., 1988. 'Consumer preferences for verbal and written medication information', *Drug Intelligence and Clinical Pharmacy*, 22, 390–96

Culyer, A.J., 1989. 'The normative economics of health care finance and provision', *Oxford Review of Economic Policy*, 5, 34–58

   1988. 'Inequality in health services is, in general, desirable?', in Green, D.G. (ed.), *Acceptable Inequalities*, London: Institute for Economic Affairs

Cummings, R.G. and Harrison, G.W., 1992. 'Homegrown values and hypothetical surveys: Is the dichotomous choice approach incentive compatible?', Department of Economics, University of New Mexico

Cummings, R.G., Brookshire, D.S. and Schulze, W.D., 1986. *Valuing Environmental Goods*, Totowa, NJ: Rowman & Allanheld

Danzig, G.B., McAllister, P.H. and Stone, J.C., 1989. 'Deriving a utility function for the US economy', *Journal of Policy Modelling*, 11, 391–424

Dardis, R., 1980. 'The value of a life: new evidence from the marketplace', *American Economic Review*, 70, 1077–82

Dasgupta, P.S and Heal, M., 1979. *Economic Theory and Exhaustible Resources*, Cambridge: Cambridge University Press

Dasgupta, P.S. and Mäler, K.-G., 1991. 'The Environment and Emerging Developing Issues', Helsinki: WIDER; *Beijer Institute Reprint Series*, 1, The Royal Swedish Academy of Sciences

Davis, R.K., 1964. 'The value of big game hunting in a private forest', in Transactions of the twenty-ninth North American wildlife conference, Washington DC: Wildlife Management Institute

Demers, M., 1991. 'Investment under uncertainty, irreversibility and the arrival of information over time', *Review of Economic Studies*, 58, 333–50

Desvousges, W.H., Johnson, F.R., Dunford, R.W., Boyle, K.J., Hudson, S.P. and Wilson, K.N., 1992. *Measuring nonuse damages using contingent valuation: an experimental evaluation of accuracy*, Research Triangle Institute Monograph, 92–1, North Carolina: Research Triangle

Dixit, A.K., 1992. 'Investment and hysteresis', *Journal of Economic Perspectives*, 6, 107–32

Dixit, A.K. and Pindyck, R.S., 1994. *Investment under Uncertainty*, Princeton, NJ: Princeton University Press

Dobbs, I.M., 1991. 'A Bayesian approach to decision-making under ambiguity', *Economica*, 58, 417–40

Dolan, P., Jones-Lee, M.W. and Loomes, G., 1993. 'Risk trade off vs standard gamble procedures for measuring health state utilities', paper presented to Health Economists' Study Group Meeting, Strathclyde, 30 June–2 July 1993

Donaldson, C., 1993. 'Theory and practice of willingness to pay for health care',

Discussion Paper, 01/93, Department of Public Health and Economics, University of Aberdeen

1990. 'Willingness to pay for publicly provided goods: a possible measure of benefit?', *Journal of Health Economics*, 9, 103–18

Drummond, M.F., 1988. *Principles of Economic Appraisal in Health Care*, Oxford: Oxford University Press

Drummond, M.F., Stoddart, G.L. and Torrance, G.W., 1987. *Methods for the Economic Evaluation of Health Care Programmes*, Oxford: Oxford University Press

Dupuit, J., 1933. *De l'utilité et de la mesure*, Turin: La Riforma Sociale; reprints of works published in 1844 and the following years

Eastaugh, S.R., 1992. *Health Economics. Efficiency, Quality, and Equity*, Westport, CT: Auburn House

1991. 'Valuation of the benefits of risk-free blood', *International Journal of Technology Assessment in Health Care*, 7, 51–7

Einarson, T.R., Bootman, J.L., McGhan, W.F., Larson, L.N., Gardner, M.E. and Donohue, M., 1988. 'Establishment and evaluation of a serum cholesterol monitoring service in a community pharmacy', *Drug Intelligence and Clinical Pharmacy*, 22, 45–8

Epple, D., 1987. 'Hedonic prices and implicit markets: estimating demand and supply functions for differentiated products', *Journal of Political Economy*, 95, 59–80

Epstein L., 1975. 'A disaggregate analysis of consumer choice under uncertainty', *Econometrica*, 43, 877–92

Evans, W. and Viscusi, W.K., 1991. 'Estimation of state-dependent utility functions using survey data', *Review of Economics and Statistics*, 73, 94–104

Finkelshtain, I. and Kella, O., 1991. 'Obtaining contingent bounds for non-contingent equivalent variations', *Economics Letters*, 36, 257–61

Fisher, A., Chestnut, L.G. and Violette, D.M., 1989. 'The value of reducing risks of death: a note on new evidence', *Journal of Policy Analysis and Management*, 8, 88–100

Fisher, A.C. and Hanemann, W.M., 1990. 'Information and the dynamics of environmental protection: The concept of the critical period', *Scandinavian Journal of Economics*, 92, 399–414

Folland, S., Goodman, A.C. and Stano, M., 1993. *The Economics of Health and Health Care*, New York: Macmillan

Freeman, M.A. III, 1979. *The Benefits of Environmental Improvement. Theory and Practice*, Baltimore: Johns Hopkins University Press

French, M.T. and Kendall, D.L., 1992. 'The value of job safety for railroad workers', *Journal of Risk and Uncertainty*, 5, 175–85

Friedman, M. and Savage, L.J., 1948. 'The utility analysis of choices involving risk', *Journal of Political Economy*, 57, 463–95

Gafni, A. and Feder, A., 1987. 'Willingness to pay in an equitable society: the case of the Kibbutz', *International Journal of Social Economics*, 14, 16–21

Garen, J., 1988. 'Compensating wage differentials and the endogeneity of job riskiness', *Review of Economics and Statistics*, 70, 9–16

Graham, D.A., 1992. 'Public expenditure under uncertainty: the net-benefit criteria', *American Economic Review*, 82, 822–46
1981. 'Cost-benefit analysis under uncertainty', *American Economic Review*, 71, 715–25
Green, C.H., Tunstall, S.M., N'Jai, A. and Rogers, A., 1990. 'Economic evaluation of environmental goods', *Project Appraisal*, 5, 70–82
Gregory, R., 1986. 'Interpreting measures of economic loss: evidence from contingent valuation and experimental studies', *Journal of Environmental Economics and Management*, 13, 325–37
Gregory, R., Lichtenstein, S. and Slovic, P., 1993. 'Valuing environmental resources: A constructive approach', *Journal of Risk and Uncertainty*, 7, 177–97
Grimes, D.S., 1988. 'Value of a negative cervical smear', *British Medical Journal*, 296, 1363
Grossman, M., 1982. 'The demand for health after a decade', *Journal of Health Economics*, 1, 1–13
1972. *The Demand for Health: A Theoretical and Empirical Investigation*, *NBER Occasional Paper*, 119, New York: National Bureau of Economic Research
Hammack, B. and Brown, G.M., Jr., 1974. *Waterfowl and Wetlands: Toward Bioeconomic Analysis*, Baltimore: Johns Hopkins University Press for Resources for the Future
Hammond, P.J., 1981. 'Ex ante and ex post welfare optimality under uncertainty', *Economica*, 48, 35–50
Handa, J., 1977. 'Risk, probabilities and a new theory of cardinal utilities', *Journal of Political Economy*, 85, 97–122
Hanemann, M.W., 1991. 'Willingness-to-pay and willingness-to-accept: how much can they differ?', *American Economic Review*, 81, 635–47
1984. 'Welfare evaluations in contingent valuation experiments with discrete responses', *American Journal of Agricultural Economics*, 66, 332–41
Hanemann, M.W. and Kriström, B., 1994. 'Current issues in discrete choice contingent valuation', in Johansson, P.-O., Kriström, B. and Mäler, K.-G. (eds.), *Current Issues in Environmental Economics*, Manchester: Manchester University Press, forthcoming
Harless, D.W., 1989. 'More laboratory evidence on the disparity between willingness to pay and compensation demanded', *Journal of Economic Behavior and Organisation*, 11, 359–79
Hartwick, J.M., 1991. 'Degradation of environmental capital and national accounting procedures', *European Economic Review*, 35, 642–9
1990. 'Natural resources, national accounting, and economic depreciation', *Journal of Public Economics*, 43, 291–304
Hausman, J.A. (ed.), 1993. *Contingent Valuation: A Critical Assessment*, Amsterdam: North-Holland
Henderson, A., 1940–1. 'Consumer's surplus and the compensating variation', *Review of Economic Studies*, 8, 117–21
Henry, C., 1974. 'Option values in the economics of irreplaceable assets', *Review of Economic Studies Symposium on Economics of Exhaustible Resources*, 89–104

Hey, J.D., 1979. *Uncertainty in Microeconomics*, Oxford: Martin Robertson

Hicks, J.R., 1945–6. 'The generalized theory of consumer's surplus', *Review of Economic Studies*, 13, 68–73

1943. 'The four consumer's surpluses', *Review of Economic Studies*, 11, 31–41

1940–1. 'The rehabilitation of consumers' surplus', *Review of Economic Studies*, 8, 108–15

1939. 'The foundation of welfare economics', *Economic Journal*, 49, 696–712

Horowitz, J.K. and Carson, R.T., 1993. 'Baseline risk and preference for reductions in risk-to-life', *Risk Analysis*, 13, 457–62

Hotelling, H., 1938. 'The general welfare in relation to problems of taxation and of railway and utility rates', *Econometrica*, 6, 242–69

Hwang, H., Reed, W.R. and Hubbard, C., 1992. 'Compensating wage differentials and unobserved productivity', *Journal of Political Economy*, 100, 835–58

Hylland, A. and Strand, J., 1983. 'Valuation of reduced air pollution in the Grenland area', Department of Economics, University of Oslo (in Norwegian)

Johannesson, M., 1992. 'Economic evaluation of lipid lowering: a feasibility test of the contingent valuation approach', *Health Policy*, 20, 309–320

Johannesson, M. and Jönsson, B., 1991a. 'Economic evaluation in health care: is there a role for cost-benefit analysis?', *Health Policy*, 17, 1–23

1991b. 'Cost-effectiveness analysis of hypertension treatment: a review of methodological issues', *Health Policy*, 19, 55–78

Johannesson, M. and Weinstein, M.C., 1993. 'On the decision rules of cost-effectiveness analysis', *Journal of Health Economics*, 12, 459–67

Johannesson, M., Johansson, P.-O. and Jönsson, B., 1992. 'Economic evaluation of drug therapy: a review article of the contingent valuation method', *PharmacoEconomics*, 1, 325–37

Johannesson, M., Jönsson, B. and Borgquist, L., 1991. 'Willingness to pay for antihypertensive therapy: results of a Swedish pilot study', *Journal of Health Economics*, 10, 461–74

Johannesson, M., Pliskin, J.S. and Weinstein, M.C., 1993. 'Are healthy-years equivalents an improvement over quality-adjusted life years?', *Medical Decision Making*, 13, 281–6

Johannesson, M., Johansson, P.-O., Kriström, B. and Gerdtham, U.-G., 1993. 'Willingness to pay for antihypertensive therapy: further results', *Journal of Health Economics*, 12, 95–108

Johannesson, M., Aberg, H., Agreus, L., Borgquist, L. and Jönsson, B., 1991. 'Cost-benefit analysis of non-pharmacological treatment of hypertension', *Journal of Internal Medicine*, 230, 307–12

Johannesson, M., Johansson, P.-O., Kriström, B., Borgquist, L. and Jönsson, B., 1993. 'Willingness to pay for lipid lowering: a health production function approach', *Applied Economics*, 25, 1023–31

Johansson, P. and Kriström, B., 1992. 'Welfare analysis in discrete choice models: an analysis of model specification', *Working Paper*, Stockholm: Stockholm School of Economics

Johansson, P.-O., 1994. 'Altruism and the value of statistical life: Empirical implications', *Journal of Health Economics*, 13, 111–18

1993. *Cost-benefit Analysis of Environmental Change*, Cambridge: Cambridge University Press

1991. *An Introduction to Modern Welfare Economics*, Cambridge: Cambridge University Press

1987. *The Economic Theory and Measurement of Environmental Benefits*, Cambridge: Cambridge University Press

Johansson, P.-O. and Löfgren, K.-G., 1994a. 'Wealth from optimal health', *Journal of Health Economics*, forthcoming

1994b. 'Comparative dynamics in health economics: some useful results, *Working Paper Series in Economics and Finance*, 17, Stockholm: Stockholm School of Economics

Johansson, P.-O., Kriström, B. and Mäler, K.-G., 1989. 'Welfare evaluations in contingent valuation experiments with discrete response data: comment', *American Journal of Agricultural Economics*, 71, 1054–56

Johansson, P.-O., Kriström, B. and Mattsson, L., 1988. 'How is the willingness to pay for moose hunting affected by the stock of moose?', *Journal of Environmental Management*, 26, 163–71

Jones-Lee, M.W., 1992. 'Paternalistic altruism and the value of a statistical life', *Economic Journal*, 102, 80–90

1991. 'Altruism and the value of other people's safety', *Journal of Risk and Uncertainty*, 4, 213–19

1989. *The Economics of Safety and Physical Risk*, Oxford: Basil Blackwell

1979. 'Trying to value a life: why Broome does not sweep clean', *Journal of Public Economics*, 12, 249–56

1976. *The Value of Life: An Economic Analysis*, London: Martin Robertson

1974. 'The value of changes in the probability of death or injury', *Journal of Political Economy*, 82, 835–49

Jones-Lee, M.W., Hammerton, M. and Philips, P.R., 1985. 'The value of safety: results of a national sample survey', *Economic Journal*, 95, 49–72

Jönsson, B., Björk, S., Hofvendal, S. and Levin, J.E., 1988. 'Quality of life in angina pectoris: a Swedish randomized cross-over comparison between transidermnitro and long acting oral nitrates', in van Eimeren, W. and Horisberger, B. (eds.), *Socioeconomic evaluation of drug therapy*, Berlin and Heidelberg: Springer-Verlag

Journal of Economic Perspectives, 8, Fall 1994. Symposia on the Contingent Valuation Method

Just, R.E., Hueth, D.L. and Schmitz, A., 1982. *Applied Welfare Economics and Public Policy*, Englewood Cliffs, NJ: Prentice-Hall

Kahneman, D. and Knetsch, J.L., 1992a. 'Valuing public goods: The purchase of moral satisfaction', *Journal of Environmental Economics and Management*, 22, 57–70

1992b. 'Reply: contingent valuation and the value of public goods', *Journal of Environmental Economics and Management*, 22, 90–4

Kahneman, D. and Tversky, A., 1979. 'Prospect theory: an analysis of decisions under risk', *Econometrica*, 47, 263–91

Kaldor, N., 1939. 'Welfare propositions of economics and inter-personal comparisons of utility', *Economic Journal*, 49, 549–52

Karlsson, G., 1991. 'Economic analysis of dental implants', *Linkoping Studies in Arts and Science*, 69. Ph.D. thesis, Linkoping: Linkoping University (in Swedish)

Karni, E. and Schmeidler, D., 1991. 'Utility theory with uncertainty', in Hildenbrand, W. and Sonnenschein, H. (eds.), *Handbook of Mathematical Economics, Vol. IV*, Amsterdam: North-Holland

Klarman, H.E., Francis, J.O.S. and Rosenthal, G., 1968. 'Cost-effectiveness analysis applied to the treatment of chronic renal disease', *Medical Care*, 6, 48–54

Knetsch, J.L. and Sinden, J.A., 1984. 'Willingness to pay and compensation demanded: experimental evidence of an unexpected disparity in measures of value', *Quarterly Journal of Economics*, 98, 507–21

Kniesner, T. J. and Leeth, J.D., 1991. 'Compensating wage differentials for fatal injury risk in Australia, Japan, and the United States', *Journal of Risk and Uncertainty*, 4, 75–90

Kohlhase, J. E., 1991. 'The impact of toxic waste sites on housing values', *Journal of Urban Economics*, 30, 1–26

Kreps, D.M., 1990. *A Course in Microeconomic Theory*, Princeton, NJ: Princeton University Press

Kriström, B., 1990a. 'Valuing environmental benefits using the contingent valuation method. An econometric analysis', *Umeå Economic Studies*, 219, University of Umeå

1990b. 'A non-parametric approach to the estimation of welfare measures in discrete response valuation studies', *Land Economics*, 66, 135–9

Krupnick, A.J. and Cropper, M.L., 1992. 'The effect of information on health risk valuations', *Journal of Risk and Uncertainty*, 5, 29–48

LaFrance, J.T. and Barney, D.L., 1991. 'The envelope theorem in dynamic optimization', *Journal of Economic Dynamics and Control*, 15, 355–85

Lancaster, K.J., 1966. 'A new approach to consumer theory', *Journal of Political Economy*, 75, 132–57

Léonard, D. and Van Long, N., 1992. *Optimal Control Theory and Static Optimization in Economics*, Cambridge: Cambridge University Press

Lindgren, B., 1981. *Costs of illness in Sweden 1964–1975*, Lund: Liber

Loomes, G. and Sugden, R., 1982. 'An alternative theory of rational choice under uncertainty', *Economic Journal*, 92, 805–24

Loomes, G., Starmer, C. and Sugden, R., 1992. 'Are preferences monotonic? Testing some predictions of regret theory', *Economica*, 59, 17–33

Lucas, R., 1988. 'On the mechanics of industrial development', *Journal of Monetary Economics*, 22, 3–48

McFadden, D.L., 1973. 'Conditional logit analysis of qualitative choice behavior', in Zacembka, P. (ed.), *Frontiers of Econometrics*, New York: Academic Press

McKenzie, G.W., 1983. *Measuring Economic Welfare: New Methods*, Cambridge: University Press

Machina, M.J., 1987. 'Choice under uncertainty: Problems solved and unsolved', *Journal of Economic Perspectives*, 1, 121–54

Mäler, K.-G., 1991. 'National accounts and environmental resources', *Environmental and Resource Economics*, 1, 1–15

1985. 'Welfare economics and the environment', in Kneese, A.V. and Sweeney, J.L. (eds.), *Handbook of Natural Resource and Energy Economics. Vol. I*, Amsterdam: Elsevier

1974. *Environmental Economics. A Theoretical Inquiry*, Baltimore: Johns Hopkins University Press

Manning, W., Keeler, E., Newhouse, J., Sloss, E. and Wasserman, J., 1989. 'The taxes of sin: Do smokers and drinkers pay their way?', *Journal of the American Medical Association*, 261, 1604–9

Marshall, A., 1920. *Principles of Economics*, 8th ed., London: Macmillan

Marshall, J.M., 1984. 'Gambles and the shadow price of death', *American Economic Review*, 74, 73–86

Mehrez, A. and Gafni, A., 1991. 'Healthy years equivalent: how to measure them using the standard gamble approach', *Medical Decision Making*, 11, 140–6

1989. 'Quality-adjusted life years, utility theory and healthy-years equivalents', *Medical Decision Making*, 9, 142–9

Menezes, C., Geiss, C. and Tressler, J., 1980. 'Increasing downside risk', *American Economic Review*, 70, 921–32

Milgrom, P., 1993. 'Is sympathy an economic value? Philosophy, economics, and the contingent valuation method', in Hausman, J.A. (ed.), *Contingent Valuation: A Critical Assessment*, Amsterdam: North-Holland

Miller, T.R., 1990. 'The plausible range for the value of life: red herrings among the mackerel', *Journal of Forensic Economics*, 3, 17–40

Milne, F. and Shefrin, H.M., 1987. 'Ex post efficiency and ex post welfare: Some fundamental considerations', *Economica*, 55, 63–79

Mishan, E.J., 1981. 'The value of trying to value a life', *Journal of Public Economics*, 15, 133–7

Mitchell, R.C. and Carson, R.T., 1989. *Using Surveys to Value Public Goods. The Contingent Valuation Method*, Washington, DC: Resources for the Future

Miyamato, J.M. and Eraker, S.A., 1985. 'Parameter estimates for a QALY utility model', *Medical Decision Making*, 5, 191–213

Mooney, G.H., 1986. *Economics, Medicine and Health Care*, Brighton: Wheatsheaf

Morey, E.R., 1984. 'Confuser surplus', *American Economic Review*, 74, 163–73

Morey, E.R., Rowe, R.D. and Watson, M., 1991. 'An extended discrete-choice model of Atlantic salmon fishing: with theoretical and empirical comparisons to standard travel-cost models', *Discussion Paper in Economics*, 91–7, Boulder, CO: University of Colorado

Mueller, D.C., 1989. *Public Choice II*, Cambridge: Cambridge University Press

Mushkin, S.J., 1962. 'Health as investment', *Journal of Political Economy*, 70, 129–57

Navrud, S. (ed.), 1992. *Valuing the Environment: the European Experience*, Oxford: Oxford University Press

von Neumann, J. and Morgenstern, O., 1947. *Theory of Games and Economic Behavior*, 2nd ed., Princeton, NJ: Princeton University Press

Ng, Y.-K., 1979. *Welfare Economics: Introduction and Development of Basic*

Concepts, London: Macmillan

NOAA (National Oceanic and Atmospheric Administration), 1994. 'Proposed regulations for natural resource damage assessments', *Federal Register*, January 7, 1994

Nyquist, H., 1992. 'Optimal designs of discrete response experiments in contingent valuation studies', *Review of Economics and Statistics*, 74, 559–62

Palmquist, R.B., 1991. 'Hedonic methods', in Braden, J.B. and Kolstad, C.D. (eds.), *Measuring the Demand for Environmental Quality*, Amsterdam: North-Holland

Pindyck, R.S., 1991. 'Irreversibility, uncertainty, and investment', *Journal of Economic Literature*, 29, 1110–48

Pliskin, J.S., Shepard, D.S. and Weinstein, M.C., 1980. 'Utility functions for life years and health status', *Operations Research*, 28, 206–24

Portney, P.R., 1981. 'Housing prices, health effects, and valuing reductions in risk of death', *Journal of Environmental Economics and Management*, 8, 72–8

Pratt, J.W., 1964. 'Risk aversion in the small and in the large', *Econometrica*, 32, 122–36

Pudney, S., 1989. *Modelling Individual Choice: The Econometrics of Corners, Kinks and Holes*, Oxford: Basil Blackwell

Querner, I., 1993. *An Economic Analysis of Severe Industrial Hazards*, Heidelberg: Physica-Verlag

Rawls, J., 1972. *A Theory of Justice*, Oxford: Clarendon Press

Ready, R., Whitehead, J. and Blomquist, G.C., 1993. 'Contingent valuation when respondents are ambivalent', mimeo

Romer, P., 1986. 'Increasing returns and long-run growth', *Journal of Political Economy*, 94, 1002–37

Rosen, S., 1988. 'The value of changes in life expectancy', *Journal of Risk and Uncertainty*, 1, 285–304

1986. 'The theory of equalizing differences', in Ashenfelter, O. and Layard, R. (eds.), *Handbook of Labor Economics*, Amsterdam: Elsevier Science Publishers

Rowe, R.D., d'Arge, R.C. and Brookshire, D.S., 1980. 'An experiment on the economic value of visibility', *Journal of Environmental Economics and Management*, 7, 1–19

Saint-Paul, G., 1992. 'Fiscal policy in an endogenous growth model', *Quarterly Journal of Economics*, 107, 1243–59

Samuelson, P.A., 1972. 'The consumer does benefit from feasible price stability', *Quarterly Journal of Economics*, 86, 476–93

1947. *Foundations of Economic Analysis*, Cambridge, MA: Harvard University Press

Savage, L.J., 1954. *The Foundations of Statistics*, New York: Wiley

Schelling, T., 1968. 'The life you save may be your own', in Chase, S.B., Jr. (ed.), *Problems in Public Expenditure Analysis*, Washington, DC: Brookings Institution

Seierstad, A. and Sydsæter, K., 1987. *Optimal Control Theory With Economic Applications*, New York: North-Holland

Selden, T.M., 1993. 'Should the government provide catastrophic insurance?',

Journal of Public Economics, 51, 241–7

Sellar, C.J., Chavas, J.P. and Stoll, J.R., 1986. 'Specification of the logit model: the case of valuation of nonmarket goods', *Journal of Environmental Economics and Management*, 13, 382–90

Shiryayev, A.N., 1984. *Probability*, New York: Springer-Verlag

Shogren, J. F. and Crocker, T.D., 1991. 'Risk, self-protection, and ex ante economic value', *Journal of Environmental Economics and Management*, 20, 1–15

Shogren, J.F., Shin, S.Y., Hayes, D.J. and Kliebenstein, J.B., 1994. 'Resolving differences in willingness to pay and willingness to accept', *The American Economic Review*, 84, 255–70

Sitter, R.R., 1992. 'Robust designs for binary data', *Biometrics*, 48, 1145–9

Smith, V.K., 1992. 'Comment: arbitrary values, good causes, premature verdicts', *Journal of Environmental Economics and Management*, 22, 71–89

1991. 'Household production function and environmental benefit estimation', in Braden, J.B. and Kolstad, C.D. (eds.), *Measuring the Demand for Environmental Quality*, Amsterdam: North-Holland

Smith, V.K. and Desvousges, W.H., 1987. 'An empirical analysis of the economic value of risk changes', *Journal of Political Economy*, 95, 89–115

Söderqvist, T., 1991. 'Measuring the value of reduced health risks: the hedonic price technique applied on the case of radon radiation', *Research Report*, The Economic Research Institute at the Stockholm School of Economics

Solow, R.M., 1986. 'On the intergenerational allocation of natural resources', *Scandinavian Journal of Economics*, 88, 141–9

Stoker, T.M., 1993. 'Empirical approaches to the problem of aggregation over individuals', *Journal of Economic Literature*, 31, 1827–76

Stokey, N.L. and Lucas, R.E., Jr., with Prescott, E.C., 1989. *Recursive Methods in Economic Dynamics*, Cambridge, MA: Harvard University Press

Suen, W., 1990. 'Statistical models of consumer behavior with heterogeneous values and constraints', *Economic Inquiry*, 28, 79–98

Sugden, R., 1993. 'A review of *Inequality Reexamined* by Amartya Sen', *Journal of Economic Literature*, 31, 1947–62

1986. 'New developments in the theory of choice under uncertainty', *Bulletin of Economic Research*, 38, 1–24

Sugden, R. and Williams, A., 1978. *The Principles of Practical Cost-benefit Analysis*, Oxford: Oxford University Press

Tahvonen, O. and Kuuluvainen, J., 1993. 'Economic growth, pollution, and renewable resources', *Journal of Environmental Economics and Management* 24, 101–18

Taylor, A.C., Evans, J.S. and McKone, T.E., 1993. 'The value of animal test information in environmental control decisions', *Risk Analysis*, 13, 403–12

Thompson, M.S., 1986. 'Willingness to pay and accept risks to cure chronic disease', *American Journal of Public Health*, 76, 392–6

Thompson, M.S., Read, J.L. and Laing, M., 1984. 'Feasibility of willingness-to-pay measurement in chronic arthritis', *Medical Decision Making*, 4, 195–215

1982. 'Willingness to pay concepts for social decisions in health', in Kane, R.L and Kane R.A. (eds.), *Values and Long Term Care*, Lexington, MA: Lexington Books

Turnovsky, S.J., Shalit, H. and Schmitz, A., 1980. 'Consumer's surplus, price instability, and consumer welfare', *Econometrica*, 48, 135–52

Ulph, A., 1982. 'The role of ex ante and ex post decisions in the valuation of life', *Journal of Public Economics*, 18, 265–76

Usher, D., 1973. 'An imputation to the measure of economic growth for changes in life expectancy', in Moss, M. (ed.), *The Measurement of Economic and Social Performance*, New York: Columbia Press

Varian, H.R., 1992. *Microeconomic Analysis*, 3rd ed., New York: W.W. Norton

Viscusi, W.K., 1993. 'The value of risks to life and health', *Journal of Economic Literature*, 31, 1912–46

1992. *Fatal Tradeoffs. Public & Private Responsibilities for Risk*, New York: Oxford University Press

1989. 'Prospective preference theory: toward an explanation of the paradoxes', *Journal of Risk and Uncertainty*, 2, 235–64

Viscusi, W.K. and Magat, W.A., 1992. 'Bayesian decisions with ambiguous belief aversion', mimeo

Viscusi, W.K. and Zeckhauser, R.J., 1976. 'Environmental policy choice under uncertainty', *Journal of Environmental Economics and Management*, 3, 97–112

Viscusi, W.K., Magat, W.A. and Forrest, A., 1988. 'Altruistic and private valuations of risk reduction', *Journal of Policy Analysis and Management*, 7, 227–45

Viscusi, W.K., Magat, W.A. and Huber, J., 1991. 'Pricing environmental health risks: survey assessments of risk-risk and risk-dollar trade-offs for chronic bronchitis', *Journal of Environmental Economics and Management*, 21, 32–51

Wagstaff, A., 1986. 'The demand for health: theory and applications', *Journal of Epidemiology and Community Health*, 40, 1–11

Wakker, P., 1994. 'Utility, qalys, and healthy-years equivalents: a discussion, a comparison, and a criticism', mimeo, Medical Decision Unit, University of Leiden

Waugh, F.W., 1944. 'Does the consumer benefit from price instability?', *Quarterly Journal of Economics*, 58, 602–14

Weber, M. and Camerer, C., 1987. 'Recent developments in modelling preferences under risk', *OR Spectrum*, 9, 129–51

Weinstein, M.C. and Stason, W.B., 1976. *Hypertension: A Policy Perspective*, Cambridge, MA: Harvard University Press

Weinstein, M.C. and Zeckhauser, R., 1973. 'Critical ratios and efficient allocation', *Journal of Public Economics*, 2, 147–57

Weisbrod, B.A., 1964. 'Collective-consumption services of individual-consumption goods', *Quarterly Journal of Economics*, 78, 471–7

1961. *Economics of Public Health*, Philadelphia: University of Pennsylvania Press

Weitzman, M.L., 1976. 'On the welfare significance of national product in a dynamic economy', *Quarterly Journal of Economics*, 90, 156–62

Williams, A., 1985. 'Economics of coronary artery bypass surgery', *British Medical Journal*, 291, 326–9

1979. 'A note on "Trying to value a life"', *Journal of Public Economics*, 12, 257–8

Willig, R.D., 1978. 'Incremental consumer's surplus and hedonic price adjustment', *Journal of Economic Theory*, 17, 227–53

1976. 'Consumer's surplus without apology', *American Economic Review*, 66, 589–97

Yunker, J.A., 1989. 'Some empirical evidence on the social welfare maximization hypothesis', *Public Finance*, 44, 110–33

Index

accident-death ratio 87
age-specific mortality risks 148
aggregation: see social welfare function
air quality 72, 77, 80, 97
altruism
 budget 133
 impure 129
 in contingent valuation studies 79, 86, 95,
  116, 127–34
 in cost–benefit analysis 130–4
 intergenerational 79
 interhousehold 63, 79, 127–30
 intrahousehold 26, 63
 paternalistic 95, 129, 130, 132
 pure or non-paternalistic 128, 129, 130,
  132
 safety-focused 95, 128, 129, 130, 132
 wealth-focused 129
ambiguous risk information 25, 88
angina pectoris 98, 159
Arrow's impossibility theorem 116
Arrow–Pratt index of
 absolute risk aversion 21
 relative risk aversion 21
averting behaviour 90, 91
Ayer curve 109

backward induction 17
baseline risk 87, 93
Bayesian learning process 88
benefit–cost ratio see cost-benefit analysis
bequests 150
Bergsonian welfare function: see social
 welfare function
Bernouli–Nash (Cobb–Douglas) social
 welfare function: see social welfare
 function
bidding approach (games): see contingent
 valuation method
blood bank 98
blood pressure 6, 10, 13, 97, 98, 100, 102,
 103, 165

Boadway paradox 125
Box–Cox transformation 114
Borel algebra 26
budget constraint (defined) 10, 14, 28

cancer 88, 139
capital income 28, 29, 30, 147
capital market 16, 36, 141
cdf: see distribution function
certainty of death 22, 47, 60, 65
cholesterol 98, 101
closed-ended approach: see contingent
 valuation method
closed-loop policy 138
comparability of utilities 117
compensating variation
 aggregate 115, 122, 123, 124, 132, 133
 and compensation tests 115, 125–6
 and complex changes 37, 143–4
 defined 35, 45
 and discrete choices 83–6
 and discrete responses 81–3
 expected 55, 64
 instantaneous 42
 non-contingent 54, 67, 68, 70, 84, 121,
  122, 123, 130, 132, 142, 143
 overall or lifetime 42, 68
 path independency of 37, 47, 50–1
 ranking properties of 39–40, 41
 and the value of statistical life 61, 69–70,
  123
 and WTP 35, 82
compensating wage 92, 93
compensation (criteria)
 actual 126
 hypothetical 115, 125–6
constant absolute risk aversion 22
contingent valuation method
 and altruism 79, 127–34
 bid vector 83, 110, 111, 112
 and bidding approach (game) 73, 98
 closed-ended 79

contingent valuation method (*cont.*)
  defined 71
  discrete/binary responses 79–83, 84–5,
    99, 103, 111
  double-bounded 169 (n. 1 to ch. 5)
  and embedding problem 77
  and experiments with real payments
    112–13
  and free rider problem 76
  and 'health' budget problem 78
  and implied value cues 76, 99, 100
  and incentives to misrepresent responses
    76
  and iterative building approach 73
  open-ended (continuous) 79, 98, 100
  and qalys/hyes 79, 155
  and scenario mispecification 77
  and starting bid 76
continuous responses: *see* contingent
  valuation method
costate variable 28, 32, 148, 149, 152
cost–benefit analysis
  and altruism 130–4
  certain loss of life 60
  and cost–benefit ratio 161–2, 165
  discounting 30, 36, 88, 89, 127, 143, 149
  intergenerational aggregation 129
  intragenerational aggregation 116–19,
    120, 126, 131
  irreversible effects 135–9
  of a large project 121–2, 130–4
  of a medical treatment 126–7
  of a small project 123, 124, 126–7, 130–4
  and risk/uncertainty 120, 130–4
  taxes in 126, 127, 130, 133
  and time-inconsistency 120
  cost–effect ratio 161–2, 165, 166
cost-effectiveness analysis 1, 2, 8, 153, 160–
  3, 165
cost function 136, 164, 165
cost-of-illness 89
cost of risk-bearing 19
cost-utility analysis 1, 2, 160
covariance 143, 168 (n. 1 to ch. 4)
CVM: *see* contingent valuation method
CV: *see* compensating variation

death intensity parameter 30, 147
death probability (risk) 4, 7, 10, 22, 28, 60,
  61, 70, 93, 135, 149
defensive expenditure 90, 91
demand functions, compensated or
  Hicksian 45, 47, 50, 51
demand functions, ordinary 10, 11, 14, 16,
  17, 31, 32, 33, 43, 44, 45, 50, 66, 112,
  140, 141, 142, 145, 150

differential equation 148
discount factor 30, 139, 147
discount rate 27, 36, 42, 139
discounting of future health (risks) 2, 69, 88
discrete responses: *see* contingent valuation
  method
distribution function (cumulative) 26, 27,
  30, 67, 69, 81, 84, 105, 110, 112, 139,
  140, 141, 143
distributional weights: *see* social welfare
  function
drug 43, 44, 47, 48, 49, 56, 76, 78, 98, 99,
  100, 137, 138, 139
dual variable 164, 165
dynamic envelope theorem 148, 149
dynamic optimization 7, 17, 148

endogenous (health) risks 25–6, 52, 61, 62,
  89, 91, 128
envelope theorem 7, 11, 148, 149
equivalent variation
  aggregate 115, 123–4, 125
  and compensation tests 115, 125–6
  and complex changes 37
  defined 36, 45
  instantaneous 42
  non-contingent 54, 55, 56, 61, 70, 105,
    121, 123, 124, 125
  overall or lifetime 42
  path independency of 37, 47, 50–1
  ranking propreties of 39–40
  and value of statistical life 61, 70
  and WTP 36, 54
essential commodity 47, 62
EV: *see* equivalent variation
exact aggregation 45
existence values 79
expectations operator 18, 23, 53, 55, 121
expected consumer surplus 4, 55, 56, 59, 64
expected costs 136
expected health 53, 54, 65, 67, 89, 112, 126
expected income 6, 19, 52, 63, 64, 65, 88,
  89, 121, 122, 126, 145
expected income and the value of life 63–5,
  88–9, 145–6
expected (indirect) utility function 66, 142
expected life time (length) 30, 146
expected payment 58
expected producer surplus 145–6
expected profitability 136
expected utility 5, 6, 17–19, 22, 23, 52–60,
  64–7, 88, 104, 106, 119–23, 126, 129,
  137, 138, 141–4, 154
expected value 19, 29, 64, 81, 88, 94, 104,
  105, 113, 137, 139, 140, 145, 146, 147

expected value of perfect information 5, 136, 138, 139
expenditure function 12
externality 79

fair bet 58
firms 91, 93
free rider problem 76
full comparability 107, 108
full health 33, 53, 154, 155, 156, 157, 159, 160
full insurance coverage 32
full measurability 117
functional status 161
future generations: *see* intergenerational altruism
future health profile 6, 15, 52, 127, 156

general equilibrium 59, 125
Giffen good 14
gross WTP 130, 133

Hamiltonian 28, 148, 149, 152
hazard (function) 30, 59, 146
hazardous waste 86, 91
health
    as a private good 6, 79, 126
    public 61, 79, 129, 134
health capital 7, 27, 28, 30, 135, 140, 146, 147, 148
health characteristics 10
health good 13, 14, 16, 25, 28, 35, 39, 43, 44, 45, 47, 48, 62, 63, 90, 140, 141, 143, 145, 151
health policy 6, 52
health production function 7, 9, 12, 13, 14, 15, 16, 17, 25, 27, 43, 47, 135, 139, 140, 141, 142, 148, 149, 151
health risk 2, 21, 24, 38, 67, 71, 81, 86, 88, 89, 90, 91, 92, 97, 143, 145, 153, 155, 163
health status 6, 7, 9, 10, 11, 13, 14, 15, 16, 19, 21, 26, 33, 38, 42, 43, 50, 52, 64, 66, 67, 89, 103, 106, 107, 112, 128, 135, 140, 141, 142, 144, 145, 154
healthy-years equivalents 2, 7, 8, 78, 79, 115, 153, 155, 156, 157, 158, 160, 161, 162, 163
hedonic wage function 91, 92, 93
Hicks' criterion 3, 125, 128
Hicksian or compensated demand function 45, 50
homothetic preferences 40
hospital 98, 136, 154, 167
house markets (and health risks) 91
household production function 49

household utility function 63, 70
human capital approach 6, 71, 88–9
hyes: *see* healthy years equivalents
hypertension 6, 97, 98, 99, 102

impure altruism 129
income distribution 125
infimum 22
infinite money measures 38–9, 41, 47, 60
information, value of 5, 7, 135, 136, 137, 138, 139
insurance 5, 9, 22, 23, 24, 25, 26, 29, 30, 32, 54, 57, 58, 81, 141, 147
interest rate 16, 29, 30, 147
intergenerational altruism 79, 129
intermediate value theorem 37, 121, 123, 131
intrahousehold altruism: *see* altruism
investment in health 7, 16–17, 27–9, 135, 146–50
irreversible effects 7, 135–9

Kaldor criterion 125
Kuhn-Tucker conditions 164

labour supply (health dependent) 144–5, 151
Lagrange function (Lagrangean) 148, 164
Lagrange multiplier 11, 31, 70, 123, 134, 150, 166
Lagrangian: *see* Lagrange function
life expectancy 68, 146
life, loss of 4, 22, 47, 59, 60, 65, 89
lifetime utility 42
likelihood ratio 108, 114
line integral 121, 131, 132 (*see also* path-independency conditions)
linear approximation 64, 65, 82, 88, 89, 105, 126
linear programming 162, 163, 164, 165, 167
linear transformation 21
log-linear 110, 111, 114
logit model: *see* probability distribution

marginal cost-effect ratio 161–2, 165, 167
marginal rate of substitution between income and risk 61, 70
marginal social utility of income 121, 122, 123, 124, 127, 131, 132, 134
marginal utility of health 11, 12, 23, 28, 64, 65, 89, 145
marginal utility of income (defined) 11
marginal utility of risk reduction 62, 63, 87
marginal welfare change measure: *see* compensating variation and equivalent variation

marginal willingness to pay for health
    (defined) 11–12 (*see also* compensating
    variation and equivalent variation)
Markov chains 66
Marshallian consumer surplus 3, 43
Marshallian consumer surplus measure 3,
    37, 43, 44, 45, 50
Marshallian or ordinary demand functions
    11, 14, 43, 44, 50
maximum likelihood estimates 107, 109–10,
    114
mean-preserving increase in variability 67,
    140, 143
mean value: *see* expected value
measurability of utilities 117
median 80, 99, 102
median voter 80
median WTP 99, 101
moments about the mean 66, 141, 142
moral hazard 59
morbidity 1, 5, 59, 61, 87, 128
mortality 1, 5, 59, 61, 87, 90, 97, 101, 128,
    148

net WTP 56
Neumann–Morgenstern household 4, 17,
    103
no-Ponzi game 29, 147
non-contingent CV: *see* compensating
    variation
non-contingent EV: *see* equivalent variation
non-essential commodity: *see* essential
    commodity
non-expected utility theories 25
non-linear programming 162, 163
non-linear regression 106
non-parametric method 99, 106, 109, 111
non-paternalistic (pure) altruism: *see*
    altruism
non-response (rate) 86, 99, 101, 103
non-stochastic compensation: *see*
    compensating variation
non-use values: *see* passive-use values
numeraire 104

odds ratio 106
open-ended method: *see* contingent
    valuation method
open-loop policy 138
opportunity cost 101, 145
optimal bid vector 111
optimal control theory 7, 27–30, 32, 68,
    135, 146–50, 152
optimal insurance 22, 26, 32, 58
optimal path (trajectory) 148, 149

Pareto criterion 116
Pareto principle 117
passive-use values 79
paternalistic altruism: *see* altruism
path-dependency issue 3
path-dependent 47, 50
path-independency conditions 37, 50–1
payment card 76
perfect substitutes 49
preference ordering 116
preference revelation 6, 71, 89
present value 16, 27, 29, 30, 31, 41, 42, 66,
    88, 127, 140, 146, 147, 148, 149, 150,
    152, 154, 162
principal–agent problem 135
private goods 6, 10, 11, 33, 35, 37, 38, 52,
    71, 72, 79, 139, 140
probability density function 30, 68, 96, 146
probability distribution
    cumulative 26, 30, 67, 69, 81, 84, 140,
        143, 146
    exponential 30
    logistic 82, 105
probability measure 26
probability space
    finite 26, 53
    uncountable 26
producer surplus 145
production function 7, 9, 12, 13, 14, 15, 16,
    17, 25, 27, 40, 43, 48, 49, 66, 135, 139,
    140, 141, 142, 146, 148, 149, 151
profit income 29
prospect theory 25, 62
public goods 63, 72, 76, 79, 163
public health 38, 61, 72
public safety ix, 54, 61, 63, 84, 87, 11, 112,
    128, 129, 133, 163

qalys: *see* quality-adjusted life-years
quality-adjusted life-years ix, 2, 7, 8, 78, 79,
    115, 153, 154, 155, 156, 157, 158, 160,
    161, 162, 163, 165
quality of life 1, 60, 146, 161
quasi-linear 4, 37, 39, 41, 45, 51, 55, 123
questionnaire: *see* contingent valuation
    method

radian measure 114
radon 90, 91
random disturbance 104
random prices 4
random prospect 19
random utility model 81
random variable 81, 105, 137, 140, 142, 143
ratio of probabilities 23, 162

ratio test 114
ratio vs difference between benefits and costs 161, 162, 165
Rawlsian welfare function: *see* social welfare function
referendum 77, 80
regret theory 25
reservation wage 144, 145
risk
  attitudes 9, 18
  aversion 19, 20, 21, 22, 23, 24, 53, 67, 143, 155
  bearing 19
  collective (household) 63
  cost 19
  of death 10, 22, 59, 60, 86, 93, 135, 149
  defined 17
  endogenous 25, 26, 62, 63, 89, 90, 91
  insurable 59
  lover 19, 20, 21, 53
  neutrality 19, 20, 21, 136
  premium 19, 91, 92
risk–dollar trade-offs 71, 153, 158, 160
risk reduction 62, 63, 69, 86, 87, 90, 91, 93, 95, 97, 98, 145, 149
risk–risk trade-offs 71, 87, 153, 158, 159, 160
risky prospect 19
Roy's identity 11

skewness 142
Social welfare function
  Bergsonian (Bergson-Samuelson) 116
  Bernouli–Nash 125
  Cobb–Douglas 125
  convex indifference curves 116
  defined 116
  egalitarian within the health sector 158
  ex ante 119–20
  ex post 119–20
  generalized utilitarian 120, 131
  and qalys 158
  Rawlsian 117–18, 125
  utilitarian 117, 120
social profitability 100, 115, 119, 122, 123, 124, 133, 134, 136, 158, 162
spread-preserving increase in the mean 67, 140, 143
standard deviation 67, 103, 104, 140, 142, 145
standard gamble 71, 101, 154–5, 159
starting point bias 76
state variable 56, 135, 147, 148, 152
states of the world 17, 18, 23, 24, 26, 53, 54, 55, 56, 57, 58, 59, 64, 69, 119, 120, 121, 124, 126, 128, 144, 145, 151

steady state 28, 29, 32
stochastic variable 26, 67, 141, 143
strategic bias 76, 99
subsidies
supply function 142, 150
supply of labour 28, 65, 141, 143
supremum 22
survey: *see* contingent valuation method
survival probability 4, 6, 7, 25, 26, 52, 59, 60, 61, 62, 63, 65, 69, 70, 81, 83, 84, 90, 128, 129, 130, 135, 146, 148

taxes 10, 33, 73, 76, 77, 80, 98, 103, 126, 127, 129, 130, 133, 134
Taylor series 64, 65, 82, 88, 89, 105, 126
time, opportunity cost of 143, 144, 145
time preference, marginal rate of 146
time trade-off method 71, 155
time-inconsistency problem 120
transformation
  affine 18, 117
  linear 21
  monotonic 18, 40
transition probability 66
treatment cost 56, 100, 103, 105, 126, 127, 161, 166

uncertainty proper 52
utilitarian welfare function: *see* social welfare function
utility function
  cardnal 18, 25, 117, 129
  Cobb-Douglas 40
  concave (in income) 19
  convex (in income) 19
  differentiable 10
  direct, introduced 9–10
  homothetic 4, 40, 51
  indirect (defined) 11
  instantaneous 27, 30, 42, 146
  intertemporal 16, 31
  lifetime 27, 30, 68, 146
  linear (in income) 19
  ordinal 9, 18, 116
  quantity-constrained 151
  quasi-concave 27
  quasi-linear 4, 37, 39, 41, 51, 55, 123
  and risk and uncertainty: *see* expected (indirect) utility function
  separable 17, 42, 159
  well-behaved 10
utility maximization
  atemporal 10, 14, 31
  and discrete choices 83–86
  and health (introduced) 14
  instantaneous 42

utility maximization (*cont.*)
  intertemporal 16–17, 28, 29, 30, 31–2, 137–8, 141, 147–8, 150, 151
  and quality changes 49
  quantity-constrained 151

value of life 4, 22, 41, 47, 48, 52, 59, 60, 62, 63, 94
value of perfect information: *see* expected value of perfect information
value of a statistical life 3, 6, 52, 59, 61, 69–70, 86, 91, 92, 93–5, 123, 128, 134, 160
variance 53, 66, 67, 92, 140, 141, 142, 143

visual-analogue scale (VAS) 10, 103, 104, 107, 112

wage differentials (and health risks) 90, 91–3
wage offer function 90
welfare function: *see* social welfare function
welfarism 116, 117
Willig formulae 45
willingness-to-pay (WTP): see compensating variation and equivalent variation
WTP: *see* willingness to pay
WTP locus 57–9